2022
SUN SIGN
BOOK

Forecasts by
Alice DeVille

Cover design by Kevin R. Brown
GettyImages.com/1179585271/© ectorplusb
GettyImages.com/1182093912/© Marina Piskunova
Interior illustration on page 19 by the Llewellyn Art Department

© 2021 by Llewellyn Publications
ISBN: 978-0-7387-6051-3
Llewellyn is a registered trademark of Llewellyn Worldwide Ltd.
2143 Wooddale Drive, Woodbury, MN 55125-2989
www.llewellyn.com
Printed in the United States of America

Contents

2022 Sun Sign Book Forecasts *by Alice DeVille*

2021

SEPTEMBER
S	M	T	W	T	F	S
			1	2	3	4
5	6	7	8	9	10	11
12	13	14	15	16	17	18
19	20	21	22	23	24	25
26	27	28	29	30		

OCTOBER
S	M	T	W	T	F	S
					1	2
3	4	5	6	7	8	9
10	11	12	13	14	15	16
17	18	19	20	21	22	23
24	25	26	27	28	29	30
31						

NOVEMBER
S	M	T	W	T	F	S
	1	2	3	4	5	6
7	8	9	10	11	12	13
14	15	16	17	18	19	20
21	22	23	24	25	26	27
28	29	30				

DECEMBER
S	M	T	W	T	F	S
			1	2	3	4
5	6	7	8	9	10	11
12	13	14	15	16	17	18
19	20	21	22	23	24	25
26	27	28	29	30	31	

2022

JANUARY
S	M	T	W	T	F	S
						1
2	3	4	5	6	7	8
9	10	11	12	13	14	15
16	17	18	19	20	21	22
23	24	25	26	27	28	29
30	31					

FEBRUARY
S	M	T	W	T	F	S
		1	2	3	4	5
6	7	8	9	10	11	12
13	14	15	16	17	18	19
20	21	22	23	24	25	26
27	28					

MARCH
S	M	T	W	T	F	S
		1	2	3	4	5
6	7	8	9	10	11	12
13	14	15	16	17	18	19
20	21	22	23	24	25	26
27	28	29	30	31		

APRIL
S	M	T	W	T	F	S
					1	2
3	4	5	6	7	8	9
10	11	12	13	14	15	16
17	18	19	20	21	22	23
24	25	26	27	28	29	30

MAY
S	M	T	W	T	F	S
1	2	3	4	5	6	7
8	9	10	11	12	13	14
15	16	17	18	19	20	21
22	23	24	25	26	27	28
29	30	31				

JUNE
S	M	T	W	T	F	S
			1	2	3	4
5	6	7	8	9	10	11
12	13	14	15	16	17	18
19	20	21	22	23	24	25
26	27	28	29	30		

JULY
S	M	T	W	T	F	S
					1	2
3	4	5	6	7	8	9
10	11	12	13	14	15	16
17	18	19	20	21	22	23
24	25	26	27	28	29	30
31						

AUGUST
S	M	T	W	T	F	S
	1	2	3	4	5	6
7	8	9	10	11	12	13
14	15	16	17	18	19	20
21	22	23	24	25	26	27
28	29	30	31			

SEPTEMBER
S	M	T	W	T	F	S
				1	2	3
4	5	6	7	8	9	10
11	12	13	14	15	16	17
18	19	20	21	22	23	24
25	26	27	28	29	30	

OCTOBER
S	M	T	W	T	F	S
						1
2	3	4	5	6	7	8
9	10	11	12	13	14	15
16	17	18	19	20	21	22
23	24	25	26	27	28	29
30	31					

NOVEMBER
S	M	T	W	T	F	S
		1	2	3	4	5
6	7	8	9	10	11	12
13	14	15	16	17	18	19
20	21	22	23	24	25	26
27	28	29	30			

DECEMBER
S	M	T	W	T	F	S
				1	2	3
4	5	6	7	8	9	10
11	12	13	14	15	16	17
18	19	20	21	22	23	24
25	26	27	28	29	30	31

2023

JANUARY
S	M	T	W	T	F	S
1	2	3	4	5	6	7
8	9	10	11	12	13	14
15	16	17	18	19	20	21
22	23	24	25	26	27	28
29	30	31				

FEBRUARY
S	M	T	W	T	F	S
			1	2	3	4
5	6	7	8	9	10	11
12	13	14	15	16	17	18
19	20	21	22	23	24	25
26	27	28				

MARCH
S	M	T	W	T	F	S
			1	2	3	4
5	6	7	8	9	10	11
12	13	14	15	16	17	18
19	20	21	22	23	24	25
26	27	28	29	30	31	

APRIL
S	M	T	W	T	F	S
						1
2	3	4	5	6	7	8
9	10	11	12	13	14	15
16	17	18	19	20	21	22
23	24	25	26	27	28	29
30						

MAY
S	M	T	W	T	F	S
	1	2	3	4	5	6
7	8	9	10	11	12	13
14	15	16	17	18	19	20
21	22	23	24	25	26	27
28	29	30	31			

JUNE
S	M	T	W	T	F	S
				1	2	3
4	5	6	7	8	9	10
11	12	13	14	15	16	17
18	19	20	21	22	23	24
25	26	27	28	29	30	

JULY
S	M	T	W	T	F	S
						1
2	3	4	5	6	7	8
9	10	11	12	13	14	15
16	17	18	19	20	21	22
23	24	25	26	27	28	29
30	31					

AUGUST
S	M	T	W	T	F	S
		1	2	3	4	5
6	7	8	9	10	11	12
13	14	15	16	17	18	19
20	21	22	23	24	25	26
27	28	29	30	31		

5

Meet Alice DeVille

Alice DeVille is known internationally as an astrologer, consultant, and writer. She has been writing articles for the Llewellyn annuals since 1998. Her contributions have appeared in Llewellyn's *Sun Sign Book*, *Moon Sign Book*, and *Herbal Almanac*.

Alice discovered astrology in her late teens when she was browsing the book section of a discount department store and found a book that had much more astrology detail in it than simple Sun sign descriptions. Bells of recognition went off immediately. She purchased the book and knew she had to have more.

Alice also held credentials as a realtor for twenty-two years in the Commonwealth of Virginia and earned Real Estate Appraisal credentials and certifications in diverse real estate specialties. Her knowledge of feng shui led to the development of numerous workshops and seminars, including those that provided realtors with tips for selling homes and working with buyers.

Alice specializes in relationships of all types that call for solid problem-solving advice to get to the core of issues and give clients options for meeting critical needs. Her clients seek solutions in business practices, career and change management, real estate, relationships, and training. Numerous websites and publications have featured her articles, including StarIQ, Astral Hearts, Llewellyn, Meta Arts, Inner Self, and ShareItLiveIt. Quotes from her work on relationships have appeared in books, publications, training materials, calendars, planners, audio tapes, and world-famous quotes lists. Often cited is "Each relationship you have with another reflects the relationship you have with yourself." Alice's Llewellyn material on relationships has appeared in *Something More* by Sarah Ban Breathnach and *Through God's Eyes* by Phil Bolsta and on Oprah's website.

Alice is available for writing books and articles for publishers, newspapers, and magazines, as well as conducting workshops and doing radio or TV interviews. Contact her at DeVilleAA@aol.com or alice.deville27@gmail.com.

How to Use This Book

by Kim Rogers-Gallagher

Hi there! Welcome to the 2022 edition of *Llewellyn's Sun Sign Book*. This book centers on Sun sign astrology—that is, the set of general attributes and characteristics that those of us born under each of the twelve particular Sun signs share. You'll find descriptions of your sign's qualities tucked into your sign's chapter, along with the type of behavior you tend to exhibit in different life situations—with regard to relationships, work situations, and the handling of money and possessions, for example. Oh, and there's a section that's dedicated to good old-fashioned fun, too, including what will bring you joy and how to make it happen.

There's a lot to be said for Sun sign astrology. First off, the Sun's sign at the time of your birth describes the qualities, talents, and traits you're here to study this time around. If you believe in reincarnation, think of it as declaring a celestial major for this lifetime. Sure, you'll learn other things along the way, but you've announced to one and all that you're primarily interested in mastering this one particular sign. Then, too, on a day when fiery, impulsive energies are making astrological headlines, if you're a fiery and/or impulsive sign yourself—like Aries or Aquarius, for example—it's easy to imagine how you'll take to the astrological weather a lot more easily than a practical, steady-handed sign like Taurus or Virgo.

Obviously, astrology comes in handy, for a variety of reasons. Getting to know your "natal" Sun sign (the sign the Sun was in when you were born) can most certainly give you the edge you need to ace the final and move on to the next celestial course level—or basically to succeed in life, and maybe even earn a few bonus points toward next semester. Using astrology on a daily basis nicely accelerates the process.

Now, there are eight other planets and one lovely Moon in our neck of the celestial woods, all of which also play into our personalities. The sign that was on the eastern horizon at the moment of your birth—otherwise known as your *Ascendant*, or *rising sign*—is another indicator of your personality traits. Honestly, there are all kinds of cosmic factors, so if it's an in-depth, personal analysis you're after, a professional astrologer is the only way to go—especially if you're curious about relationships, past lives, future trends, or even the right time to schedule an important life event. Professional astrologers calculate your birth chart—again, the "natal" chart—based on the date, place, and exact time of your birth—which allows for a far more personal and specific reading. In the meantime, however, in addition to reading up on your Sun sign, you can use the tables on pages 8 and 9 to find the sign of your Ascendant. (These tables, however, are approximate and tailored to those of us born in North America, so if the traits of your Ascendant don't sound familiar, check out the sign directly before or after.)

There are three sections to each sign chapter in this book. As I already mentioned, the first section describes personality traits, and while it's fun to read your own, don't forget to check out the other Sun signs. (Oh, and do feel free to mention any rather striking behavioral similarities to skeptics. It's great fun to watch a Scorpio's reaction when you tell them they're astrologically known as "the sexy sign," or a Gemini when you thank them for creating the concept of multitasking.)

The second section is entitled "The Year Ahead" for each sign. Through considering the movements of the slow-moving planets (Jupiter, Saturn, Uranus, Neptune, Pluto), the eclipses, and any other outstanding celestial movements, this segment will provide you with the big picture of the year—or basically the broad strokes of what to expect, no matter who you are or where you are, collectively speaking.

The third section includes monthly forecasts, along with rewarding days and challenging days, basically a heads-up designed to alert you to potentially easy times as well as potentially tricky times.

At the end of every chapter you'll find an Action Table, providing general information about the best time to indulge in certain activities. Please note that these are only suggestions. Don't hold yourself back or rush into anything your intuition doesn't wholeheartedly agree with—and again, when in doubt, find yourself a professional.

Well, that's it. I hope that you enjoy this book, and that being aware of the astrological energies of 2022 helps you create a year full of fabulous memories!

Kim Rogers-Gallagher has written hundreds of articles and columns for magazines and online publications and has two books of her own, *Astrology for the Light Side of the Brain* and *Astrology for the Light Side of the Future.* She's a well-known speaker who's been part of the UAC faculty since 1996. Kim can be contacted at KRGPhoenix313@yahoo.com for fees regarding readings, classes, and lectures.

Ascendant Table

Your Sun Sign	6–8 am	8–10 am	10 am– Noon	Noon– 2 pm	2–4 pm	4–6 pm
			Your Time of Birth			
Aries	Taurus	Gemini	Cancer	Leo	Virgo	Libra
Taurus	Gemini	Cancer	Leo	Virgo	Libra	Scorpio
Gemini	Cancer	Leo	Virgo	Libra	Scorpio	Sagittarius
Cancer	Leo	Virgo	Libra	Scorpio	Sagittarius	Capricorn
Leo	Virgo	Libra	Scorpio	Sagittarius	Capricorn	Aquarius
Virgo	Libra	Scorpio	Sagittarius	Capricorn	Aquarius	Pisces
Libra	Scorpio	Sagittarius	Capricorn	Aquarius	Pisces	Aries
Scorpio	Sagittarius	Capricorn	Aquarius	Pisces	Aries	Taurus
Sagittarius	Capricorn	Aquarius	Pisces	Aries	Taurus	Gemini
Capricorn	Aquarius	Pisces	Aries	Taurus	Gemini	Cancer
Aquarius	Pisces	Aries	Taurus	Gemini	Cancer	Leo
Pisces	Aries	Taurus	Gemini	Cancer	Leo	Virgo

Your Sun Sign	Your Time of Birth					
	6–8 pm	8–10 pm	10 pm–Midnight	Midnight–2 am	2–4 am	4–6 am
Aries	Scorpio	Sagittarius	Capricorn	Aquarius	Pisces	Aries
Taurus	Sagittarius	Capricorn	Aquarius	Pisces	Aries	Taurus
Gemini	Capricorn	Aquarius	Pisces	Aries	Taurus	Gemini
Cancer	Aquarius	Pisces	Aries	Taurus	Gemini	Cancer
Leo	Pisces	Aries	Taurus	Gemini	Cancer	Leo
Virgo	Aries	Taurus	Gemini	Cancer	Leo	Virgo
Libra	Taurus	Gemini	Cancer	Leo	Virgo	Libra
Scorpio	Gemini	Cancer	Leo	Virgo	Libra	Scorpio
Sagittarius	Cancer	Leo	Virgo	Libra	Scorpio	Sagittarius
Capricorn	Leo	Virgo	Libra	Scorpio	Sagittarius	Capricorn
Aquarius	Virgo	Libra	Scorpio	Sagittarius	Capricorn	Aquarius
Pisces	Libra	Scorpio	Sagittarius	Capricorn	Aquarius	Pisces

How to use this table: 1. Find your Sun sign in the left column.

2. Find your approximate birth time in a vertical column.

3. Line up your Sun sign and birth time to find your Ascendant.

This table will give you an approximation of your Ascendant. If you feel that the sign listed as your Ascendant is incorrect, try the one either before or after the listed sign. It is difficult to determine your exact Ascendant without a complete natal chart.

Astrology Basics

Natal astrology is done by freeze-framing the solar system at the moment of your birth, from the perspective of your birth place. This creates a circular map that looks like a pie sliced into twelve pieces. It shows where every heavenly body we're capable of seeing was located when you arrived. Basically, it's your astrological tool kit, and it can't be replicated more than once in thousands of years. This is why we astrologers are so darn insistent about the need for you to either dig your birth certificate out of that box of ancient paperwork in the back of your closet or get a copy of it from the county clerk's office where you were born. Natal astrology, as interpreted by a professional astrologer, is done exactly and precisely for you and no one else. It shows your inherent traits, talents, and challenges. Comparing the planets' current positions to their positions in your birth chart allows astrologers to help you understand the celestial trends at work in your life—and most importantly, how you can put each astrological energy to a positive, productive use.

Let's take a look at the four main components of every astrology chart.

Planets

The planets represent the needs or urges we all experience once we hop off the Evolutionary Express and take up residence inside a human body. For example, the Sun is your urge to shine and be creative, the Moon is your need to express emotions, Mercury is in charge of how you communicate and navigate, and Venus is all about who and what you love—and more importantly, how you love.

Signs

The sign a planet occupies is like a costume or uniform. It describes how you'll go about acting on your needs and urges. If you have Venus in fiery, impulsive Aries, for example, and you're attracted to a complete stranger across the room, you won't wait for them to come to you. You'll walk over and introduce yourself the second the urge strikes you. Venus in intense, sexy Scorpio, however? Well, that's a different story. In this case, you'll keep looking at a prospective beloved until they finally give in, cross the room, and beg you to explain why you've been staring at them for the past couple of hours.

Houses

The houses represent the different sides of our personalities that emerge in different life situations. For example, think of how very different you act when you're with an authority figure as opposed to how you act with a lover or when you're with your BFF.

Aspects

The aspects describe the distance from one planet to another in a geometric angle. If you were born when Mercury was 90 degrees from Jupiter, for example, this aspect is called a square. Each unique angular relationship causes the planets involved to interact differently.

Meet the Planets

The planets represent energy sources. The Sun is our source of creativity, the Moon is our emotional warehouse, and Venus describes who and what we love and are attracted to—not to mention why and how we go about getting it and keeping it.

Sun

The Sun is the head honcho in your chart. It represents your life's mission—what will give you joy, keep you young, and never fail to arouse your curiosity. Oddly enough, you weren't born knowing the qualities of the sign the Sun was in when you were born. You're here to learn the traits, talents, and characteristics of the sign you chose—and rest assured, each of the twelve is its own marvelous adventure! Since the Sun is the Big Boss, all of the other planets, including the Moon, are the Sun's staff, all there to help the boss by helping you master your particular area of expertise. Back in the day, the words from a song in a recruitment commercial struck me as a perfect way to describe our Sun's quest: "Be all that you can be. Keep on reaching. Keep on growing. Find your future." The accompanying music was energizing, robust, and exciting, full of anticipation and eagerness. When you feel enthused, motivated, and stimulated, that's your Sun letting you know you're on the right path.

Moon

If you want to understand this lovely silver orb, go outside when the Moon is nice and full, find yourself a comfy perch, sit still, and have a nice, long look at her. The Moon inspires us to dream, wish, and sigh, to reminisce, ruminate, and remember. She's the Queen of Emotions, the astrological purveyor of feelings and reactions. In your natal chart, the condition of the Moon—that is, the sign and house she's in and the connections she makes with your other planets—shows how you'll deal with whatever life tosses your way—how you'll respond, how you'll cope, and how you'll pull it all together to move on after a crisis. She's where your instincts and hunches come from, and the source of every gut feeling and premonition. The Moon describes your childhood home, your relationship with your mother, your attitude toward childbearing and children in general, and what you're looking for in a home. She shows what makes you feel safe, warm, comfy, and loved. On a daily basis, the Moon describes the collective mood.

Mercury

Next time you pass by a flower shop, take a look at the FTD logo by the door. That fellow with the wings on his head and his feet is Mercury, the ancient Messenger of the Gods. He's always been a very busy guy. Back in the day, his job was to shuttle messages back and forth between the gods and goddesses and we mere mortals—obviously, no easy feat. Nowadays, however, Mercury is even busier. With computers, cell phones, social media, and perhaps even the occasional human-to-human interaction to keep track of—well, he must be just exhausted. In a nutshell, he's the astrological energy in charge of communication, navigation, and travel, so he's still nicely represented by that winged image. He's also the guy in charge of the five senses, so no matter what you're aware of right now, be it taste, touch, sound, smell, or sight—well, that's because Mercury is bringing it to you, live. At any rate, you'll hear about him most when someone mentions that Mercury is retrograde, but even though these periods have come to be blamed for all sorts of problems, there's really no cause for alarm. Mercury turns retrograde (or, basically, appears to move backwards from our perspective here on Earth) every three months for three weeks, giving us all a chance for a do-over—and who among us has never needed one of those?

Venus

So, if it's Mercury that makes you aware of your environment, who allows you to experience all kinds of sensory sensations via the five senses? Who's in charge of your preferences in each department? That delightful task falls under the jurisdiction of the lovely lady Venus, who describes the physical experiences that are the absolute best—in your book, anyway. That goes for the music and art you find most pleasing, the food and beverages you can't get enough of, and the scents you consider the sweetest of all—including the collar of the shirt your loved one recently wore. Touch, of course, is also a sense that can be quite delightful to experience. Think of how happy your fingers are when you're stroking your pet's fur, or the delicious feel of cool bed sheets when you slip between them after an especially tough day. Venus brings all those sensations together in one wonderful package, working her magic through love of the romantic kind, most memorably experienced through intimate physical interaction with an "other." Still, your preferences in any relationship also fall under Venus's job description.

Mars

Mars turns up the heat, amps up the energy, and gets your show on the road. Whenever you hear yourself grunt, growl, or grumble—or just make any old "rrrrr" sound in general—your natal Mars has just made an appearance. Adrenaline is his business and passion is his specialty. He's the ancient God of War—a hot-headed guy who's famous for having at it with his sword first and asking questions later. In the extreme, Mars is often in the neighborhood when violent events occur, and accidents, too. He's in charge of self-assertion, aggression, and pursuit, and one glance at his heavenly appearance explains why. He's The Red Planet, after all—and just think of all the expressions about anger and passion that include references to the color red or the element of fire: "Grrr!" "Seeing red." "Hot under the collar." "All fired up." "Hot and heavy." You get the idea. Mars is your own personal warrior. He describes how you'll react when you're threatened, excited, or angry.

Jupiter

Santa Claus. Luciano Pavarotti with a great big smile on his face as he belts out an amazing aria. Your favorite uncle who drinks too much, eats too much, and laughs far too loud—yet never fails to go well above and beyond the call of duty for you when you need him. They're all perfect examples of Jupiter, the King of the Gods, the giver of all things good, and the source of extravagance, generosity, excess, and benevolence in our little corner of the Universe. He and Venus are the heavens' two most popular planets—for obvious reasons. Venus makes us feel good. Jupiter makes us feel absolutely over-the-top excellent. In Jupiter's book, if one is good, it only stands to reason that two would be better, and following that logic, ten would be just outstanding. His favorite words are "too," "many," and "much." Expansions, increases, and enlarge-ments—or basically, just the whole concept of growth—are all his doing. Now, unbeknownst to this merry old fellow, there really is such a thing as too much of a good thing—but let's not pop his goodhearted bubble. Wherever Jupiter is in your chart, you'll be prone to go overboard, take it to the limit, and push the envelope as far as you possibly can. Sure, you might get a bit out of control every now and then, but if envelopes weren't ever pushed, we'd never know the joys of optimism, generosity, or sudden, contagious bursts of laughter.

Saturn

Jupiter expands. Saturn contracts. Jupiter encourages growth. Saturn, on the other hand, uses those rings he's so famous for to restrict growth. His favorite word is "no," but he's also very fond of "wait," "stop," and "don't even think about it." He's ultra-realistic and quite pessimistic, a cautious, careful curmudgeon who guards and protects you by not allowing you to move too quickly or act too recklessly. He insists on preparation and doesn't take kindly when we blow off responsibilities and duties. As you can imagine, Saturn is not nearly as popular as Venus and Jupiter, mainly because none of us like to be told we can't do what we want to do when we want to do it. Still, without someone who acted out his part when you were too young to know better, you might have dashed across the street without stopping to check for traffic first, and—well, you get the point. Saturn encourages frugality, moderation, thoughtfulness, and self-restraint, all necessary habits to learn if you want to play nice with the other grown-ups. He's also quite fond of building things, which necessar-ily starts with solid foundations and structures that are built to last.

Uranus

Say hello to Mr. Unpredictable himself, the heavens' wild card—to say the very least. He's the kind of guy who claims responsibility for lightning strikes, be they literal or symbolic. Winning the lottery, love at first sight, accidents, and anything seemingly coincidental that strikes you as oddly well-timed are all examples of Uranus's handiwork. He's a rebellious, headstrong energy, so wherever he is in your chart, you'll be defiant, headstrong, and quite unwilling to play by the rules, which he thinks of as merely annoying suggestions that far too many humans adhere to. Uranus is here to inspire you to be yourself—exactly as you are, with no explanations and no apologies whatsoever. He motivates you to develop qualities such as independence, ingenuity, and individuality—and with this guy in the neighborhood, if anyone or anything gets in the way, you'll 86 them. Period. Buh-bye now. The good news is that when you allow this freedom-loving energy to guide you, you discover something new and exciting about yourself on a daily basis—at least. The tough but entirely doable part is keeping him reined in tightly enough to earn your daily bread and form lasting relationships with like-minded others.

Neptune

Neptune is the uncontested Mistress of Disguise and Illusion in the solar system, beautifully evidenced by the fact that this ultra-feminine energy has been masquerading as a male god for as long as gods and goddesses have been around. Just take a look at the qualities she bestows: compassion, spirituality, intuition, wistfulness, and nostalgia. Basically, whenever your subconscious whispers, it's in Neptune's voice. She activates your antennae and sends you subtle, invisible, and yet highly powerful messages about everyone you cross paths with, no matter how fleeting the encounter. I often picture her as Glinda the Good Witch from *The Wizard of Oz*, who rode around in a pink bubble, singing happy little songs and casting wonderful, helpful spells. Think "enchantment"—oh, and "glamour," too, which, by the way, was the old-time term for a magical spell cast upon someone to change their appearance. Nowadays, glamour is often thought of as a rather idealized and often artificial type of beauty brought about by cosmetics and airbrushing, but Neptune is still in charge, and her magic still works. When this energy is wrongfully used, deceptions, delusions and fraud can result—and since she's so fond of ditching reality, it's easy to become a bit too fond of escape hatches like drugs and alcohol. Still, Neptune inspires romance, nostalgia, and sentimentality, and she's quite fond of dreams and fantasies, too—and what would life be like without all of that?

Pluto

Picture all the gods and goddesses in the heavens above us living happily in a huge mansion in the clouds. Then imagine that Pluto's place is at the bottom of the cellar stairs, and on the cellar door (which is in the kitchen, of course) a sign reads "Keep out. Working on Darwin Awards." That's where Pluto would live—and that's the attitude he'd have. He's in charge of unseen cycles—life, death, and rebirth. Obviously, he's not an emotional kind of guy. Whatever Pluto initiates really has to happen. He's dark, deep, and mysterious—and inevitable. So yes, Darth Vader does come to mind, if for no other reason than because of James Earl Jones's amazing, compelling voice. Still, this intense, penetrating, and oh-so-thorough energy has a lot more to offer. Pluto's in charge of all those categories we humans aren't fond of—like death and decay, for example—but on the less drastic side, he also inspires recycling, repurposing, and reusing. In your chart, Pluto represents a place where you'll be ready to go big or go home, where investing all or nothing is a given. When a crisis comes up—when you need to be totally committed and totally authentic to who you really are to get through it—that's when you'll meet your Pluto. Power struggles and mind games, however—well, you can also expect those pesky types of things wherever Pluto is located.

A Word about Retrogrades

"Retrograde" sounds like a bad thing, but I'm here to tell you that it isn't. In a nutshell, retrograde means that from our perspective here on Earth, a planet appears to be moving in reverse. Of course, planets don't ever actually back up, but the energy of retrograde planets is often held back, delayed, or hindered in some way. For example, when Mercury—the ruler of communication and navigation—appears to be retrograde, it's tough to get from point A to point B without a snafu, and it's equally hard to get a straight answer. Things just don't seem to go as planned. But it only makes sense. Since Mercury is the planet in charge of conversation and movement, when he's moving backward—well, imagine driving a car that only had reverse. Yep. It wouldn't be easy. Still, if that's all you had to work with, you'd eventually find a way to get where you wanted to go. That's how all retrograde energies work. If you have retrograde planets in your natal chart, don't rush them. These energies may need a bit more time to function well for you than other natal planets, but if you're patient, talk about having an edge! You'll know these planets inside and out. On a collective basis, think of the time when a planet moves retrograde as a chance for a celestial do-over.

Signs of the Zodiac

The sign a planet is "wearing" really says it all. It's the costume an actor wears that helps them act out the role they're playing. It's the style, manner, or approach you'll use in each life department—whether you're being creative on a canvas, gushing over a new lover, or applying for a management position. Each of the signs belongs to an element, a quality, and a gender, as follows.

Elements
The four elements—fire, earth, air, and water—describe a sign's aims. Fire signs are spiritual, impulsive energies. Earth signs are tightly connected to the material plane. Air signs are cerebral, intellectual creatures, and water signs rule the emotional side of life.

Qualities
The three qualities—cardinal, fixed, and mutable—describe a sign's energy. Cardinal signs are tailor-made for beginnings. Fixed energies are solid, just as they sound, and are quite determined to finish what they start. Mutable energies are flexible and accommodating but can also be scattered or unstable.

Genders
The genders—masculine and feminine—describe whether the energy attracts (feminine) or pursues (masculine) what it wants.

The Twelve Signs

Here's a quick rundown of the twelve zodiac signs.

Aries
Aries planets are hotheads. They're built from go-getter cardinal energy and fast-acting fire. Needless to say, Aries energy is impatient, energetic, and oh-so-willing to try anything once.

Taurus
Taurus planets are aptly represented by the symbol of the bull. They're earth creatures, very tightly connected to the material plane, and fixed—which means they're pretty much immovable when they don't want to act.

Sequence	Sign	Glyph	Ruling Planet	Symbol
1	Aries	♈	Mars	Ram
2	Taurus	♉	Venus	Bull
3	Gemini	♊	Mercury	Twins
4	Cancer	♋	Moon	Crab
5	Leo	♌	Sun	Lion
6	Virgo	♍	Mercury	Virgin
7	Libra	♎	Venus	Scales
8	Scorpio	♏	Pluto	Scorpion
9	Sagittarius	♐	Jupiter	Archer
10	Capricorn	♑	Saturn	Goat
11	Aquarius	♒	Uranus	Water Bearer
12	Pisces	♓	Neptune	Fish

Gemini

As an intellectual air sign that's mutable and interested in anything new, Gemini energy is eternally curious—and quite easily distracted. Gemini planets live in the moment and are expert multitaskers.

Cancer

Cancer is a water sign that runs on its emotions, and since it's also part of the cardinal family, it's packed with the kind of start-up energy that's perfect for raising a family and building a home.

Leo

This determined, fixed sign is part of the fire family. As fires go, think of Leo planets as bonfires of energy—and just try to tear your eyes away. Leo's symbol is the lion, and it's no accident. Leo planets care very much about their familial pride—and about their personal pride.

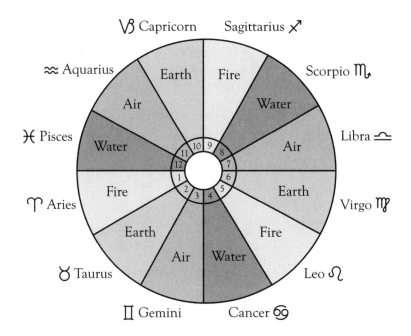

Virgo

Virgo is mutable and therefore easily able to switch channels when necessary. It's part of the earth family and connected to the material world (like Taurus). Virgo energy loves to work, organize, and sort, but most of all, to fix what's broken.

Libra

This communicative air sign runs on high. It's cardinal, so when it comes to making connections, Libra is second to none. Libra planets are people pleasers and the honorary cruise directors of the zodiac, and are as charming and accommodating as the day is long.

Scorpio

Scorpio is of the water element and a highly emotional creature. Scorpio energy is fixed, too, so feelings are tough to shake and obsessions are easy to come by. Planets in this sign are devoted and determined and can be absolutely relentless.

Sagittarius

Sagittarius has all the fire of Aries and Leo but, due to its mutable nature, tends to be distracted, spreading its energy among projects and interests. Think of Sagittarius energy as a series of red-hot brush fires, firing up and dying down and firing up again in a new location.

Capricorn

As the third earth sign, Capricorn is concerned with reality and practicality, complete with all the rules and regulations it takes to build and maintain a life here on Planet Number Three. Capricorn energy takes charge and assumes responsibility quite easily.

Aquarius

The last of the three communicative air signs, Aquarius prefers mingling and interacting with a group via friendships. Freedom-loving Aquarius energy won't be restricted—not for long, anyway—and is willing to return the favor, in any and all relationships.

Pisces

Watery Pisces runs on its emotions—and even more so on its intuition, which is second to none. This mutable, flexible sign is aptly represented by the constant fluctuating movements of its symbol, the two fish.

Aspects

Astrological aspects describe the relationships between planets and important points in a horoscope chart. Basically, they're the mathematical angles that measure the distance between two or more planets. Planets in square aspect are 90 degrees apart, planets in opposition are 180 degrees apart, and so forth. Each of these aspect relationships seems to link energies in a very different way. For example, if two planets are in square aspect, think of what you know about "squaring off," and you'll understand exactly how they're interacting. Think of aspects as a way of describing the type of conversation going on between celestial bodies.

Here's a brief description of the five major aspects.

Conjunction

When two planets are within a few degrees of each other, they're joined at the hip. The conjunction is often called the aspect of "fusion," since the energies involved always act together.

Sextile

Planets in sextile are linked by a 60-degree angle, creating an exciting, stimulating astrological "conversation." These planets encourage, arouse, and excite each other.

Square

The square aspect is created by linking energies in a 90-degree angle—which tends to be testy and sometimes irritating but always action-oriented.

Trine

The trine is the "lazy" aspect. When planets are in this 120-degree angle, they get along so well that they often aren't motivated to do much. Trines make things easy—too easy, at times—but they're also known for being quite lucky.

Opposition

Oppositions exist between planets that are literally opposite one another. Think about seesaws and playing tug-of-war, and you'll understand how these energies get along. Sure, it can be a power struggle at times, but balance is the key.

2022 at a Glance

The year starts off with the planet of disruption, Uranus, retrograde in Taurus until January 18, when it moves direct at 10 degrees and shakes up the world of Taurus folks born between April 30 and May 10. Those born in the middle degrees of Aquarius, Leo, and Scorpio will receive a jolt or two during this cycle that is bound to affect the status of careers, plans, and relationships before the chaotic planet goes retrograde again on August 24, reinforcing its surprising hold until it goes direct again in January 2023. Another planet emerging in retrograde motion is the personal planet Venus, now in Capricorn and affecting the love lives of those born with planets in the middle degrees of Capricorn until the planet of harmony moves direct on January 29 and shifts the direction of romantic interplay. On January 14, Mercury, the messenger of the gods, makes its first retrograde station of the year in Aquarius, throwing a few curve balls to your personal, travel, and work plans for the next three weeks by delaying the flow of progress you anticipated.

Jupiter, the planet of prosperity and expansion, covers considerable territory in 2022 in two different signs. The year begins with Jupiter in Pisces renewing connections with its old ruler while feeling a strong sense of spiritual awakening as the people on the planet recover from the disruptive aftermath of the global coronavirus pandemic. In late May, Jupiter's rapid trip through Pisces ends as it moves into Aries for five months and interacts assertively with family, friends, and work colleagues until July 28, when the planet of expansion turns retrograde and steadily makes its way back into Pisces territory in late October before going direct again on November 23.

Saturn in Aquarius moves direct from 12 degrees to 25 degrees in the sign until June 4, when the planet of restrictions, lessons to learn, and inconvenient constraints goes retrograde until October 23. You'll have a chance to review your finances, get treatment for and improve your health, and make important decisions about household matters, employment contracts, politics, and relationship stability. Many on the planet believe the December 2020 conjunction of Jupiter and Saturn in Aquarius foreshadowed the attempted overthrow of the US Capitol on January 6, 2021, and the change of political party control with validation of the results of the 2020 presidential election. While the country continues to seek stability and nationwide peace, the population is adjusting to new policies and learning to trust again.

With the journey of Neptune in Pisces, in its own home turf, we've had a couple of years of dealing with the fog of uncertainty connected to coronavirus and efficacy of treatment for it, record-breaking unemployment, the closing of schools, and the inability to see family and loved ones at a distance. In 2022 Neptune will be retrograde from June 28 to December 3. Pluto in Capricorn is advancing toward completing its first cycle on the planet since its discovery in 1930. Depending on where this dwarf planet falls in your natal chart, you have opportunities to release any doubts and fears that create unwanted baggage in your life and prevent you from manifesting goals. Take the lead in acknowledging what generates stress and enjoy the healthy attitude that follows. Pluto's retrograde cycle runs from April 29 to October 8. All four eclipses in 2022 fall in two fixed signs, Taurus and Scorpio. Two are solar and two are lunar. The closer they are to a planet in your chart, the greater the impact.

2022 SUN SIGN BOOK

Forecasts by
Alice DeVille

Aries

The Ram
March 20 to April 19

♈

Element: Fire

Quality: Cardinal

Polarity: Yang/masculine

Planetary Ruler: Mars

Meditation: I build on my strengths

Gemstone: Diamond

Power Stones: Bloodstone, carnelian, ruby

Key Phrase: I am

Glyph: Ram's head

Anatomy: Head, face, throat

Colors: Red, white

Animal: Ram

Myths/Legends: Artemis, Jason and the Golden Fleece

House: First

Opposite Sign: Libra

Flower: Geranium

Keyword: Initiative

The Aries Personality

Strengths, Talents, and the Creative Spark

Giving others a chance to see the way your personality unfolds is a vital part of your individuality. After all, Mars is the ruler of your sign and you take leadership and decision-making seriously. You love being in charge. Planets that appear in the first house of your birth chart accentuate the Aries traits describing your approach to life and your identity, which you are proud to demonstrate to those who are in your circle. The more planets that reside in your first house, the greater the tendency toward self-promotion. If someone says, "Show me what you've got," you'll give them the best expression of your gifts and more. This momentum may include taking the wheel, as driving and owning sports cars agrees with your style. Being action-oriented is a trait you're proud of and one you are likely to pass on to your children with shining examples.

Your rapidly firing mind is a lot like your walk—energetic, engaging, and eager to arrive at your destination. Whether you're seeking a quick solution to a problem that creeps up on you or working out a plan for a long-term project that needs major tweaking, your optimism elevates the spirit of the undertaking. Teams that work with you appreciate your no-nonsense approach to getting to the core of the plan and delegating assignments that mesh with the mission. As a self-proclaimed idea person, you want to identify strategies and the meat of the work but prefer to have others do the grunt work, like crunching numbers, keeping the timeline, and doing the research. Once you near the finish line, you may get bored. Celebrating success for a job well done is part of your style that allows you to share the limelight with others as you make the transition to a welcome new opportunity.

Intimacy and Personal Relationships

Life is an adventure for you since you are not the type of person to settle into a routine that repeats the same cycle every week. Your socializing choices may include attending ball games, concerts, drag races, golf matches, parties, and weddings. You place considerable emphasis on having fun. With every attraction you might find in an amusement park, you'll want to give your date, family member, or friend the ultimate enjoyable experience. Intimate partners and friends are likely to include members of the fire signs (Aries, Leo, Sagittarius) and air signs

(Gemini, Libra, Aquarius). Rub elbows with them and you could find the perfect romantic partner who treasures your warmth and passion.

You'll get into a few shouting matches with fire sign partners, yet you'll kiss and make up quickly and look for ways to celebrate the finer points of your relationship. If your partner is an air sign, you are likely to spend considerable time debating differing points of view. When the object of your affection becomes a permanent fixture in your life, you hold on tight and shower this special treasure with abundant affection and loyalty. If you detect signs of waning interest from a partner or a wandering eye, you're apt to pull away and withdraw from further intimacy. Finding your soulmate is a major quest that is a special part of your emotional well-being.

Values and Resources

A positive self-image means the world to you. No one but you can own or protect your turf more effectively. A fearless player, you thrive on self-sufficiency, building a world where you drive the engine. As an affirmed risk-taker, you don't sit around wringing your hands and worrying about fatal mistakes when you make a decision. With your impulsive nature, you often have to go back and correct a few oversights after leaving room for creative error. You're known for grabbing the lion's share of responsibility and show reluctance when it comes to asking for help. It all boils down to trust, and you believe you are the best one for the job—the one with the plan and the answers. You are fussy about assigning team members. You admire those who say what's on their mind, argue, and then let it go. Once you let others into your inner circle, you share the limelight judiciously, making sure your colleagues possess the requisite commitment to demonstrate innovation and persistence. You enjoy the company and working style of individuals who express their unique individuality and shy away from hiring employees who are clones in need of constant direction.

Blind Spots and Blockages

Prestige, salary, and glory often drive your attraction when considering career choices. A major life lesson is sure to involve times when you make a spontaneous decision about accepting a new job before you have asked the right questions. Once you realize you've made a mistake, you often have to live with the consequences far longer than you prefer as you wrestle with critical responsibilities. If you're the one who makes staffing selections, you've been known to lament the impulsive hiring of someone who seemed to have an engaging personality and sense of humor, only to discover the constant joking was actually a foil for marginal accomplishment and low performance levels. Your temper can get in the way of productivity and amicable relationships. Add impatience to the mix and you come across as battle-ready when you're just blowing off steam. For some of you, a similar scenario unfolds in your personal life and leads to disillusionment if you haven't accurately assessed the strength of intimate relationships, leading to an inevitable breakup.

Goals and Success

Nothing pleases you more than a hot new project that puts you in charge of the details and gives you the autonomy to set the parameters, develop the main points, and showcase the accomplishments when the work is done. Your brand of enthusiasm makes you incredibly good at selling the big picture to the executive branch and engaging the interest of employees who are passionate about opportunities to gain experience and meet the targets of major timelines. You're good at figuring out who needs more formal or on-the-job training and generously approve educational opportunities that add to the skills diversity of the team. Your internal radar has you scanning the horizon for signs of challenges that stand in the way or hinder progress. That's when you identify contingencies and build a wish list that includes a cadre of experts to ensure an open path to developing strategies that net desired results. Trailblazing looks so good on you—enjoy the victory as you scope out the next major initiative.

Aries Keywords for 2022
Charisma, cheerfulness, confidence

The Year Ahead for Aries

As you charge into 2022 with optimistic expectations about your fate and fun this year, remember that the networks you have built are expanding to include more challenging opportunities to showcase your personality. The year starts out with Venus retrograde in your solar tenth house of career and authority, suggesting you examine workplace relationships and preferences carefully so you know what to expect after the planet goes direct on January 29. If there is any emotional baggage surrounding assignments, be sure to address it. On January 14,

Mercury makes its first retrograde motion of the year in Aquarius and your solar eleventh house. Be on the lookout for mix-ups surrounding meetings and appointments with friends, groups, and organizational events. Details are likely to change, and possibly leadership too on various levels. Uranus in Taurus has been retrograde since August 19, 2021, and turns direct in your solar second house of income and resources on January 18. This movement could bring the release of funds that have been held back, a promotion, financial changes, or a surprise windfall.

The warrior in many of you has surfaced over the last few years, possibly connected with the COVID-19 pandemic that spread to most parts of the world. With little known about how to combat the gravity of the coronavirus, you may have joined forces with initiatives led by the CDC Foundation and worldwide watchdog agencies. Perhaps you raised funds or led teams to supply personal protective equipment, medical supplies, and emergency staffing for healthcare workers. Be sure to embrace your power in 2022 and step into a world of exciting new opportunities.

Jupiter

For most of the year, with the exception of a retrograde and a sign-change period, Jupiter occupies your solar twelfth house in Pisces, until it moves into Aries and your solar first house on December 20 for a long tour of duty in 2023. Every member of your sign benefits from Jupiter's presence in the complex twelfth house as you contemplate future moves that are growing from ideas you have been entertaining for months. Dream big and watch them come true. In the intervening months while Jupiter is in Aries and your solar first house, Jupiter stimulates energetic periods of activity related to your goals and helps you attract powerful contacts offering support and interest in successful ventures—yours or stimulating collaborative efforts. Be sure to take full advantage of your most important networks to generate interest in your creative work. This transit may also amp up your social life and bring with it increased opportunities to eat rich foods, desserts, and too many party appetizers. Why not add a longer workout routine to combat any tendency to put on weight? On July 28 Jupiter will turn retrograde in your solar first house in Aries, moving back into Pisces and your solar twelfth house on October 28, until it goes direct on November 23 for the remainder of the year. Those of you born between March 20 and 30 will see the most action from Jupiter while it is in Aries and occupies your solar first house. You'll discover clues on how to expand important areas in your world, fulfill your dreams, and experience exciting adventures. While in Pisces, Jupiter creates opportunities to brainstorm and research innovative concepts and ideas behind the scenes that you'll execute in 2023. Savor the desired outcome and put those visions on your dream sheet.

Saturn

Saturn, the taskmaster planet, has been occupying your solar eleventh house since December 17, 2020, in Aquarius. These days, the demand for your presence is so high that you don't seem to have any downtime. While this is not usually a complaint from a highly energetic Aries, you could feel mentally taxed and short on patience. When transiting your solar eleventh house, Saturn could demand that you wear two hats, hold two or more jobs, or settle into a new position, the result of a well-deserved promotion. Additionally, your replacement will be relying on you heavily for training and orientation. Since Saturn entered Aquarius, you have seen increased activity with professional groups, organizational affiliations, and friendships. At times, interactions with authorities in charge have revealed the depth of ambitious goals intended to expand the influence of these groups. Meanwhile, ponder what role you would like to play in implementing new directions. Responsibility could escalate if you are asked to take the lead in one or more complex initiatives. Conversely, you could be having second thoughts about the resources affiliated with your job, noting any deficiency that may prevent you from achieving your career goals.

A Saturn transit through the eleventh house highlights where you could benefit from critical changes in your plans and why you think there are missing parts that could make your journey smoother. This house represents your hopes and dreams and the most important plans you have for your future. It deserves a critical look at details that contribute to desired outcomes. If your priorities line up with your goals, you'll have significant success via collaborative efforts while building rapport with individuals and groups. Saturn's retrograde period during 2022 occurs from June 4 through October 23. During this period, avoid making purchases of big-ticket items like vehicles, homes, pricey jewelry, and other luxury items unless you ask your astrologer to thoroughly check your natal chart. Seek loans and settle mortgages on days that work best for prevailing conditions in your chart. Clear insight leads you to your dreams!

Uranus

What's it like in your solar second house of developmental opportunities, financial outlook, income, resources, and values since the planet of chaos first showed its face here in May 2018, giving you a taste for what a seven-year passage through Taurus might bring? In 2022 Uranus turns direct here in your solar second house on January 18, making it possible to implement financial changes, discard accumulating material goods that have outlived utility, and eliminate unsavory practices that brought upheavals to your work environment. If you have planets in this house, you no doubt have had some chaos and a shock or two that rocked your world. Some Aries may have been fired from a job or placed on a furlough, suspending the fluidity of a steady paycheck. Others may have reaped the benefits of demonstrating excellent performance practices in the form of a promotion, raise, or generous bonus. If you lost a job connected with the upheavals of the COVID-19 pandemic, you may have changed careers after taking qualifying coursework online and getting certified in a new field. Many a charismatic Aries started a new business and welcomed the challenge of a refreshing change of pace. Those of you born between April 1 and 9 experience the greatest activity this year from Uranus in Taurus and your solar second house. The unpredictable planet will move into retrograde motion on August 24 and go direct on January 22, 2023. Enjoy innovative interludes.

Neptune

As a watery, slow-moving planet, Neptune advances only four to five degrees a year and has occupied your solar twelfth house since April 2011. This location represents themes that include atonement, grief, self-imposed confinement, or recovery after medical setbacks. You may get heavily involved in charitable work or visit hospitals to see relatives and friends or because you are undergoing tests or treatments. With Jupiter in Pisces also in your solar twelfth house, you are reminded to take care of yourself and not let overwork prevent you from scheduling critical health exams. A fitness routine scores big points in giving you the energy you need to cope with your hectic schedule. Some of you may organize benefits to help those who are struggling to survive the aftermath of recent economic and health upheavals. COVID-19 hit hard and had an impact on so many. Comfort those who suffered losses. With Neptune in this private and even secretive house, you could be considering a career move and take a sabbatical so you can study in privacy to obtain qualifications for a new job. Bosses of some Aries could confide details of upcoming changes, including reorganizations or reengineering the job structures. You could be asked to do some key work on the project and work from home to make sure no leaks of important details occur prematurely. With Neptune active in your solar twelfth house, look for intuitive insight if you are searching for a new set of wheels. A deal could come your way out of the blue via a mysterious messenger, and your quick mind will take the hint and act on it. Those of you born between April 10 and 15 will experience the most Neptunian action during 2022. The planet of illusion will be retrograde from June 28 to December 3.

Pluto

You are not a sign known for having copious amounts of patience. With Pluto firmly planted in your solar tenth house of career, ambition, people in high places, recognition, and the status quo since January 2008, you are ready to say goodbye to the planet of slow but total transformation. You survived a barrage of transiting planets and eclipses in this house in recent years that pummeled your nerves and threw your comfort zone into overdrive. The last of the outer planets is Pluto, still creating blocks to productivity and success for late-born Aries (April 14-19) this year as it moves along on its journey through Capricorn. Those of you born on these dates are most affected by the transit. As the finish line approaches in late March of 2023, when Pluto gets its feet wet in Aquarius, you will experience the full effect of goal attainment and freedom. In 2022, certain Aries may get an early start on a bailout via a decision for retirement or accepting a battery-charging new job. Only if you've learned to demonstrate self-confidence, eliminate baggage that has kept you stuck in non-palatable circumstances, or dropped any lingering fear patterns will you be ready to embrace a solid, much deserved change.

How Will This Year's Eclipses Affect You?

In 2022 a total of four eclipses occur: two solar (New Moon) and two lunar (Full Moon) eclipses, which create intense periods that start to manifest a few months before their actual occurrence. All four of them occur in your chart's solar money houses. Eclipses unfold in cycles involving all twelve signs of the zodiac and usually occur in pairs about two weeks apart. Never fear eclipses—think of them as opportunities that allow you to release old and outworn patterns. Sometimes they stimulate unexpected surprises and windfalls. The closer an eclipse is to a planet or point in your chart, the greater the importance of it in your life. Those of you born with a planet at the same degree as an eclipse are likely to see a high level of activity in the house where the eclipse occurs.

The first Solar Eclipse of 2022 occurs on April 30 in Taurus and your solar second house of assets, earnings, personal development, money you receive, and valued resources. This eclipse could be an eye-opener since it shares space with transiting Uranus in Taurus and could affect financial holdings, planned purchases, retirement accounts, and anticipated raises. Unanticipated offers or wins may also occur to sweeten your outlook on security.

On May 16, 2022, the first Lunar Eclipse of the year takes place in Scorpio and your solar eighth house of joint funds, debts, investments, estates, wills, sex, birth, death, and transformation. This eclipse brings opportunities to review your debt load and make plans with your partner to pay it down and develop a viable savings plan that meets your mutual goals. Some of you may take on a second job or consider supplemental work to accelerate your plans to reduce what you owe. A partner may be the recipient of a raise that helps meet your needs.

The second Solar Eclipse of 2022 takes place on October 25 in Scorpio and your solar eighth house of joint savings and income, debt, karmic conditions, psychological matters, mental depth, and executing duties tied to other people's money. Matters that were percolating in May could come to a head and require your attention or a joint decision to resolve them. You may be paying off a mortgage or settling an estate, receiving a generous dividend from an investment, or opening a bank account or college fund for an infant. A new income stream is possible for you or a partner that brings a welcome financial boost.

The year's final eclipse is a Lunar Eclipse on November 8 in Taurus and your solar second house of money, resources, how you spend your money, and what you value. Even though you may be wary of the presence of Uranus in Taurus in this house, you could be feeling very relieved after paying down a chunk of debt during the year. Since Uranus is conjunct this eclipse degree, you are wise to be on the lookout for sudden repairs to your home, vehicle, or electronic equipment or to unanticipated shake-ups in your employment zone. Contractors could be vulnerable to clauses in contracts that affect funding issues, so double-check wording. Maintain cheerfulness as you navigate new directions and celebrate the successes you earn along the way.

Aries | January

Overall Theme

Entertain friends and family early in the month and savor the delightful rapport you share. Next take a critical look at your career and work world when you return from the holiday celebrations. Spread cheer and learn all you can about promotion opportunities that are about to emerge.

Relationships

Show gratitude for meaningful friendships and cherish the camaraderie you have with trusted confidants. Enjoy winter getaways with close friends or family. New people show up in your life through network connections. You and your partner show practical mental attunement and communicate harmoniously on the 24th. What a good time to review your budget and set 2022 financial goals.

Success and Money

Make sure you sign contracts or shop for appliances at the winter sales before Mercury goes retrograde on the 14th. Meetings start on a serious note and get the ball rolling with unified enthusiasm for emerging goals. Uranus goes direct on the 18th and could mean a release of anticipated funds or a notice that a loan you applied for went through or your quoted mortgage interest rate dropped.

Pitfalls and Potential Problems

Avoid peevish contacts and arguments that lead to confusion on the 11th. Intensity prevails at home on the Full Moon of January 17. Do whatever you can to get to the bottom of a stubborn streak that threatens to disrupt the prevailing peace. Children may clash with your preferences on the 19th.

Rewarding Days

3, 4, 18, 24

Challenging Days

11, 17, 19, 26

Aries | February

Overall Theme

Maybe you've been thinking the world needs more love. Check out some of the days this month that speak volumes about the state of your love life, and share your feelings with loved ones. Then keep your eyes open for challenges that lead you to help those less fortunate. You'll be touched by what you learn about others and how simple acts of kindness make a difference in a person's life.

Relationships

All the love planets line up favorably on the 8th and the 12th. Exude your famous charisma and toast your significant other as you pay tribute and celebrate your personal milestones. The Moon in Cancer on Valentine's Day is perfect for an intimate party at home centered around sharing a favorite dish and a decadent dessert.

Success and Money

Mercury goes direct on the 3rd and brings stability to financial undertakings that have been on hold since mid-January. Take a new look at planned expenses in case you want to juggle priorities. Your bargaining power increases on the 8th and puts you in a favorable position for getting a good deal on furniture, jewelry, and vehicles.

Pitfalls and Potential Problems

Don't get yourself into a position where you wallow in regret over working too much, feeling guilty about shortchanging the time you spend with your children. Admit that you could use more sleep, and be more vigilant about taking care of your health. Avoid arguments on the 6th and 13th.

Rewarding Days

4, 8, 12, 27

Challenging Days

1, 6, 13, 25

Aries | March

Overall Theme

The New Moon on the 2nd in Pisces and your solar twelfth house creates a private think tank for you to mull over the dominant Aquarius planets that pop up in your solar eleventh house all month. The emphasis is on analysis of emerging issues, smooth communication with professional associates, and goal alignment to reach an agreement. Compliment team players on the quality of their work.

Relationships

Romance is in the air. A friendship with a colleague could take a romantic turn when Venus and Mars travel together in Aquarius from March 7 through the end of the month. The 19th promises to be the perfect date night, giving you a chance to talk the night away and cuddle as you marvel over your newfound closeness.

Success and Money

Performance discussions with authority figures give you a chance to state your preferences regarding the location of your work environment. Speak up and show your boss that you are amenable to telecommuting or accepting a detail to learn new facets of your work. Accomplishments bring benefits, applause, and respect.

Pitfalls and Potential Problems

Hide your credit cards on the 7th, when challenging aspects could lead to overspending. Emotional drama on the 12th could lead to a tension-filled weekend that stifles open communication. The Full Moon on the 18th brings out opposition opinions aggravated by confusing information that has not been properly vetted. Table decisions until the following week.

Rewarding Days

2, 5, 19, 30

Challenging Days

7, 12, 18, 25

Aries | April

Overall Theme
Relationships seem to dominate the landscape this month. You'll be hearing from siblings, cousins, and neighbors who are excited about getting together and extending invitations for a reunion or party. Expect more contact than usual via calls, text messages, e-mail, and social media.

Relationships
Lock in the 9th for family gatherings. Enjoy the rapport and do some exploring to find out what types of vacations appeal to loved ones this year, especially after the prolonged period of social distancing and virtual studies that tried your patience. Pursue fun and relationship building as you share favorite entertainment venues. Check in on a cousin who may need your help.

Success and Money
The first Solar Eclipse of 2022 occurs on the 30th in your solar second house of income and assets. Meet with bankers, mortgage brokers, and realtors right after that day to explore deals and learn about the financial advantages these professionals offer and the estimated timing of completed transactions.

Pitfalls and Potential Problems
Avoid arguments on the 12th with children who may be annoyed over some type of restriction you placed on them for staying out too late or not doing chores. Don't let them pit parent against parent in the hope of getting you to cave and restoring their privileges prematurely. A night out could get unnecessarily expensive on the 15th if you don't know what you are getting into when trying a new restaurant or entertainment venue.

Rewarding Days
6, 9, 27, 30

Challenging Days
4, 12, 15, 22

Aries | May

Overall Theme

Although the month starts off with several planets in dreamy, romantic Pisces and your solar twelfth house, playtime and bonding work out best during the first week of May. Venus moves into Aries by the 3rd, and later in the month, so does Mars, giving you plenty of energy and passion for your love life and for the work demands that pull you in multiple directions.

Relationships

Honor your mom on Mother's Day, May 8, and show your nurturing side to family and dear friends on the 6th. A family dinner is a big hit with invited guests when you personalize details and adorn the table with festive china, flowers, and favors. A serious talk gets off on the wrong foot when Mercury goes retrograde on May 10 in your solar third house of communication if you insist on that date for a showdown.

Success and Money

Look for announcements that favor your role in the workplace. A new assignment is in the works. Details surface in the next month or two. You learn about financial increases in your retirement investments this month and use a much deserved raise to add a higher percentage to your account.

Pitfalls and Potential Problems

Avoid harsh words with someone at home base who is feeling ultra-sensitive on the 7th. Conditions remain sensitive for about a week, especially if your spouse is involved. Don't launch a major initiative or schedule a critical work meeting on the 19th, when key players are absent or ill.

Rewarding Days

3, 11, 16, 30

Challenging Days

7, 13, 19, 27

Aries | June

Overall Theme
The spotlight this month is on education, communication, and local travel. A child's accomplishments give you something to smile about as the school year draws to a close. Stay flexible to accommodate sudden twists and turns as Mercury stations to move direct in Taurus on the 3rd and Saturn goes retrograde in Aquarius on the 4th. Each Mercury retrograde occurs in air signs this year.

Relationships
With Venus in Taurus for most of the month, you and your significant other touch each other's heart and soul emotionally and sensually. Mars in your sign of Aries adds passion and close encounters to the mix. Siblings contact you and share family news. Make plans for a summer get-together. Let cheerfulness be a binding quality in getting family together.

Success and Money
Work assignments put the attention on stellar teamwork with colleagues and collaborators. The quality of the work gives everyone a boost in morale. The effort to accelerate meeting timeline goals could lead to a shared bonus or raise. A negotiated contract spells out favorable terms and a winning solution for outmoded practices.

Pitfalls and Potential Problems
Tension and arguments prevail on the home front, especially between June 2 and 9. You could be called out for keeping secrets or holding out on plan details. Disagreements over money priorities get solved only after parties listen to both sides of the issue. Vast differences of opinion in a group endeavor surface on the 18th and leave meeting participants stymied over solutions.

Rewarding Days
4, 12, 22, 27

Challenging Days
2, 9, 18, 19

Aries | July

Overall Theme

Jupiter in Aries shines on travelers this month. Is there a vacation in your future? What could possibly be more patriotic than celebrating the 4th of July with your family? Enjoy the celebrations and the fireworks. Then extend the playtime by another week or two to bask in the sun and salty air at the beach.

Relationships

Children and their preferences for recreation and favorite amusements dominate the first ten days of July. Relatives and contacts at a distance schedule bonding time and reunions around the 11th. Friends extend invitations for meals at mid-month and put out feelers for hosting larger get-togethers based on availability.

Success and Money

Early discounts on the price of a vehicle may attract your attention. Follow up on a random contact to maximize purchasing power. You could be in the right place at the right time and feel your confidence soar when the ideal auto, product, or cherished luxury item occupies the limelight and tempts you to buy. Go with your gut.

Pitfalls and Potential Problems

Comments could be misinterpreted on the 13th, leading to workplace friction that may fester until someone realizes the gravity of the mistake. Jupiter turns retrograde on July 28 on the same day of the New Moon in Leo. Travel plans are more successful earlier in the month, even though the aspects work favorably for those born in the early degrees of Aries.

Rewarding Days

2, 11, 16, 22

Challenging Days

1, 7, 13, 25

Aries | August

Overall Theme
A couple gallons of paint go a long way toward adding sparkle to a room in your home when you're ready to redecorate. Then take a breather and spend an adventurous week in the wilderness, in the mountains, or on a ranch beginning on the 8th. Listen to your inner voice and invite a love interest to join you.

Relationships
You value connections more than ever this month due to satisfying interactions with the coworkers who compliment your style and show appreciation for your original ideas. Relatives at a distance, including in-laws, demonstrate love and affection for the caring way you welcome them into your life and include them in your plans.

Success and Money
Outstanding completion of projects with workmates gains the attention of management. Cost savings and efficiency measures are impressive. When reports of accomplishments are made available, recommendations are likely to include the promise of a salary increase for contributors. Single Aries could meet a new romantic interest connected to professional dealings during the first few days of the month.

Pitfalls and Potential Problems
Be wary of challenging your significant other or intimidating business partners with confrontational words when lunar aspects create tension with Mars and Uranus. Steer clear of showdowns on the 11th, when group members engage in heated discussions at meetings. Apply safety precautions while traveling when Uranus goes retrograde in Taurus on the 24th.

Rewarding Days
2, 8, 15, 24

Challenging Days
4, 11, 19, 29

Aries | September

Overall Theme

A mix of social gatherings dominates the landscape this month, including parties, reunions, vacations, and visits with relatives and friends. As long as you return before the Pisces Full Moon occurs on the 10th and Mercury in Libra goes retrograde on the 9th, it's a go for long-distance or foreign travel over the first eight days of September.

Relationships

Rapport with children and their teachers, professors, and academic faculty gets the school year off to a positive, inspiring start. By seeking a second opinion from a new medical care practitioner, you notice immediate improvement in the treatment of a long-term ailment. You bond romantically and spiritually with your significant other around the New Moon on the 25th.

Success and Money

Successful networking opens doors to new entrepreneurial ventures. Funding for projects comes from new sources around the 8th. You may be collaborating with financial planners and financial analysts to develop a new budget and assess the need to hire more employees to meet staffing goals.

Pitfalls and Potential Problems

If you're planning to take a few days off to extend the long holiday weekend, your boss may call you back on the 6th to help resolve a management problem that cancels your plans. You could be a bit edgy on the 12th and start the workweek off with petty complaints and nitpicking. Watch what you say at meetings and how you deliver a message to workmates.

Rewarding Days

3, 8, 20, 25

Challenging Days

6, 10, 12, 23

Aries | October

Overall Theme

Educational matters are on the table this month with Mars in the intellectual sign of Gemini. Self-development via the perfect online course leads to new career opportunities to build credentials in your chosen field. Hire a tutor to give a child extra help with complex subjects and notice the surge in enthusiasm for learning.

Relationships

Spend quality time with your love partner and consider a date night on the 15th to stir the passion you feel and cherish your loved one's company. Single Aries may be suddenly attracted to someone you encounter at the workplace. Keep your emotions in check and think about the consequences if you decide to pursue this individual.

Success and Money

Performance incentives show up in your paycheck, giving you a reason to appreciate steady employment and the commitment you have to showcasing your talent. Use extra cash that comes your way near the Solar Eclipse on October 25 to pay down debt. You may have some of it left to put aside for holiday spending or to add to your savings fund.

Pitfalls and Potential Problems

Planetary shifts occur all month. Mercury goes direct in Virgo on the 2nd, followed by Pluto in Capricorn on the 8th and Saturn in Aquarius on the 23rd. Avoid travel or making sudden decisions on these dates. Mars turns retrograde in Gemini on the 30th in your solar third house and could upset the start date for travel, deliveries, and contracts.

Rewarding Days

4, 15, 20, 25

Challenging Days

1, 3, 9, 16

Aries | November

Overall Theme

With a Lunar Eclipse in Taurus on November 8 in your solar second house of earnings, you'll be tempted to open your wallet to get an early start on buying holiday gifts and purchasing decorations for your home. Careful planning and strategic shopping trips help you meet goals. Put text alerts on your phone to monitor sales.

Relationships

Several days this month favor gatherings with family and friends. The 14th is perfect for scheduling a pre-holiday game night for your family with food and fun on the menu. Depart for a trip home for Thanksgiving on November 20, when cordial vibes prevail and you beat the holiday rush. Expect lots of calls from loved ones who can't join you, especially on the 23rd and 24th.

Success and Money

Bargain hunting lets you satisfy the requests on the wish lists of favorite people. When shopping online, look for free delivery from reliable vendors and have the company send gifts directly to recipients' addresses. Jupiter goes direct on the 23rd, the day of the Sagittarius New Moon, and favors plans for holiday travel.

Pitfalls and Potential Problems

After assessing the debt load you discover on November 1 and the list of planned purchases for the coming months, wisely shop for sales and cut back on items that will put you over the top of your available budget. Solve a work environment problem on the 19th by scoping out the source of confusion and defusing temper flare-ups.

Rewarding Days

4, 14, 20, 23

Challenging Days

1, 8, 19, 25

Aries | December

Overall Theme

How delightful that your Sun is compatible with the Sun, Mercury, and Venus in Sagittarius as they travel playfully in early December to give your month a jovial boost. These orbs get support from compatible Saturn in Aquarius too, making you want to take a break from the grindstone and plan a rejuvenating getaway to a favorite destination.

Relationships

Connections with the executive team at your workplace blossom, netting you invitations to holiday parties and gatherings. Be sure to attend with a favorite partner. The Full Moon on the 7th in Gemini could bring phone calls and messages from siblings that have a serious health or financial undertone. The situation improves by the 9th.

Success and Money

Neptune in Pisces goes direct in your solar twelfth house on the 3rd and clears up ambiguity over pending financial matters that could not be completed. Interest rates are more favorable than you anticipated. You can move ahead with plans that are on your bucket list, too. Schedule personal medical exams between the 9th and 15th.

Pitfalls and Potential Problems

Health matters come to a head for a relative on the 16th, leading to an important discussion with medical professionals. This date is also one you should avoid when scheduling personal medical procedures. Moodiness prevails on the 23rd if last-minute work requests interfere with scheduled time off for the holidays.

Rewarding Days

4, 9, 25, 30

Challenging Days

2, 7, 16, 23

Aries Action Table

These dates reflect the best—but not the only—times for success and ease in these activities, according to your Sun sign.

	JAN	FEB	MAR	APR	MAY	JUN	JUL	AUG	SEP	OCT	NOV	DEC
Move	24					4			3			
Romance		12	19	27				24		15		4
Seek counseling/ coaching			30				11		25		20	
Ask for a raise	18				3			15			14	
Vacation				6			2			20		9
Get a loan		8			30	12						

Taurus

**The Bull
April 19 to May 20**

♉

Element: Earth

Quality: Fixed

Polarity: Yin/feminine

Planetary Ruler: Venus

Meditation: I trust myself
and others

Gemstone: Emerald

Power Stones: Diamond, blue
lace agate, rose quartz

Key Phrase: I have

Glyph: Bull's head

Anatomy: Throat, neck

Color: Green

Animal: Cattle

Myths/Legends: Isis and Osiris,
Ceridwen, Bull of Minos

House: Second

Opposite Sign: Scorpio

Flower: Violet

Keyword: Conservation

The Taurus Personality

Strengths, Talents, and the Creative Spark

Your sign has major concerns over what you receive, value, or seek in life, three concepts that are strongly affiliated with your natural habitat, the second house of the zodiac. Reliability is an asset that draws employers to you to handle the details of large projects because you never lose sight of the big picture. You're enthusiastic about earning every perk that brings you satisfaction and a comfortable life. Few can match your undaunted display of determination when you're given a task. No one stands a chance to divert you from your chosen path once you have decided on your life work. The options are many, such as the world of banking, financial management, real estate, sales, and creative expression in diverse forms. When you make a promise to a loved one or a boss, you do all that you can to keep it, as your conscience drives your dedication and hard work.

Rulership of your sign comes under Venus, the love goddess of balance, beauty, and harmony. You like to work with your hands, and many of you are adept at baking, hairdressing, healing modalities, pottery, and sewing. Not surprisingly, you are drawn to careers that allow you to express your artistic talent (painting, sculpture, tile work, etc.), design, decorating, floral arrangement, gardening, and landscaping. Another of your gifts is your beautiful voice, which you express via public speaking, lecturing, teaching, and singing. You have a gifted ear for appreciating melodious notes. Musical instruments are a draw. Many a Taurus is skilled at playing one or more of them, often making a career of teaching students how to play instruments such as the piano and organ. Even the Taurus who prefers to get a musical fix at a concert rather than taking music lessons will find a home for a grand piano in their living space. It makes a great statement for a status-conscious Taurus.

Intimacy and Personal Relationships

Since you take love seriously, the department of love and devotion holds a special place in your heart. You don't give your heart away without putting out feelers to make sure the one who attracts you is capable of staying the course and demonstrating mutual love and affection. You've been burned once or twice and learned the painful lesson that the outer package is not always accurate. You can be tenacious, possessive, and patient, sometimes to a fault. When you don't recognize the signals that a romance is not working, you often stay too long, hoping it can be healed. Ditto for friendships that have lost their luster. Now you have to learn to trust and build confidence in seeking a soulmate while you study everything about a prospective partner to make sure they have the total package. Otherwise they won't know what to do with a sensual, tactile, and passion-driven Taurus who believes in romance, wining and dining, and sharing an endless supply of love. Wait until they see how much you enjoy moonlight, candles in the dark, the smell of exotic flowers, sexy perfume, and tender cuddling. You seldom get tired of demonstrating your devotion and loyalty to your significant other or to cherished friends. Look for love among the reliable earth signs Virgo and Capricorn or from nurturing Cancer or adoring Pisces. Enjoy the possibilities.

Values and Resources

It has been said that your lists have lists, and you use them routinely to check the boxes displaying tasks and accomplishments. You value routines and enjoy the privacy of working alone most of the time even though you are a supportive team player. Opportunities to close the door and burn the midnight oil appeal to you—the quiet feeds your fertile brain and fortifies your energy to produce your desired output. Research is always part of your analytical expertise, allowing you to put your heart and soul into gathering the important facts and comparing probable outcomes. Organization plays a big role in your operating style, beginning with finances, storage, and retrieval of clothing, groceries, household goods, materials, and important documents. That preference for precise care follows you into your work world, where you put aside time to get everything you need in its proper place, creating a safety valve to ensure efficiency in future undertakings. Self-development is high on your list of priorities, whether it comes from a degreed program, certification, on-the-job training, workshops, or online venues. You believe that every day yields a teachable moment and take pride in recognizing the spark when it occurs. Lingering debt makes you feel unsettled. You wisely prefer to repay college tuition loans quickly.

Blind Spots and Blockages

As task-oriented and conscientious as you are, you sometimes show a stubborn streak that prevents you from listening to the other side of the argument or from hearing feedback from key players in your life, including bosses, teammates, and your significant other. Predictability is important to you; change is not a preference in your lifestyle. At times you don't recognize that your inflexibility causes you to sacrifice the quality time you need to create life balance. Those of you who are die-hard workaholics learn lessons through failed relationships when you relentlessly pursue the acquisition of money over leisure time with partners and family. With Uranus in Taurus crashing through your sign this year and causing upsets, you have to be careful not to ignore your feelings that could reflect low self-esteem or depression. Avoid anger build-up and take a day off for a mental health break when problems seem to mount. You won't be letting anybody down by temporarily withdrawing from the rat race. Instead you'll recharge your stamina and refresh your objective problem-solving skills.

Goals and Success

The words "I'm no quitter" were probably coined by a Taurus. You attribute your success to studying every angle of your work and perfecting your product so it is worthy of approval and praise. Compensation is one of your drivers, because you like to surround yourself with comfort and fine-quality goods and want to be able to afford them. You work hard for and expect a generous salary and raises in return for your precise work and devotion to your job. Whatever effort it takes to buy the home of your dreams, you'll make that goal a priority and will take great pride in furnishing it with elegant furniture and accessories. Another personal mantra is "slow and steady wins the race," which to you means security and not having to rush through the familiar routines you prefer, thus allowing time for quality control. You pace yourself in your quest to acquire the finer things in life and won't rush out to purchase things that merely fill a space and give you little satisfaction. That's why you will save up for that piece of fine art and picture the wall in your home that it will someday adorn and draw compliments for your fine taste.

Taurus Keywords for 2022
Temperance, tenacity, tenderness

The Year Ahead for Taurus

Nothing going on in the universe is as powerful as the thunderbolt planet, Uranus, making a conjunction to your Sun this year in Taurus and giving your personal world a wake-up call. Use this time to examine situations that have you in a rut and could benefit from a little chaos to get you to move forward and away from old patterns. Uranus starts 2022 in retrograde motion in your solar first house and moves direct on January 18, giving you a chance to exercise your options for using new skills and signature tools you have at your disposal to create a brighter, more spontaneous future as you meet your cherished goals. At the start of the new year, love planet Venus is retrograde in Capricorn in your solar ninth house of travel, people at a distance, education, spirituality, and publishing. Residual circumstances over the last couple of years may have forced you to separate from individuals and conditions that were a vital part of your life. When Venus resumes direct motion on January 29, you may be making decisions regarding a love interest or career move that could change the direction of your life. On January 14, Mercury makes its first retrograde motion of the year in Aquarius in your solar tenth house of authority, ambition, career, and status quo. Plans that were heading in a certain direction may be put on hold due to a change in management, organizational priorities, or funding.

Saturn in Aquarius occupies your solar tenth house of achievements and restrictions again this year. Over the past two years, your work schedule and mission may have undergone temporary changes to accommodate concerns about the worldwide COVID-19 pandemic. Work as you know it may still be going through a new phase of retraining employees and adjusting the mission to accommodate safety concerns, emerging staffing needs, and the way individuals perform their work. Teammates may have suffered illness, loss of life, or financial hardships and need workable solutions. Perhaps you could play a role in showing sensitivity to those who are still recovering by initiating a program that offers emotional relief and ideas for restoring fiscal stability. Show your inner tenderness and compassion to those who desire a new lease on life.

Jupiter

This year Jupiter makes a home in Pisces and occupies your solar eleventh house of goals, wishes, dreams, associations, friends, groups, your employer's assets, and humanitarian endeavors. With the exception of both a retrograde and a sign-change period, Jupiter occupies this space until December 20, when it moves into Aries for a challenging assignment in 2023. You'll find out this year how much "people need people" when you contact your networks and widen your circle through clubs, neighborhood associations, professional memberships, peer groups, and volunteer initiatives engaged in delivering services to food banks, teachers' organizations, schools, people without housing, and seniors. Invitations from diverse sources will be plentiful. You'll have to decide how many you can accommodate due to your highly demanding work schedule. On July 28, Jupiter will turn retrograde in Aries and your solar twelfth house, moving back into Pisces in your solar eleventh house on October 28 before it goes direct again on November 23 through the end of 2022. Expand your goals and work on those you want to achieve this year. Jupiter loves Pisces, its traditional ruler, and magic seems to happen when it occupies this sign. Apply for scholarships and grant money or accept available funds from your employer if a higher education dream interests you and enables you to enroll in courses. Note that expansive Jupiter forms a conjunction with Neptune in Pisces in April that favors the activities of individuals born the first few days of Taurus.

Saturn

What a year to have the planet of restriction hanging out in Aquarius and your solar tenth house of career, ambition, authority figures, government, maturity, and standards of excellence, where it has been since December 2020. You're still working on post-pandemic recovery and sorting through newly enacted rules and regulations designed to ensure workplace safety and implement changing work practices that more closely reflect current conditions for conducting business. You'll be sorting through the consequences and limitations of the shifts, including delays, as you work around the red tape in an attempt to reframe goals and adapt to emerging views. One of your challenges will be that you are working too much, which could lower your vitality. Since you tend to be a workaholic when extremely stressful conditions prevail, you'll need to make adjustments to stay healthy. You're determined to showcase your tenacity and show that taskmaster Saturn what makes you tick. Protect your immune system by getting more sleep and eating well or you won't be able to maintain the high level of energy you desire. Saturn's retrograde period occurs from June 4 through October 23. Venus and Mars in Aquarius line up here for most of March and part of April, making for a lively interplay in your area of employment and status in life. Could there be raises, rewards, and romance in the mix? Saturn usually brings you what you deserve when it makes contact with your Sun.

Uranus

How would you describe the feeling you have after nearly four years of Uranus in Taurus moving through your solar first house of action, assertiveness, enterprise, individuality, and passion? Would you say the journey has been easy-peasy, queasy, or breezy so far? With two eclipses also landing in this house in 2022, be prepared for a jolt or two. The seven-year cycle of this transit is approaching the halfway mark. Uranus wants credit for getting the job done of shaking up the status quo, deviating from routine patterns, bringing new people or unanticipated visitors into your life, and making sure you witness your share of bizarre behavior and sudden blow-ups. Uranus moving through your solar first house can be very tough on partners who don't know what to make of your sudden mood shifts, change in outlook, and attitude toward risk-taking, which is far from the predictable Taurus personality they have come to depend on and love. Taurus folks born between May 1 and 10 feel the most noticeable pressure from Uranus this year. The planet of chaos will move into retrograde motion on August 24 and go direct on January 22, 2023.

Neptune

Your driven Taurus personality needs a break from the 24/7 work patterns and finds a change of pace when Neptune comes calling. Have you noticed the calm that is nipping at your heels lately? The watery planet of compassion, psychological health, and secrets has occupied your solar eleventh house of associates, friendships, and goals since April 2011. Under the spell of this dreamy, psychic planet, you'll experience a greater degree of intuitive insight and may bond with members of metaphysical and spiritual groups where you feel at home in the arcane world of mystical themes. Through dedication and focused attention, you'll internalize so much of the psychic gift you have that you will understand that you "just know" what is going on before anyone confirms it. All you have to do is just sit back and wait for validation to amp up your confidence to use your talent freely and judiciously. If you are available, you might even meet a romantic partner through these connections as you exude tenderness and savor quiet moments. You'll enjoy sharing confidences, discoveries, and mystical dreams that are likely to show up with greater frequency, especially while transiting Jupiter in Pisces occupies this house. The eleventh house also represents humanitarian initiatives that attract you to projects that champion the underdog, support voting rights, supply goods to food banks, and collect clothing and household goods for those without a home. Since you care about the health and welfare of others, you may be active in volunteer services for hospitals and veterans groups, including teaching meditation, yoga, or reiki to individuals who benefit from alternative healing modalities. Neptune moves only four to five degrees each year. In 2022 it most affects those of you born between May 10 and 16. The retrograde period for Neptune will be from June 28 to December 3 this year.

Pluto

Pluto, the planet of deep transformation, has been firmly planted in Capricorn and your solar ninth house since late January 2008 and relates to advanced education, foreign countries and cultures, your higher mind, in-laws, philosophy, publishing, religion, relocation, and long-distance travel. Even if you don't experience blocks in each of these areas, people around you might be meeting challenges connected with these themes. You'll find that hidden elements come to light as the year unfolds. For example, in-laws can be having serious issues with their marriage and make you privy to their secret; you have writer's block and can't seem to get your manuscript ready for publication; buried stress is affecting your will and eroding your supply of temperance, causing you to overeat, satisfy your sweet tooth, and subsequently gain weight; a child may have fears about gaining admission to a preferred university; or you're worried that financial cutbacks at work may force you to relocate to an area that has little opportunity for career growth. You can expect change this year if your birthday falls between May 15 and 20, the dates most affected now by Pluto's ability to uncover hidden baggage and help you release what's in your subconscious mind that you no longer need to protect. Say goodbye to phobias and hello to new directions. In 2022 Pluto in Capricorn goes retrograde on April 29 and moves direct on October 8.

How Will This Year's Eclipses Affect You?

Your sign features prominently in the eclipses of 2022. A total of four eclipses occur: two solar (New Moon) and two lunar (Full Moon), which bring intense periods that start to manifest about two months before they actually occur. All four of them take place in two of your solar chart's angular houses, the first and seventh, putting the spotlight on action from you and from partnerships. Eclipses manifest in cycles involving all twelve signs of the zodiac and usually occur in pairs about two weeks apart. Never be afraid of eclipses—think of them as opportunities that allow you to face old, outworn patterns and release them. Eclipses may trigger unexpected revelations, surprises, and windfalls. The closer an eclipse is to a planet or point in your chart, the greater the importance it plays in your life. Those of you born with a planet at the same degree as an eclipse are likely to see a high level of activity in the house where the eclipse occurs.

The first Solar Eclipse of 2022 occurs on April 30 in Taurus and your solar first house of appearance, assertiveness, character, enterprise, image, individuality, personality, and self-development. The pressure is on you to keep your goals and promises on track, to deliver what you said you would accomplish on time, and to make any adjustments to your work and play habits that will contribute toward achieving life balance. If your physical appearance and health have been problematic, this eclipse will remind you to seek solutions and get counsel from medical specialists, dieticians, and behavioral consultants.

Two weeks later, the first Lunar Eclipse of the year occurs on May 16 in Scorpio and your solar seventh house of relationships that include partners, spouses, business collaborators, roommates, advisors, consultants, legal or medical professionals, open enemies, and the public. If you have planets located in this house, expect revelations of any problem areas with principal players to come to light. If connections are positive, you'll benefit from strengthening bonds and fulfilling goals. Should you be experiencing challenges, any rough spots will hit you head-on and call for discussion and possible solutions.

On October 25, the second Solar Eclipse of 2022 takes place in Scorpio and your solar seventh house of business and personal partners, spouses, collaborators, roommates, doctors, lawyers, therapists, advisors, consultants, enemies, and the public. When this eclipse hits after months of examining what you found regarding relationships back in May, you will know whether remedial action had the desired results or whether the relationships or affiliated issues need more attention.

The year's final eclipse is a Lunar Eclipse on November 8 in Taurus and your solar first house of action, assertiveness, passion, and self-interest. Hanging out close to this degree is transiting Uranus in Taurus, so if this eclipse falls opposite your birthday on May 6–8, stay safe, keep your emotions in check, expect some drama, and celebrate the feeling of liberation. Be sure to nurture your body, mind, and spirit.

Taurus | January

Overall Theme

Breathe and settle down. The year starts out with Uranus in Taurus going direct in your solar first house, giving you the go-ahead to proceed with long-distance matters that were put on hold last summer. Pace yourself in taking action if the situation involves a love interest, because Mercury is going to go retrograde on the 14th.

Relationships

People at a distance, especially women, are ready for a talk and a reunion. Encounters with work colleagues increase due to changing employment conditions and the need to reorganize staffing patterns that could be tied to better economic conditions. Love partners are in a bonding mood and show a romantic side around the time that Venus goes direct on the 29th.

Success and Money

Good news revolves around an influx of cash that promises solid employment and overdue raises as the economy shows solid signs of improvement after the suspended operations related to the COVID-19 pandemic. By the 24th, you'll be singing cheerful praises to the enthusiasm you encounter as a member of your company team.

Pitfalls and Potential Problems

A routine weekend happy hour could be a bust if the expected number of friends don't show up for the gathering on the 7th. Although you encounter an attractive offer to buy merchandise you're seeking on the 14th, just as Mercury goes retrograde, give yourself a few days to research product details. The 17th could find you emotionally drained from engaging in difficult discussions with needy people.

Rewarding Days

2, 5, 24, 27

Challenging Days

7, 10, 14, 17

Taurus | February

Overall Theme

The Aquarius New Moon on the 1st puts the spotlight on your career in your solar tenth house and indicates your boss is all business about pivoting to new revenue streams or seeking federal aid to get the momentum back on track. Expect to be in demand for your analytical and fiscal expertise. Recruit a talented team to help.

Relationships

Check on the health of a parent who is ailing on the 6th or grab some extra rest after an intense workweek leaves you exhausted. Celebrate Cupid's month by attending an early Valentine's Day party on the 4th with favorite friends. Entertain your children with a treat they'll enjoy on the 18th, and don't forget to save the 23rd for a romantic date with your partner.

Success and Money

Meeting new people through networking helps you identify potential collaborators and teammates. Be sure to pass on resumes and contact information to hiring authorities, especially after Mercury goes direct on the 3rd. A lottery scratcher purchase around the 18th brings unexpected cash, allowing you to treat family and friends to an elegant dinner.

Pitfalls and Potential Problems

Keep your wallet at home on the 11th, a day that could lead to impulse spending on something that is overpriced. Stressful encounters may come to a head at home base when the Full Moon in Leo on the 16th leaves an emotional footprint. Talk things out peacefully or you face more of the same on the 21st.

Rewarding Days

4, 6, 18, 23

Challenging Days

1, 11, 16, 21

Taurus | March

Overall Theme

Job demands put you in the spotlight when new directions lead to organizational change. Use tact and the power of persuasion to win over reluctant employees who are on the fence about staying. Security, something you fully understand, is at the heart of the reservations. Be sure to mention benefits and cost savings and highlight the value of esprit de corps.

Relationships

The relationship you have with yourself gets a boost of confidence in your employment arena from your management team and coworkers citing outstanding accomplishments. Friends want to celebrate with you and plan a special meal or invite you to a party on the 4th. You may surprise your sweetheart with a meaningful jewelry gift on the 9th.

Success and Money

Financial investments pay off and give you a good feeling when you look at your bank statements and dividends. Conditions are favorable for seeking a loan to refinance your mortgage or opt for a home equity loan to fund a remodeling project. Look for good deals on new windows.

Pitfalls and Potential Problems

On the 18th, challenging aspects to the Virgo Full Moon from Mercury, Jupiter, and Neptune curb your enthusiasm for taking a gamble on a proposal, making a quick trip to a casino or vacation destination, or going overboard to buy expensive gifts. A lingering sore spot could put a damper on a romantic interlude with your partner on the 22nd, when the Moon makes harsh aspects to love planets Venus and Mars.

Rewarding Days

1, 4, 9, 24

Challenging Days

6, 15, 18, 22

Taurus | April

Overall Theme

You experience the New Moon in your chart twice this month. When it happens on the 1st, the Moon is in Aries and your solar twelfth house and you feel a bit under the weather. By the time it appears in Taurus and your solar first house on the 30th, making a conjunction aspect with Uranus, you get a big boost of energy from the first Solar Eclipse of the year. Expect revelations and a livelier pace.

Relationships

Teachers and instructors play a greater role in your life now through learning opportunities you're pursuing. To obtain the desired credentials, you demonstrate commitment and determination to fulfill a cherished goal. Spend quality time with partners and friends who enjoy music and dance the night away, especially on the 13th or 18th.

Success and Money

After hearing rumors on the 7th of imminent job expansion, you listen for news of exciting opportunities to improve your cash flow through applying for a new job or pursuing a high-visibility work project. Tenacity pays off when you get the good news that you made the cut on the list of candidates.

Pitfalls and Potential Problems

Steer clear of testy conversations with relatives or neighbors on the 10th, when comments seem like weapons of mass destruction. Bow out, insist you are not familiar with the controversial theme, and refuse to weigh in on a verbal ambush. Stress is high when you uncover an accounting mistake on the 20th and need a couple of days to resolve the error.

Rewarding Days

1, 7, 18, 30

Challenging Days

10, 16, 20

Taurus | May

Overall Theme

Household projects that beautify your home highlight the primary activity this month. Get these major undertakings and disruptions out of the way so you can plan ahead for a much deserved summer vacation. Dramatic designs and color choices showcase the good taste you and your significant other share. Dress up your front door.

Relationships

Family members excitedly bond over ideas for maximizing space in your home through redecorating, making furniture selections, and adding complementary accessories. Children weigh in on their choices. Be sure to consider feng shui conventions. Around the time of the Lunar Eclipse on the 16th, you and your significant other grow closer and share fond memories of your early days as a couple.

Success and Money

Satisfaction comes from seeing your blueprints come to life, whether you are building a home or remodeling your kitchen. Begin your household projects by May 2 to make sure they are underway before Mercury turns retrograde on the 10th. Take delight in the perk your contractor offers to add value to the job.

Pitfalls and Potential Problems

Nobody saw it coming when a professional contact stretches the truth around the 4th or confuses issues by stating "facts" without providing sufficient research to back them up. Don't make a spending decision on the 18th, when project costs escalate considerably over original estimates. Shipping costs and foreign manufacturing firms could be blamed for construction delays.

Rewarding Days

2, 8, 16, 30

Challenging Days

4, 10, 18, 19

Taurus | June

Overall Theme

Venus stars in your sign this month, Taurus, prompting you to pay greater attention to the loves in your life. Call them, pamper them, and schedule a date. If you're available and looking for a sweetheart, the 16th is a good day to meet someone new, particularly if you are on vacation. June vibrates when Mercury goes direct on the 3rd and Saturn and Neptune station to move retrograde.

Relationships

Heartfelt talks lead to stability in intimate connections and close the gap on uncertainty that has lingered over recent unsettling comments. Through the 15th, children relish the extra attention you give them and savor the participation in playtime, fun, and games that include the whole family. Add a few surprises to the mix and you'll be the hero of the month.

Success and Money

The cost of travel has escalated, making you glad you put aside bonus money to fund satisfying getaway options. Be glad you have recently benefited from successful contracts that boosted your income while Mercury, Venus, and Uranus unite in your solar first house this month. Share opportunities for emerging projects with your networks at a business lunch around the 21st.

Pitfalls and Potential Problems

Avoid acquiring battle scars on the 4th, when Saturn turns retrograde in Aquarius and could lead to an intense verbal exchange. Neptune in Pisces clashes with the Moon in Gemini as it turns retrograde on the 28th, diminishing the value of a desired transaction and putting a damper on planned purchases.

Rewarding Days

3, 8, 16, 21

Challenging Days

6, 12, 23, 28

Taurus | July

Overall Theme

Get out the air mattresses—company is coming! The holiday celebrations take on new meaning this year when visitors join you at home base for special gatherings. Many of your favorite people show up a few days early to reminisce, eat delicious food, compete in pie-eating contests, attend ballgames, and watch the 4th of July parade.

Relationships

Relatives fill your home and backyard with laughter and good cheer after greeting guests with smothering rounds of hugs and kisses. Animated chatter fills the air as grandparents and cousins take turns sharing recent news, welcoming babies and new family members to the clan, and tasting a smorgasbord of delicious dishes. Bonding festivities take place between July 3 and 9, with room for a couple sight-seeing day trips.

Success and Money

Business partners or those responsible for your paycheck announce welcome pay increases, while those on commission learn details of new incentive splits after the 9th. Monday the 18th brings news of planned alliances, reorganizations, and awards ceremonies at scheduled business meetings. Certain groups are recruiting for help at benefits or for charity drives.

Pitfalls and Potential Problems

Too many last-minute demands on your time may surface on the 1st and could interfere with plans you're making for the holiday weekend. Negotiate for more realistic terms. Table legal discussions on the Full Moon on the 13th, when communication related to your pending issues hits a sour note. Early the following week looks much better.

Rewarding Days

3, 9, 18, 27

Challenging Days

1, 5, 13, 22

Taurus | August

Overall Theme

All systems are go for increasing activity in your social life, dating if you are single, and planning enjoyable outings with your partner and children. Short weekend vacations work well to treat the family to a change of scenery. The days between the 15th and the 20th may net the sweetest deals and maximize spending power with options that satisfy loved ones.

Relationships

Your significant other holds the cards and your attention when identifying the ideal spot to chill out, go sightseeing, take a cruise, or seek the perfect spot for a romantic escape. Consider booking an all-inclusive cruise that begins at the time of the New Moon on the 27th to whisk you away to an island paradise. Treat young children to amusement parks and older children to concerts.

Success and Money

A good part of the month revolves around paying tuition for children's education or for classes that you are taking to earn additional job credentials. Meet with a seasoned counselor to discuss the higher education options for one of your children or for you if you have not yet completed your own degree.

Pitfalls and Potential Problems

Face work challenges with an open mind on the 3rd, when clashes occur over two diverse strategies for completing a major milestone. Expect more testy discussions through the 7th, a day when it is better to listen than to argue. The Full Moon on the 11th exacerbates tension in your workplace for a few more days.

Rewarding Days

1, 15, 20, 27

Challenging Days

3, 7, 11, 23

Taurus | September

Overall Theme

Make your presence known in business and social circles this month while the Sun in Virgo forges compatible aspects to your solar first house. Networking has strong possibilities for locating competitive talent to staff emerging projects. Travel right after the holiday to make your case and excite potential candidates looking for new professional opportunities.

Relationships

Connecting with a budget officer is a priority to ensure that work initiatives are fully funded and satisfy stakeholders that plans are a go. In-laws schedule time for a visit and plan a few surprises to entertain you and the family. Open your heart to words of love and pursue romance the last week of the month.

Success and Money

You have much to contribute in terms of successful strategies for working remotely and collaborating with others to complete critical projects. Accept an invitation to share how-to steps with the team and show them how to get from point A to point B to meet important deadlines. Incorporate zoom meetings or video chats. Monetary rewards leap into your future.

Pitfalls and Potential Problems

Be cautious when Mercury turns retrograde in Libra on the 9th in your solar sixth house of daily routines and delays activity along with clear communication. The 6th also caters to your health and gains prominence around the time of the Libra New Moon on the 25th. Schedule medical exams or tests. Be sure to discuss weight gain or nutrition issues with your physician.

Rewarding Days

4, 7, 14, 25

Challenging Days

2, 20, 27

Taurus | October

Overall Theme

Excessive frustration is about to end. Abundant planetary activity drives this month's focus, which starts out with Mercury going direct on the 2nd in Virgo (let's start talking), followed by Pluto moving direct on the 8th in Capricorn (dump the baggage) and Saturn turning direct in Aquarius on the 23rd (implement those plans). Monitor spending and hold back the sarcasm when energetic Mars in Gemini makes a retrograde station in your solar second house on the 30th.

Relationships

From the 5th onward, camaraderie with the management team and colleagues soars to favorable heights at your workplace. Leadership and team contributions elicit an achievement-oriented work culture determined to accomplish goals. Family members show love and support for pressing time commitments. Light romantic fires during the Solar Eclipse in Scorpio on the 25th.

Success and Money

You value collaboration that motivates you to go to work each day in a positive state of mind, not an easy thing to do with erratic outbursts from Uranus in your sign this month. Acknowledgment of performance excellence on the job manifests in celebratory meals, recognition, cash bonuses, and promotions.

Pitfalls and Potential Problems

After planets return to direct motion, take a breath to collect your thoughts before finalizing transactions. Financial advice misses the mark on the 2nd and 8th, prompting you to check sources and develop new numbers. On the 19th, check investment proposals and contracts that may not contain material you need to make a decision.

Rewarding Days

5, 11, 14, 25

Challenging Days

2, 8, 12, 27

Taurus | November

Overall Theme

Vitality could be flagging on the 8th when a Lunar Eclipse settles in your solar first house and drains your energy. Give yourself a mental health break and take sick leave. Start a new exercise program when you feel better. Swimming might be a fine way to tone unused muscles. Check security programs and update software and passwords.

Relationships

Contact increases with friends and professional associates looking for commitments to attend meetings, parties, and holiday fundraisers. Siblings put out feelers to line up gatherings for the upcoming holidays. Community organizers look for volunteers to distribute clothing, food, and gifts to neighborhood members in need. You have ideas for funding holiday gifts and share the plan with your partner right before Thanksgiving.

Success and Money

An unexpected return on an investment puts more money in your checkbook, adding to your desire for financial security. Although you start looking for a new vehicle, your intuition wisely tells you to sleep on it. Join work colleagues for a holiday get-together a few days prior to the feast.

Pitfalls and Potential Problems

Jupiter goes retrograde on November 23. Just as you reap the benefits of a cash windfall, you may have to part with some of it to replace a broken appliance or pay for repairs to a household item. Children disclose holiday plans that interfere with the ones you scheduled during Thanksgiving week. Arguing continues on and off from the 19th through the 27th.

Rewarding Days

3, 14, 15, 20

Challenging Days

1, 8, 19, 23

Taurus | December

Overall Theme

The first few days of December, spend reflective time counting your blessings and the benefits you reaped during this successful year. Once Venus and Mercury line up in your solar ninth house of long-distance matters, your thoughts go to travel plans and visiting those you love for the holidays.

Relationships

Implement your plan to work with a favorite children's charity mid-month to spread holiday cheer and boost the spirit of those who are ill or without the means to afford holiday festivities. Schedule a day to make ornaments or bake cookies. Kindness makes a difference in sharing the spirit of the season. Show your significant other how much your tender loving heart cares.

Success and Money

With Saturn transiting your solar tenth house all year, you stepped up to the challenges of increased responsibility and received much deserved rewards. Enjoy them now. You have the magic formula for creating the perfect holiday and do all the budgeting, planning, and shopping for gifts and food supplies ahead of time. Your grateful family appreciates your love.

Pitfalls and Potential Problems

You may encounter unreliability among friends or mix-ups over lunch dates the first few days of the month. Confusion reigns and plans can't be easily rescheduled. Keep your eye on credit cards when shopping or treating friends to a holiday happy hour on the 9th. Table travel on the 29th, when Mercury goes retrograde in Capricorn.

Rewarding Days

4, 15, 20, 25

Challenging Days

1, 9, 18, 29

Taurus Action Table

These dates reflect the best—but not the only—times for success and ease in these activities, according to your Sun sign.

	JAN	FEB	MAR	APR	MAY	JUN	JUL	AUG	SEP	OCT	NOV	DEC
Move				13		16		1	7		14	
Romance		18			16		9			25		
Seek counseling/coaching		23				3			25			15
Ask for a raise	5		9					20		5		
Vacation	2			27			27					25
Get a loan			24		30						20	

Gemini

The Twins
May 20 to June 21

♊

Element: Air

Quality: Mutable

Polarity: Yang/masculine

Planetary Ruler: Mercury

Meditation: I explore my
inner worlds

Gemstone: Tourmaline

Power Stones: Ametrine, citrine,
emerald, spectrolite, agate

Glyph: Pillars of duality,
the Twins

Anatomy: Shoulders, arms,
hands, lungs, nervous system

Colors: Bright colors, orange,
yellow, magenta

Animals: Monkeys, talking birds,
flying insects

Myths/Legends: Peter Pan,
Castor and Pollux

House: Third

Opposite Sign: Sagittarius

Flower: Lily of the valley

The Gemini Personality

Strengths, Talents, and the Creative Spark

No better multitasker exists than versatile Gemini. Early in life you decided that very few limits hold you back and nothing can stop you from expanding your consciousness. You're here to facilitate high-quality communication when you write, speak, or use body language. The talent you possess shows others how to think on their feet and encompasses your excellent presentation skills, motivational acumen, and enthusiastic, positive attitude. The sheer energy of lively communication stimulates the air you breathe. Not only do you thrive on having a voice in the process, but you also firmly believe that silence was meant to be broken with the words of wisdom that seem to come so easily to you. Wherever you find a forum for disseminating information, you'll be networking and giving your lungs a workout. You're a huge fan of using a mobile network and employ most available technologies to keep current and stay accessible in a variety of settings. During the recent COVID-19 pandemic, you acted like the spirit guide of the media world, helping the onslaught of telecommuters suddenly displaced from their work spaces due to social-distancing mandates. No doubt your employer is grateful that you not only know what to do but also quickly develop guidelines and bring the team up to speed via online instruction.

Your sign's ruler is Mercury and the third house is your domain, the space where your mind shows what it's made of—how rapidly it expresses concepts, stimulates creative thinking, and processes information. Preferred learning methods shine in this space and increases your desire for higher education. A good number of Geminis are perpetual students. This department also covers the way you like to get around. Geminis enjoy driving and prefer sporty cars with all the bells and whistles. Siblings, at least one of them, hold a special place in your heart. You probably confer or visit regularly with them, depending on the bonding memories you have from your childhood. The perfect job environment would include employment at a high-energy organization that hires people with good presentation skills who know how to generate enthusiasm and have a gift for motivating teams. You absolutely must have work that keeps you stimulated or you lose interest and spend too much time on trivia, gaming, and surfing the internet.

Intimacy and Personal Relationships

Before you declare that you have found a significant other, you prefer to date a variety of individuals to determine what makes them unique. A discussion-ready diva or a man of many words describes a partner who appeals to you. You strongly desire mental stimulation and are happiest in the company of those who enjoy intellectual talks and excel at spontaneous repartee. Very few Geminis are looking for a couch potato with a set routine. You enjoy the freedom of an active social life, the draw of parties, neighborhood gatherings, and local travel. A partner who joins you, shares your interests, appreciates the opportunity to learn new topics, and enjoys the prospect of mind expansion is a keeper. Anyone you date should understand that you love to talk, never seem to run out of things to say, and will cherish the one who listens and enjoys asking questions to test your considerable knowledge. You thrive on engaging in conversations that focus on newsmaking items, entertainment gossip, politics, health breakthroughs, games like Jeopardy, and books on the bestseller list. Find a partner with a sharp sense of humor that matches your quick wit and load your calendar with exciting adventures.

Values and Resources

Acquisition of knowledge is your jam, and you treasure it as a preferred resource. Collecting books, subscribing to publications, visiting bookstores, and browsing the internet keeps you up-to-date on current events, new trends, medical breakthroughs, politics, and every facet of show business. You value innate intelligence and possess the ability to absorb information swiftly. People who get to know you may refer to you as "the Brain" because you know a lot about many topics and can easily converse or write about them. This asset makes you an excellent teacher, trainer, or facilitator. A position that calls for travel is an excellent fit for your nervous-energy-burning personality that thrives on multitasking and learn-as-you-go experiences. Known as an eloquent speaker, you may have also mastered one or more foreign languages and value the opportunity to practice your skills with native speakers or while traveling to other countries for business or pleasure.

Blind Spots and Blockages

Normally you're a stickler for using proper grammar in the spoken and written word, an absolute necessity for producing quality work. On the rare occasion that you haven't done your homework, you'll mispronounce a word or experience a disastrous slip of the tongue. You learned the hard way that you can't fake it with the pros or those with expertise in the world of communication. If you want to be the lord of the podium, you have to learn to check your facts and the spelling of names and new words. Sometimes you're caught in a Mercury retrograde loop and can easily lose track of time, forget a due date, or ramble on during a talk instead of ending it smoothly. A frequent blind spot involves hogging the podium and forgetting to give others a chance to express their opinion or deliver their report. Refrain from interrupting other speakers inappropriately when they are presenting. Avoid blasting others with ill-timed insults that you disguise as a joke. Become a better listener and you'll learn more about how other brilliant minds work.

Goals and Success

Mercury, the messenger of the gods, is the ruler of your sign and also one of your worthy role models. You use adaptability, diplomacy, and a polished product to excel at your craft as you present material that is clear and accurate. Your mission may involve communication that relates to instructional, oral, or written material. No wonder you're called the Great Communicator for the passion you put into delivering a message. Audiences love you when you energize their attention span by varying the tone, pitch, pace, and body language while successfully breathing life into topics for discussion. If you have a flair for comedy, use your humor effectively to break the ice and get attendees warmed up. You'll be a sought-after speaker, emcee, or subject-matter specialist.

Gemini Keywords for 2022
Communication, concepts, creativity

The Year Ahead for Gemini

As you leave 2021 behind, you're wrapping up a year that saw you in the role of change agent, wearing several analytical hats as you navigated through the disruptions in workplace practices and routines stimulated by the COVID-19 pandemic. You likely traveled considerably or worked in more than one place most of the year. Eclipses in your solar first and seventh houses brought an abundance of visibility your way, calling attention to partnership matters as well. In 2022, you're ready to regroup while you use some time behind the scenes to strategize. That won't be easy with Uranus in Taurus starting out the year retrograde in your solar twelfth house, where it turns direct on January 18 and nudges you to take ownership of a new role. Two eclipses show up here in Taurus to highlight the state of your health, the welfare of others, privacy, secrets, and books or articles you might be working on for future publication. As the year begins, love planet Venus is retrograde in Capricorn in your solar eighth house of rebirth, intimacy, death, and other people's money. If anything is out of kilter with you and your partner or the state of your finances, now is the time to work on the issues since Venus turns direct on January 29 and demands clarity to manage sensitive subjects. After coping with the lineup of Capricorn planets here in recent years, your lone aggravator is Pluto in Capricorn in late degrees giving you space to unload any karma that gets in the way of physical or spiritual progress.

On January 14, the planet of communication, Mercury, becomes the first planet to turn retrograde this year in Aquarius, occupying your solar ninth house of travel, higher education, and philosophy. You will notice that travel demands will not be as prolific. This feeling will be further validated by the presence of transiting Saturn also in Aquarius and your ninth house, indicating fiscal restrictions in the midst of organizational recovery from economic and staffing shortages resulting from the pandemic's toll on the planet. Be on the lookout for new employment opportunities as you broaden your field of expertise.

Jupiter

With the exception of a retrograde and a sign-change period this year, Jupiter occupies your solar tenth house in Pisces until December 20, when it moves to Aries for all of 2023. What a good place to be if you're looking for a new job, a promotion, or a career change. Recognition from authority figures for past efforts is inevitable. Plan for a change of focus in your work via details, courses, certification, or degree programs. COVID-19 may have led to directed reassignment of duties and schedule changes. How you handled them brought accolades that elevated your stellar reputation. Be sure to add the experience you acquired to your resume. Jupiter travels rapidly through Pisces until May 10, when it moves into Aries and your solar eleventh house of groups and goals and generates a long teaser period in that sign. On July 28, Jupiter will turn retrograde in your solar eleventh house in Aries, moving back into Pisces and your solar tenth house on October 28 until it goes direct on November 23 through the end of the year. If the fields of communication and technology that include advertising, comedy, cyber security, emceeing, instructing, journalism, linguistics, professional driving, public speaking, speech pathology, and writing match your area of expertise, look into opportunities that pop up through your diverse networks. Note that Jupiter connects with transiting Neptune in Pisces in April, an asset that favors an interest in and creation of metaphysical materials.

Saturn

In December 2020, Saturn entered Aquarius and your solar ninth house of foreign cultures, higher education, in-laws, religion, long-distance travel, and writing. Planets in Aquarius work very well with Gemini placements and add discipline and an analytical focus to the work you seek and projects you manage. If you write for a living, market demand calls for development of articles or books that discuss the shift in direction that has affected the health of world citizens, the economic, business, and personal ramifications of imposed social distancing, and how restrictions in the last few years affected the way we do business. Look for universal studies in the pipeline that examine the social impact of living through a pandemic. These opportunities create new jobs and require a close examination of the capabilities of our health and welfare systems. Become a vital part of teams that study these conditions. Jump on the bandwagon and put your curious, versatile mind to the test by exploring these concepts. Although restrictions may be imposed on your travel schedule due to safety and budgetary mandates, some of you will take to the international skies to work with experts in other countries who examine critical conditions and seek solutions that benefit the world. Along the way, you may have to forego travel for pleasure since your calendar is about to fill up with challenging assignments again. This year Saturn touches the lives most intensely of Geminis born between June 1 and 18. Brush up on your language and diplomacy skills before packing your bags for a demanding year of adventure.

Uranus

How is your solar twelfth house of seclusion holding up after another year of hosting transiting Uranus in Taurus? If you have any natal planets in Taurus, you've learned that they are generally unfriendly with transiting Saturn in Aquarius, which has put a damper on your solar ninth house of travel. Uranus is ready to break free and take to the land, sea, and air, and needs a liberator. With two eclipses in Taurus in 2022 in your solar twelfth house, you have a couple of conspirators that may help you beat the odds of staying confined for another year. If you were born between May 30 and June 10, Uranus, the planet of chaos and disruption, has the greatest impact on your complex mind and mundane routines. Even if you planned to hole up and work on a secret project, heal from a health injury or illness, or hide out until you're sure that COVID-19 is behind you, it's time to put out feelers to your network. Connect with potential employers that have positions matching your valuable skills. The planet of the unexpected will move into retrograde motion on August 24 and go direct on January 22, 2023. Be ready for the shake-up call and put your lightning-quick brain to the test.

Neptune

Planets in dreamy Pisces tend to clash with those in mentally focused Gemini, sending confusing messages and wasting valuable time that could be better spent on analytical pursuits. By now you know the drill, Gemini, since Neptune has been in Pisces and your solar tenth house of career, ambition, authority, and organizational matters since April 2011. With this long transit in place, you may be spending more time than usual comforting work colleagues dealing with life-and-death matters. Your golden tongue lets the right words come easily to you, convincing others there is a big job to do. Sometimes you want to forge ahead with plans to revamp the look of the workplace or rewrite the mission statement in a week, but Neptune in this house of advancement entices you to daydream or distracts you from getting the job done efficiently. Look on the bright side: if you want to give a concept or product a new perspective, work with Neptune to stimulate ideas, create a different vision, or adapt to coworkers whose work styles offer a less structured approach. Those of you born between June 10 and 18 will experience the most challenging Neptune action in 2022. The planet of dreams, illusion, and mystical mornings will be retrograde from June 28 to December 3. Review your goals as you sail a creative ship and launch new concepts for change in the year ahead.

Pluto

Pluto, the karma cleaner of the zodiac, made its first appearance in your solar eighth house of birth, sex, death, wills and estates, joint income and assets, debts and mortgages, rebirth, psychological depth, and mysteries back in 2008. The dwarf planet has been in Capricorn during this long passage, moving slowly through those issues you stored in this complex house, making sure you understand the fear you have buried in your subconscious, and stimulating your deep psyche to let go. How is Pluto affecting your life now? What baggage have you been hauling around all these years? Was it fear of intimacy, too much debt, not expressing what is on your mind, or fear of anger and what you might do if you couldn't control your temper? What else has been eating away at you? What would it look like if you didn't have the problem?

Pluto has a reputation for creating very intense situations in relationships that show up as power struggles. For example, it can make a marriage or partnership woefully unbearable even if the couple stays together. Financial challenges can magnify the unpleasant continuing drama, leading to distrust of the partner. Any number of circumstances represent the death of painful matters, not just an actual physical death of you or someone you know. Then comes rebirth of the life and the soul. Pluto is slipping into the final degrees of this long transit, which wraps up in 2025. It forms an inconjunct aspect to your Sun this year if you were born between June 16 and 20, the dates most affected by this transit. In 2022 Pluto in Capricorn's retrograde period begins on April 29 and lasts until October 8. Seize the day and make clear communication a priority.

How Will This Year's Eclipses Affect You?

In 2022 a total of four eclipses occur. Two are solar (New Moon) and two are lunar (Full Moon), which create intense periods that start to manifest a few months before their actual occurrence. All four of these eclipses occur in your chart's solar twelfth and sixth houses. Eclipses unfold in cycles involving all twelve signs of the zodiac and usually occur in pairs about two weeks apart. Think of eclipses as opportunities to release old patterns and conditions that have outlived their usefulness. Have no fear of them since they may also bring you unexpected surprises and windfalls. The closer an eclipse is to a degree or point in your chart, the greater its importance is likely to be in your life. If you were born with a planet at the same degree as an eclipse, you are likely to see a high level of activity in the house where the eclipse occurs. An eclipse's impact may last six months to a year or more.

The first Solar Eclipse of 2022 occurs on April 30 in Taurus and your solar twelfth house of healing, private matters, hospital visiting, meditation, hidden enemies, psychic insight, and charities. You could be healing from emotional setbacks or taking steps to reclaim your power after dealing with unplanned career or relationship dilemmas. Overwork brought about by sudden changes in direction may have left you exhausted or forced a sabbatical. Now you're ready to hit the trail, clean up lingering problems, and get back to the action. Inspiration comes to you out of the blue with Uranus in this house.

On May 16, the first Lunar Eclipse of the year takes place in Scorpio and your solar sixth house of daily routines, fitness, health, organization, nutrition, pets, and teamwork. Your workload is likely to increase when managers assign you to tasks involving your spot-on communication skills that include problem-solving, editing, and writing. Be sure to schedule medical and dental checkups and have your physician assess the viability of any medications you are currently taking.

The year's second Solar Eclipse takes place on October 25 in Scorpio and your solar sixth house. By this time, your entire work routine will have changed, as well as the colleagues you collaborate with and the types of projects assigned to you. If you have contracts to write books or articles, the deadlines are looming and the pace picks up, leaving you with little downtime in the fall. Manage stress with yoga, meditation, and helpful mind-mapping techniques. Calm down by adopting an adorable little animal companion who takes your mind off the stressful work pace and welcomes you each day with love.

The year's final eclipse on November 8 is a Lunar Eclipse, again in Taurus and your solar twelfth house of recovery, regrouping, healing, hospital visiting, metaphysics, enemies, psychic insight, secrets, and charities. The sabbatical you took earlier in the year brought you to a good place to clear the air and make compatible choices for future experiences. Just looking at the matters connected with your solar twelfth house is a writer's dream. You have your pick to develop human interest stories, write about medical cures, provide insight into the pandemic, and explore the depths of the metaphysical and spiritual world. Time to get out of bed and seek new outlets for your talent. Knowing you, Gemini, you'll hold out for two choices and give each of them a visible path.

Gemini | January

Overall Theme

Matters of intimacy are on your mind this month with Venus and Pluto in your solar eighth house stoking the fires of passion. Mars throws in some spicy moments as it races through your solar seventh house of partners, inspiring the two of you to plan a private vacation around the 5th that allows you to ignite a few sparks in your romantic life. Welcome the year with a blast of enthusiastic energy.

Relationships

The focus this month is on your family and partner. Gatherings cater to game night and movies everyone enjoys. Ask parents to join you, too. Let the kids help with preparation of snacks and quick meals. Children share their thoughts on what they want most in the new year. Plan a surprise around their wishes on the 24th.

Success and Money

Venus rules the money you make and how you spend it. You started the month with reserve cash from your holiday bonus, and entertain options for spending it. Part of you has your eyes on a new car and thinks the extra cash would make a good down payment. Don't part with it while Venus is retrograde through January 29.

Pitfalls and Potential Problems

Your ruling planet, Mercury, will turn retrograde on January 14 in Aquarius, and the Moon is in your solar first house as well—not a good day for signing a contract. Erratic Uranus goes direct on the 18th, after generating months of anxious moments while retrograde in your solar twelfth house.

Rewarding Days

3, 5, 21, 24

Challenging Days

1, 10, 17, 26

Gemini | February

Overall Theme

Major announcements fill the workplace with an air of expectancy after a tough year of adjusting to economic recovery and a more balanced job market. Celebratory vibes fill you with hope for creative, meaningful work as options manifest and encourage you to jump aboard, work on your resume, and take action after Mercury goes direct on the 3rd.

Relationships

Right after the New Moon in Aquarius on February 1, objective leaders, seasoned analysts, and impassioned colleagues come together, setting the tone for the year as they embrace new directions and a plan of work. Genuine camaraderie surfaces as employees bond. Family members offer help and understanding along with a sounding board to encourage you to make important life decisions as employment prospects surface.

Success and Money

For many Geminis, a new salary offer is on the table this month, along with a change in duties and an increased level of responsibility. Venue-changing expectations align with your brilliant communication skills and lead to creative contributions and important alliances.

Pitfalls and Potential Problems

Plans with friends fizzle out the first weekend of the month, and annoyance sets in over getting a late cancellation notice. Seek reimbursement for any reservation costs you have to eat as a result. You can shop now, but please don't purchase a car on the second weekend of the month. The deal won't be as sweet as the one you find a week later.

Rewarding Days

3, 8, 11, 18

Challenging Days

5, 13, 19, 20

Gemini | March

Overall Theme

The New Moon in Pisces on the 2nd shines in your solar tenth house of career and organizational direction. Important business travel to a resort area may give you an opportunity to arrive early, allowing time to enjoy a few attractions before the rest of your colleagues gather for serious discussions.

Relationships

Venus and Mars in Aquarius travel in harmony with your sign, facilitating romantic opportunities most of the month. While basking in the presence of your significant other, spend quality time showing your loving and cherishing nature. If you're single, create opportunities to mix and mingle at social gatherings during the third weekend of the month, where you'll meet eligible prospects.

Success and Money

Jupiter in Pisces highlights your career sector and prospects for expansion that are calling attention to your spot-on flair for successfully negotiating contracts and motivating the team to accomplish goals. Your boss responds by giving you more responsibility in the company and acknowledges your performance with a salary increase or bonus.

Pitfalls and Potential Problems

The Virgo Full Moon on the 18th puts a damper on interactions at home. Skip discussions about making expensive purchases. On the 24th, don't overreact to phone calls from parents or estranged spouses who bombard you with complaints. Listen patiently and schedule a less volatile time to work on solutions.

Rewarding Days

1, 2, 9, 20

Challenging Days

6, 10, 17, 24

Gemini | April

Overall Theme

With your preference for variety and the spice it adds to the stuck places in life, your restless spirit is ready for a new beginning. In response, two New Moons appear this month. The first one is in Aries on April 1 in your solar eleventh house, and the second is a Solar Eclipse in Taurus and your solar twelfth house on April 30.

Relationships

With the New Moon on April 1 occurring in your solar eleventh house, you'll be socializing with members of professional groups at meetings or luncheons. Bring your engaging sense of humor, shoot the breeze, and lighten the air. Just don't pull any awkward April Fools' jokes on friends or colleagues who may be blindsided by your unexpected antics.

Success and Money

The 9th is an opportune day for investing your money in the stock market with backup support from your broker. This date favors visiting a mortgage lender to discuss attractive rates for a mortgage or home equity line of credit. Positive feedback pours in from collaborators regarding current work projects and puts your boss in a gracious mood.

Pitfalls and Potential Problems

You'll be in a good mood and ready for action on the 7th until you uncover a financial mistake that could be costly and needs correction before you can move forward with plans. Too much weekend partying could leave you fatigued on the 18th.

Rewarding Days

1, 9, 13, 27

Challenging Days

4, 7, 18, 20

Gemini | May

Overall Theme

Action from the eclipses is on your mind and interferes with your best-laid plans. The April 30th Solar Eclipse in Taurus just hit transiting Uranus in your solar twelfth house, revealing secrets and highlighting medical issues. On the 16th, a Lunar Eclipse in Scorpio occurs in your solar sixth house of health and daily environment, necessitating a doctor visit or a round of tests for you, a loved one, or a key player at work.

Relationships

Heartfelt communication is the star this month that bridges the gap in expressing feelings. The Lunar Eclipse in Scorpio on May 16 brings coworkers together who share their concerns about the welfare of a colleague. You and your partner find comfort in forging stronger bonds while discussing solutions to address the health of a loved one.

Success and Money

Jupiter moves into Aries on the 10th and favors expanding networks, hiring additional staff, and examining organizational resources to tap the money that supports initiatives. You receive funds for home projects or personal expenses on the 7th, yet execution of these plans is more successful after mid-June.

Pitfalls and Potential Problems

Your ruling planet, Mercury, is about to go retrograde in Gemini on the 10th and affects education plans, the timing of construction work, and financial investments. Pluto turned retrograde in Capricorn in your solar eighth house on April 29, compatibly aspected to the April 30th Taurus eclipse. Although delays affect your plans, they will work out.

Rewarding Days

2, 7, 14, 18

Challenging Days

4, 11, 16, 19

Gemini | June

Overall Theme

Finances represent the root of activity this month. The Moon shows up in Cancer twice, on the 1st and again on the 28th, when the New Moon occurs in your solar second house. Assess resources and take inventory of debts on the 3rd and 16th. Be sure you don't make impulsive decisions about accelerating a repayment schedule or you could wind up short of cash to cover planned expenses.

Relationships

Cousins, siblings, and neighbors contact you and compete for time on your calendar. Unfinished household tasks and pressing work projects preclude you from making firm plans until after Venus moves into your sign the last weekend of the month. Then clear some space around the 27th for a few days of rest and recreation and hit the beach or mountain trails for some well-deserved fun.

Success and Money

As long as you continue to make wise financial decisions, your money picture is solvent and your income shows promising increases. You will have to watch for blocks or confusion to your Sun from transiting Jupiter in Pisces in your solar tenth house career sector.

Pitfalls and Potential Problems

Mercury goes direct on the 3rd, while delay-oriented Saturn slips into retrograde motion on the 4th in Aquarius, throwing a curve ball into family plans that will have to be modified. On the 28th, Neptune turns retrograde in your solar tenth house until December 3 and calls for clarification of new business proposals with the management team.

Rewarding Days

3, 6, 16, 27

Challenging Days

2, 8, 14, 30

Gemini | July

Overall Theme
Looks like the planets will line up to treat you to a happy 4th of July celebration with loved ones ready to join you for a week of fun and games!
Reunite with siblings, invite your parents, and ask close neighbors to
attend festive gatherings at your home. Accept invitations for family outings and make the most of downtime.

Relationships
Bond with children over short, enjoyable trips to favorite recreation
spots. Alternately, find sports venues, amusement parks, or a dude ranch
to give everyone a unique experience to stretch their comfort zone. Siblings and their families may decide to join you when you cue them in to
your new ideas for fun.

Success and Money
Paid vacations are a big help when it's time to take off to recharge your
batteries, and the best is yet to come. If you will be away during the early
part of the month, your boss may surprise you with an offer of a new job
or a lead to a challenging assignment when you return. Look for esteem-
elevating messages on the 28th.

Pitfalls and Potential Problems
Don't be discouraged when the Full Moon in Capricorn opposes Mercury in Cancer on the 13th and sends mixed signals your way. It's not
the right time to buy luxury items or jewelry. Jupiter turns retrograde on
the 28th in Aries and your solar eleventh house of goals, discouraging
you from making risky purchases.

Rewarding Days
2, 8, 18, 28

Challenging Days
5, 10, 13, 22

Gemini | August

Overall Theme

The month gets off to an earthy start with the Moon in performance-oriented Virgo in your solar fourth house making a trine aspect to transiting Mars and Uranus in sensuous Taurus and a sextile to emotional Venus in Cancer. That combination sparks a romantic tone in your home, rekindles passion,, and puts you in the mood to reminisce fondly about old times. Light candles, dine at home, and feast on fancy food.

Relationships

Your perceptions about workplace dynamics have been spot-on lately. Noting the increased compatibility among team members and adherence to pressing deadlines, you consider nominating employees for a group award. Your thoughtful gesture pleases your boss, who may recommend you for a management training program.

Success and Money

When outstanding performances roll in, the money rolls out in the form of bonuses and raises. A leadership role you take on attracts the attention of the management group, who appreciate the motivation and extra effort. The entire team benefits from stellar productivity that exceeds deadlines.

Pitfalls and Potential Problems

Expect a few jolts of electrifying energy when Uranus in Taurus goes retrograde until January 22, 2023, in your solar twelfth house of seclusion. Depending on planetary placements in your natal chart, certain Geminis may hear of job cutbacks.

Rewarding Days

1, 6, 20, 24

Challenging Days

3, 8, 11, 27

Gemini | September

Overall Theme

Take action cautiously. Do your homework first. Four planets are retrograde this month and Mercury is about to join them, making its third appearance this year in that state on September 9 in Libra and your solar fifth house of children, risk-taking, romance, and vacations. You know the drill. One of the best things you can do instead of initiating new activities is to clean up what you have already started.

Relationships

Lucky you! Your love partner joins you for a getaway over the Labor Day holiday that could include foreign travel. Be sure your passport is up to date. Attend events related to your children—sporting events, debates, open houses, and PTA meetings. Schedule a pizza night out or treat children to a favorite amusement.

Success and Money

Schedule an appointment with your attorney on the 8th to make revisions to your will and update estate details. Circumstances may have changed and call for vigilance. Review documents from bankers and financial analysts on the 19th. Note any aspects that seem questionable and schedule a meeting in early October to make changes.

Pitfalls and Potential Problems

Exhaustion sets in as you scramble to tie up loose ends on the 1st prior to traveling over the holiday. Pace yourself and don't try to do the impossible. The Full Moon on the 10th may test the compatibility between you and your partner if you engage in hostile behavior.

Rewarding Days

3, 8, 19, 27

Challenging Days

1, 10, 12, 18

Gemini | October

Overall Theme

The final Solar Eclipse of 2022 occurs in your solar sixth house in Scorpio on October 25. You could be dealing with two areas that trigger the renowned Gemini adrenaline that rushes through your nervous system: multitasking and losing your voice. New responsibilities shift the focus of work assignments.

Relationships

You form new relationships with people at a distance that become a critical part of your workday. Travel is vital to helping you understand cultural and professional differences. In-laws and other relatives extend an invitation to visit. Work with publishers that has been cyclical increases in scope based on demand for emerging topics.

Success and Money

Energetic Mars spends most of the month in Gemini and your solar first house, making sure you complete every assigned task in record time. Important meetings with attorneys or consultants reassure you that your finances are in top shape and your assets are safe. Intensity is part of the work environment when additional assignments double your workload.

Pitfalls and Potential Problems

It looks like a planetary rush with three planets going direct again this month and the fiery planet Mars going retrograde in Gemini on October 30. Mercury moves direct in Virgo on the 2nd, followed by Pluto in Capricorn on the 8th and Saturn in Aquarius on the 23rd. Let the energy pass before you take action on items you had on hold.

Rewarding Days

4, 5, 19, 25

Challenging Days

2, 8, 12, 17

Gemini | November

Overall Theme

Your youthful spirit comes alive with plans for holiday shopping, gatherings, and helping those less fortunate realize their dreams. You won't be getting much sleep as you anticipate every thrill the universe has lined up in this thankful season. On the same date as the New Moon in Sagittarius, Jupiter in Pisces goes direct on the 23rd, just in time to lend a hand to late-arriving visitors.

Relationships

People travel from distant places to sit at your holiday table. It's a multi-generational gathering that calls for a feast to please many palates while including traditional favorites. Ask each guest to talk about a cherished Thanksgiving memory or mention their favorite dish from childhood.

Success and Money

Early in the month your work leader shows appreciation for your contributions by giving you a generous incentive bonus. Wise saving habits and performance awards supply you with the money to shop for cherished gifts, surprise children, write Christmas cards, and mail packages early.

Pitfalls and Potential Problems

The Lunar Eclipse on the 8th falls in Taurus and your solar twelfth house, reminding you to review your intentions for healing your heart and mind. Avoid conflicts with inner fears on this date while the Moon and Uranus are conjunct. Since Uranus in Taurus has temporary lodgings in your solar twelfth house, weather conditions (mental and physical) could affect your outlook and travel plans. Stay safe.

Rewarding Days

4, 14, 21, 23

Challenging Days

1, 8, 11, 19

Gemini | December

Overall Theme

This month is about sharing your spirit. Early holiday gatherings start popping up on the 4th, the day after Neptune goes direct in Pisces and your solar twelfth house. Enjoy the company of dear friends and members of groups. Pay generosity forward by funding meals for food banks and soup kitchens. Buy a gift for an angel tree to help a child celebrate the season with a cherished toy.

Relationships

Inspirational events spark your desire to help those less fortunate. Cook a meal every few weeks for someone recovering from an illness, buy groceries for those who can't drive, or run errands for others. Enjoy memorable moments with your significant other, your children, and loved ones who gather to celebrate the holidays and ring in the new year with you.

Success and Money

Jupiter lingers in your solar tenth house until the 20th, when it enters Aries and reminds you what a prosperous year you've had in your career sector, earning new respect from authority figures. Unusual gifts come your way in the form of stocks, checks, and the sale of shares from an investment.

Pitfalls and Potential Problems

The year's only Full Moon in your sign occurs on December 7 conjunct retrograde Mars in Gemini. Be on the lookout for careless drivers, drinkers who have had too much, and individuals who want to argue. Don't plan travel on the 29th, when Mercury goes retrograde in your solar eighth house.

Rewarding Days

4, 7, 13, 25

Challenging Days

1, 10, 17, 23

Gemini Action Table

These dates reflect the best—but not the only—times for success and ease in these activities, according to your Sun sign.

	JAN	FEB	MAR	APR	MAY	JUN	JUL	AUG	SEP	OCT	NOV	DEC
Move	24		1				2		8		21	
Romance		8		1	18			1		19		13
Seek counseling/coaching		3				6			27			
Ask for a raise					6		18				4	
Vacation	9		20					24				25
Get a loan				9		16				4		

Cancer

The Crab
June 21 to July 22

Element: Water

Quality: Cardinal

Polarity: Yin/feminine

Planetary Ruler: The Moon

Meditation: I have faith in the promptings of my heart

Gemstone: Pearl

Power Stones: Moonstone, Chrysocolla

Key Phrase: I feel

Glyph: Crab's claws

Anatomy: Stomach, breasts

Colors: Silver, pearl white

Animals: Crustaceans, cows, chickens

Myths/Legends: Hercules and the Crab, Asherah, Hecate

House: Fourth

Opposite Sign: Capricorn

Flower: Larkspur

Keyword: Receptivity

The Cancer Personality

Strengths, Talents, and the Creative Spark

The gift of intuition drives your personality and keeps you tuned in to everything that is going on around you, even when you don't let on that you're aware of each nuance. You walk into a room and can pick up on the vibrations, often getting clues for what may have happened before you entered. Instant radar computes. For example, you can look into the eyes of someone who is speaking and if what they are saying does not resonate well, you can tell whether what they are saying is the truth. No wonder individuals who know you call you psychic. Combine these assets with your phenomenal ability to remember birthdays, historical moments, and trivia and you have the winning formula for landing a job, making yourself invaluable to your employing organization, and creating a loyal following. Marveling at your memory, those in your circle may label you "The Encyclopedia" and throw timeline questions your way. Usually up for the challenge, you enjoy matching wits with other brainiacs.

Cancer is the second cardinal sign in the zodiac, and the water element rules your ruler, the Moon. Because you were born with a tremendous amount of sensitivity and responsiveness to others' plights, certain contacts may see you as a pushover, easily used by those with a sob story. My, how they misunderstand your inner strength. You live up to your mission of being action-oriented and deliver on your promises. A well-developed sixth sense combines with your gifts of compassion and sympathy to highlight your nurturing personality, which leads you toward helping others solve their problems while you see inside their souls. That Cancerian receptivity also means you have to learn to protect yourself so you don't absorb too much of another's trauma.

Intimacy and Personal Relationships

An ideal romantic outcome for you is finding your soulmate, yet you know that does not always happen quickly. It is not unusual for you to have more than one marriage or engagement in your quest to find the perfect mate. When loves walks into your life, you feel the impact deeply. You may not act on it immediately because your complex sensitivity needs time to retreat into your protective shell while you examine your heart's responses. Once you decide you have found the person of your dreams, you thrive on the intimacy of this relationship. For a successful partnership, Cancers often choose their opposite sign, Capricorn, or resonate with another water sign, Scorpio or Pisces, or earthy Taurus or Virgo. You're a keeper, and if the right person is in your life, your heart chakra opens, allowing you to enjoy a long and happy union. Family and friends have a special place in your life and are most important to you. The strong ties of these relationships give you the security you desire and run deep, forming an intimate circle that you treasure forever. It is very hard on your psyche when relationships are troubled, especially if they become severed. It leads to heartache for you if you are unable to heal the estrangement. When you say "I love you," you mean it.

Values and Resources

People represent treasures in your life, whether they are family, friends you treat like family, or bosses and workmates you collaborate with, learn to rely on, and trust. Not one to forget a kindness someone has shown you, you'll fondly recall incidents from childhood and reflect on the details throughout your life. Conversely, old slights or injustices come up out of the blue when similar conditions arise in current reality, reminding you of the reasons why you creatively avoid certain people and seek protection from further hurts. You love your children and value the role of a parent, enjoying every nurturing moment while you dote on your offspring and guide them toward meaningful learning opportunities and successful careers. You display welcoming vibes with open arms and big hugs while going out of your way to make others feel comfortable in your home or place of employment. Nothing fits your personal style more than preparing and offering delicious food to visitors, whether at an elegantly set dining room table or the patio barbecue. Surprise parties are one of your specialties when you host a birthday honoree, a milestone anniversary, or a wedding shower. Cancers of all genders enjoy cooking and appreciate lovely homes with state-of-the-art kitchens equipped with every tool to facilitate use of your extensive culinary art.

Blind Spots and Blockages

Even though you are fully aware of what is going on around you, you don't always take action to put a stop to bad behavior others display or the way they take advantage of your generosity either at work or at home. Eventually the Cancerian crabbiness comes out when you try to stuff too much angst inside. The longer you postpone addressing what is eating at you, the louder your stomach growls looking for relief and an outlet for frustration. Instead of burying yourself in your work or doing someone else's chores, you can put an end to resentment by having a focused conversation with the one who offends you. Not everyone is a mind reader. Sulkiness only leads to uneasy relationships with associates. While your reputation for being sentimental is exceptional, you may go overboard in keeping mementos and old papers and files. Just think of the monumental task you'll have when it's time to purge. Why not shred a pile weekly to make room for your latest acquisitions?

Goals and Success

Cardinal-sign initiative is highly evident in your career, where you develop several skills that qualify you for more than one area of specialization. You have what it takes to invest the energy needed to achieve your goals using your excellent financial acumen and talent for making money. A leadership role is a must to maximize internal happiness and satisfy your need for security. Since you're very service-oriented, you may find that prerequisite in a government position that gives you the latitude to develop your unique management style and master the art of problem-solving. You're likely to create opportunities for yourself by capitalizing on your expertise and running your own business, an enterprise that may range from operating a restaurant or catering business to starting a consulting company that improves work performance and includes developing and conducting situation-specific workshops and seminars.

Cancer Keywords for 2022

Impression, internalization, intuition

The Year Ahead for Cancer

An abundance of relationship changes affected your life in 2021 that came about through illnesses, marriages, employment or lack of it, death, and coping with the COVID-19 pandemic. Whatever happened in your solar fourth house of home and family as a result of the coronavirus and the fallout from the presidential election left you with deep impressions of your inner world and what lies ahead in 2022 to facilitate healing. Jupiter's entry into Pisces and your solar ninth house could step up the pace of your travel schedule after the low-key emphasis and social-distancing factors that limited activity in the last two years. By late May, Jupiter's rapid road trip moves into Aries for five months and interacts with authority figures and your career-oriented solar tenth house. Saturn in Aquarius transits your solar eighth house, driving home the message that partners benefit most from managing finances agreeably and keeping to a debt-reduction plan. Socializing with friends and special interest groups or members of clubs and associations takes up considerable space on your calendar as you pursue humanitarian causes. Surprises and a few shock waves accompany these gatherings thanks to the presence of retrograde Uranus in Taurus in your solar eleventh house of associates. This planet will move direct on January 18, generating more interest in ideas for members to solve critical issues.

Neptune's dreamy vibes hold court in your solar ninth house of the higher mind, lending inspiration to your creative ideas, which include a well-deserved vacation to break the monotony of an enforced rigid routine. As you enter 2022, note that transiting Pluto in Capricorn is still in your solar seventh house of partners, giving subtle reminders of any traces of baggage that are ripe for removal. On January 14, Mercury makes its first retrograde station of the year in Aquarius and your solar eighth house. Be sure to keep an eye on financial records, especially expenses, for the following three weeks.

Jupiter

With the exception of a retrograde and a sign-change period, Jupiter occupies your solar ninth house, until it moves into Aries on December 20 for a nearly yearlong transit of your solar tenth house. Cancers benefit from Jupiter's presence in the solar ninth, the house that rules writing and publishing, spirituality, your higher mind (more classes, anyone?), taking a sabbatical or a long-distance journey, interactions with in-laws or people from another country, and legal or medical matters. Jupiter travels swiftly through Pisces until May 10, when it gives you a long teaser period in the sign of Aries until the wee hours of October 28, when it slips back into Pisces. Move full steam ahead on your goals in matters associated with this house, and contact your networks to showcase your intuitive ideas. Jupiter in Pisces is compatible with your sign and paves the way for a successful enterprise that could lead to collaborative opportunities. On July 28, Jupiter will turn retrograde in Aries and your solar tenth house after stimulating your appetite for a career change and then moving back into Pisces in your solar ninth house in October. Those of you born between June 22 and 29 experience the most action from Jupiter while it is in Aries, making you uncomfortable with the status quo and filling you with ideas for initiating the vision for a new career role. Enjoy the creative fulfillment, study the options, and put your plan in motion in 2023.

Saturn

Since December 17, 2020, Saturn in Aquarius has been occupying your solar eighth house of partnership assets, joint income, money you and/or a partner owe (such as mortgage, credit card, or personal debt), investments, retirement funds, estates, wills, birth, sex, karma, death, taxes, and deep psychological matters. Known as a stern taskmaster, Saturn has been stirring the pot the last few years to encourage you to pay down debt, add to your savings funds, address partnership disagreements that affect security, and truly look at complex conditions that limit your freedom. Either you or a partner may have been juggling two jobs to stay afloat financially the last few years. One of you may have lost your job or been relocated to home base for your physical work space in light of social-distancing requirements. Cancers with school-age children may have taken on additional duties involving home schooling and a requirement to stay flexible with a revolving school schedule. That means you do double duty in maintaining a workable calendar and meeting family needs. Those of you born between July 2 and 19 are most affected by this Saturn transit in 2022.

A Saturn transit through your solar eighth house shows where you could benefit from stabilizing resources, taking inventory of your assets, planning for the future, and working compatibly with your significant other to achieve financial goals. Forge a collaborative alliance to succeed and seek the help of experts if you feel stuck. Goal alignment helps you see the big picture. Saturn's retrograde period during 2022 occurs from June 4 through October 23. Do your homework if you anticipate any large purchases of homes, vehicles, or recreational property. Take a look at the fine print of any refinances or mortgage loans for a new purchase. Pay down debt, add to savings, and thoroughly check your chart with your astrologer before signing papers. Validate your impressions when you feel you need more information and find your way to a clear vision.

Uranus

You'll have little downtime in your solar eleventh house of goals, plans and wishes, fondest dreams, associations, friendships, groups, and organizations with transiting Uranus in Taurus in residence for another year, putting demands on your time and the way you interact with others. This passage through Taurus has brought new connections into your life since May 2018, when it laid the groundwork for challenges and increased responsibilities related to memberships in compatible groups. The eleventh house represents your employer's resources, which may have been stretched thin during the COVID-19 crisis when conferences, meetings, and seminars were canceled due to spatial restrictions that limited physical interaction with attendees. The world of online meetings emerged as a critical link for keeping the workforce communicating. You may have been instrumental in setting up the details for your company, which no doubt has made changes to the way business practices are carried out. Jupiter in Pisces travels compatibly with Uranus and may aid you in securing rewarding work and promotions and accommodating a smooth change of pace. Even if you are going to bail this year and start a business of your own, you have what it takes to make adjustments effortlessly. You'll also be looking at plans with friends and assessing whether you will be able to keep commitments. The planet of chaos has the greatest impact this year on Cancers born between July 1 and 12, pushing them into action that syncs with important needs.

Neptune

Wherever you find Neptune, you meet up with illusion and the possibility that not everything is what it appears to be. This year is no exception, when the slow-moving watery planet advances a few more degrees through Pisces in your solar ninth house of advanced education, higher-mind thinking, philosophy, foreign countries and cultures, business or personal travel, in-laws, politics, publishing, and writing. You took a big break from routine to sleep through or daydream over how the plans you laid out in 2020 missed the mark due to circumstances beyond your control (the coronavirus pandemic), and you've been playing catch-up ever since. If you took a gap year in your university pursuits, now is the time to enroll to complete your degree. Cancers who underwent a career shift or job change are going to travel more or set up conferences with communication services that bring remotely situated employees into the loop, as telework becomes the norm. Visits from family and friends at a distance pick up and keep your social calendar lively and rewarding as loving reunions take place. Those of you who spent quality time tapping into Neptune in Pisces have written books, articles, guides, journals, and romantic novels that are ready for publication. Neptune has occupied your solar ninth house since April 2011, encouraging spiritual growth and expanding your perspective of the planet. Those of you born between July 12 and 19 will benefit most from Neptune's action during 2022.

Pluto

Since January 2008, Pluto, the planet of transformation and rebirth, has been deeply entrenched in Capricorn and your solar seventh house, reminding you of any lingering areas connected to business and personal partners that need to be addressed before you are finally free of emotional angst. No doubt you have learned a lot about people who enter your life, challenge you with an important lesson, and then leave in matters related to intimacy, collaboration, shared roles and responsibilities, or cooperative agreements. The seventh is a public house, and the quality of your relationships has an impact on how others view your actions, your image as a team, and how much you and partners value social interactions. After fourteen years of dealing with the karma cleaners associated with Pluto, you have a pretty good handle on what generates stress in relationships, whether you have solved any of the problems you have been internalizing, and how well you have acknowledged the successful outcomes that make you happy in intimate or professional alliances. What are you going to be this year: a keeper or a killjoy? Those of you born between July 17 and 22 see the most activity in manifesting healing, with transiting Pluto opposing your Sun and challenging you to speak up and tell the truth.

How Will This Year's Eclipses Affect You?

The signs Taurus and Scorpio dominate the eclipse cycles of 2022. A total of four eclipses occur: two solar (New Moon) and two lunar (Full Moon), which bring intense periods that start to manifest about two months before they actually occur. All four of them take place in two of your solar chart's succedent houses, the eleventh and fifth, putting the spotlight on activities associated with friends, groups, and goals as well as situations involving your social and romantic life, children, sports, and speculation. Eclipses manifest in cycles involving all twelve signs of the zodiac, usually occurring in pairs about two weeks apart. Never fear eclipses—think of them as opportunities that allow you to face old, outworn patterns and release them. Eclipses trigger unexpected revelations, surprises, and windfalls. The closer an eclipse is to a planet in your chart, the greater the importance it plays in your life. Those of you born with a planet at the same degree as an eclipse may see a high level of activity in the house where the eclipse occurs.

The first Solar Eclipse of 2022 occurs on April 30 in Taurus and your solar eleventh house of goals, plans, wishes, fondest dreams, associations, friendships, groups and organizations, humanitarian interests, and your employer's resources. The pressure is on you to keep goals on track, balance work with activities that involve memberships reflective of your personal philosophy, and lead initiatives that serve the greater good. Transiting Uranus in Taurus is also present to keep you alert to chaotic conditions.

Two weeks later, the first Lunar Eclipse of the year occurs on May 16 in Scorpio and your solar fifth house of children and their interests, romance, amusements, sports, and speculative ventures. If you have planets located in this house, expect revelations regarding problem areas with people connected to this house to come to light. If connections are positive, you'll benefit from strengthening bonds and fulfilling goals. Should you be experiencing challenges, any rough spots will hit hard and call for discussion and workable solutions. A lack of sleep from working too many hours could mean trouble for your health. Find ways to have fun, relax, and enjoy life.

The second Solar Eclipse of 2022 takes place on October 25 in Scorpio and your solar fifth house of entertainment, vacations, children, coaching, teaching, romance, social life, and risk-taking. When this eclipse hits after months of working on what you found regarding affiliations back in May, you will know whether the actions you took netted the desired results. You could be headed for an engagement if single or walking away from a dying romance.

The year's final eclipse is a Lunar Eclipse on November 8 in Taurus and your solar eleventh house of friends, groups, and goals. In close proximity to this degree is transiting Uranus in Taurus, so be sure to take stock of weak links in memberships in professional organizations and decide whether you want to continue or find a more compatible affiliation to show your support for local and global initiatives.

Cancer | January

Overall Theme

The month looks promising for interactions with spouses and professional partners, thanks to mutual admiration for the rapport you share. Travel is a good option in the first half of January, when Jupiter in Pisces joins the Moon and encourages participation in quality relaxation time.

Relationships

You are sentimental about close relationships and have a chance to show how much you cherish the bonds of intimate and professional partnerships. Create opportunities for much deserved getaways and include romantic gestures meaningful to your significant other. Be sure to include some downtime mid-month to recharge your batteries for your return to the work world.

Success and Money

Make sure you set aside time to review your budget and finalize 2022 financial goals, especially those that involve purchase decisions important to you and your partner. Sign agreements before Mercury goes retrograde on the 14th, and finish planned shopping for sale items before that date. Uranus goes direct on the 18th in your solar eleventh house, stimulating connection with friends who want to reconnect during the last weekend of the month after a long absence.

Pitfalls and Potential Problems

Arguments that surface on the 1st generate confusion and could push your blood pressure up a notch or two. Intense discussions at work lead to impasses on the 10th that can't be settled until the air clears later in the week. Partners balk at plans on the 26th and demand an alternative.

Rewarding Days

2, 7, 14, 30

Challenging Days

1, 10, 17, 26

Cancer | February

Overall Theme

Sentimental Cancer thinks ahead to Valentine's Day, planning a surprise and quality time for celebrating with your significant other. Seek more love as well, reaching out to others in distant places to reconnect and express affectionate greetings. Humanitarian plights leave an impression on you to do something to help those in need. Jump at the chance to get involved.

Relationships

A meeting of kindred spirits on the 9th sets the tone for a new initiative to benefit individuals with food, clothing, and shelter shortages. Accept a leading role in jump-starting plans. Valentine's Day presents opportunities to host a dinner and celebrate while sharing love stories, delicious food, and fond memories with guests.

Success and Money

Mercury goes direct on the 3rd, stabilizing the dynamics of personal and business relationships that have seemed erratic since mid-January. A weekend trip refreshes your psyche and restores enthusiasm for tackling planned projects when you return. Partnership funds show an unexpected increase around the 27th that favors purchasing power.

Pitfalls and Potential Problems

Business discussions net mixed results at best on February 6. You're too tired to develop a sales pitch on the 11th and feel guilty because you need a mental health break from overwork. The Full Moon in Leo on the 16th zaps energy and makes you aware of the need to consider your health. Steer clear of money arguments on the 16th and 21st.

Rewarding Days

3, 9, 14, 27

Challenging Days

6, 11, 16, 25

Cancer | March

Overall Theme

With the New Moon in Pisces in your solar ninth house on the 2nd, you use creative energy to work on material you're writing, hoping to incorporate research and development into relevant themes. A weekend retreat inspires you to write without interruption. You recognize that communication with teams improves goal congruity and nets a unified effort to meet timelines.

Relationships

Celebrate success. Business associates and coworkers demonstrate productivity and deserve acknowledgment for a job well done. Medical professionals show a special interest in your health improvement on the 24th. Cherish a romantic interlude with your partner around the 7th, with Venus and Mars in Aquarius and your solar eighth house.

Success and Money

Raises or bonuses are on the agenda after the middle of the month. Use a portion of your windfall to seed a short vacation or purchase an item on your wish list. Your creative way with words pays off in bringing new work your way and stabilizes your desire for a steady paycheck. Listen to your intuition. Compete for the new project.

Pitfalls and Potential Problems

If all you do is talk about work problems that are on your mind on the 6th, you'll end up having words with your significant other, who prefers a lighthearted agenda. A lunch date could hit a rocky road on the 7th, leading to hurt feelings. A phone call from a sibling on the Full Moon in Virgo on the 18th could bring up old baggage. Punt on heavy discussions.

Rewarding Days

4, 13, 24, 28

Challenging Days

6, 18, 22

Cancer | April

Overall Theme

The New Moon in Aries on the 1st speaks volumes about the energy you are pouring into your work as you assimilate facets of newly acquired responsibilities. At home you have your eye on the garden beds to plant some herbs and veggies, but the phone keeps ringing for your professional services and interferes with taking a day off.

Relationships

Add a little spontaneity to your weekend around the 22nd by planning some fun and relaxation with your significant other. The bonds you share deserve memorable interludes that result in renewed love and affection. Relatives at a distance extend invitations and suggest entertainment options that meet group needs.

Success and Money

The first Solar Eclipse of 2022 occurs on the 30th in Taurus and your solar eleventh house of friends, memberships, goals, and leadership initiatives. Start working on agenda items mid-month for upcoming business lunches, so you have plenty of discussion items to attract commitment of diverse attendees.

Pitfalls and Potential Problems

Expect disagreements in organizational gatherings to occur early in the month. You may uncover sore feelings over membership roles that need a resolution and crop up all month. Pluto goes retrograde on the 29th, followed by the Solar Eclipse on the 30th, which could generate misunderstandings if goals have not been clarified. Avoid a tug-of-war over credit card use for personal items that seem excessive from the 12th to the 14th.

Rewarding Days

1, 7, 22, 27

Challenging Days

4, 12, 16, 30

Cancer | May

Overall Theme

The compatible Pisces planets that are present in your solar ninth house early this month suggest that you take time to play, go on vacation, or give your full attention to romance. Venus moves into Aries by the 3rd, and later in the month, so does Mars, moving considerable attention to your career. Work demands may present challenges.

Relationships

Mother love is a strong Cancerian trait, and if yours is alive, you'll dedicate time to show her you care on May 8. If your mom is gone, you fondly remember her nurturing spirit as you share important memories with family. Friends who share similar goals meet to discuss mutual plans and interests early in the month. Enjoy a nice reunion lunch with old friends.

Success and Money

Members of your work team pull together despite stressful circumstances and possibly staff vacancies to unite in developing all of the pieces of a presentation that reflects the group's expertise. Enjoy the accolades your boss heaps on you for the role you have played in completing assigned projects. The promise of a promotion or raise lifts your spirits.

Pitfalls and Potential Problems

Mercury goes retrograde on the 10th in Gemini and your solar twelfth house and has you scrambling for the right words. Take a breath. The Lunar Eclipse on the 16th occurs in your solar fifth house, possibly leading to worry about competition with a romantic prospect.

Rewarding Days

1, 6, 18, 26

Challenging Days

4, 11, 13, 20

Cancer | June

Overall Theme

The spotlight is on substantial planetary activity this month. Mercury goes direct on the 3rd in Taurus and your solar eleventh house and favors group meetings this month featuring important announcements. Saturn goes retrograde in Aquarius on the 4th, and Neptune in Pisces follows suit on the 28th. Well-thought-out directives lighten the workload via streamlined procedures.

Relationships

Venus spends most of the month in Taurus and your solar eleventh house, favoring plans with friends, partners, siblings, or neighbors. Schedule fun gatherings before the Full Moon on the 14th. Afterward, work priorities involving assignments with new hires could absorb a significant amount of your time, especially if you are tasked with conducting training or orientation. Catch up with family news around the 8th.

Success and Money

Enjoy the good news about your health and congratulate yourself for working on your blood pressure and lowering cholesterol numbers. You're feeling more organized after making physical changes in arranging furniture at home. Celebrate birthdays with other Cancers in your workplace. Make birthday plans for lunch with a neighbor.

Pitfalls and Potential Problems

Mars in Aries in your solar tenth house clashes with work plans and affects schedules, resulting in mandatory overtime to stay on track. Money disagreements add tension on the home front. Review planned purchases before going out on a limb impulsively. Sensitive feelings surface around the 12th on a date with a romantic connection.

Rewarding Days

3, 8, 14, 23

Challenging Days

6, 9, 12, 28

Cancer | July

Overall Theme

Jupiter turns retrograde in Aries and your solar tenth house on July 28. Could its presence signal a delay in the start of your vacation plans? If you schedule time away from the 2nd through the 10th, the outcome will be much more satisfactory. Give some intuitive thought to your goals for the year ahead as you celebrate your 2022 Solar Return.

Relationships

Long-distance travel to see relatives or take a bucket-list trip is possible on the 18th, as long as no travel or health restrictions limit options. July is a good month to strengthen family ties and include close relatives in exciting adventures. If you are home over the 4th of July, host a cookout.

Success and Money

By setting aside funds for recreation and amusement earlier in the year, you snag the best bargains on airfare, park admissions, sight-seeing tours, and musical venues. Certain Cancers may win all-expenses-paid trips or tickets to favorite sporting events. Include the preferences of each immediate family member in your plans.

Pitfalls and Potential Problems

Instructions for completing a task may be misconstrued around the 12th, leading to confusion and delays in meeting deadlines. Clarify contractual terms with authority figures on the 20th to avoid overstepping boundaries. Jupiter turns retrograde on July 28, the same day as the New Moon in Leo. Delay travel plans by a day for best results.

Rewarding Days

2, 7, 18, 28

Challenging Days

5, 12, 13, 20

Cancer | August

Overall Theme

Your financial picture looks rosy, especially from the 1st to the 12th. Spend some of your cash on home improvements, especially kitchen design or appliances. Look over contract terms and schedule desired work. Plan a short getaway around the 14th to check out real estate prospects and potential living conditions.

Relationships

You'll spend more time than usual this month with mortgage brokers, financial advisors, and realtors who offer products, property, and services that interest you. Networking leads to valuable connections in distant locations and may draw you to a different lifestyle. Include your partner in planned trips, especially if you can mix business with pleasure.

Success and Money

Superior credit nets you the most desired loan for a home purchase, vacation residence, or refinance of your existing property. Shop for the best terms early in the month if you're ready to make a move. The 14th shows promise, even though you have to avoid impulsiveness in decision-making. Discuss first impressions with your partner, along with the cost and value of transactions.

Pitfalls and Potential Problems

Avoid conflict at home base on the 4th, when feelings seem fragile and tempers short. Confrontations in the workplace could occur and rattle team spirit around the 8th. Get tension under control before you meet with management on the 16th to show a unified front in work performance. Resolve differences before Uranus goes retrograde in Taurus on the 24th.

Rewarding Days

1, 12, 14, 24

Challenging Days

4, 8, 16, 27

Cancer | September

Overall Theme

Extend the long holiday weekend by a few extra days to enjoy a surprise adventure with your significant other that strengthens your shared love bond. Work could get demanding by the 12th, but you anticipate the deluge and get organized. The Pisces Full Moon on the 10th occurs right after Mercury in Libra goes retrograde on the 9th, alerting you to table travel and get both your physical space and your office environment in order.

Relationships

Partnership ventures shine this month, in both your personal and business worlds. Acknowledge the strength of collaborative project efforts and look for ways to combine the talents of others who have relevant skills and could enhance productivity. Renewed passion helps you bond romantically with your love partner the last weekend of the month.

Success and Money

You and your partner combine resources to pay for household improvements that lift your spirits and make you want to stay in your home instead of listing it for sale. When you learn the accelerating value of your home, you may want to shop for another property and use the equity to land a lucrative deal.

Pitfalls and Potential Problems

Children's interests clash with plans right before the holiday weekend, forcing a disappointing schedule change. Work with key players to resolve the problem so you can salvage part of the trip. Keep a low profile on the 20th, when the Moon is in your sign and your "crabby" face emerges.

Rewarding Days

6, 12, 17, 22

Challenging Days

2, 10, 20, 25

Cancer | October

Overall Theme
Mars in Gemini in your solar twelfth house creates ample opportunity to pursue studies and write articles or books and gives you space to create inspiring content. If report writing is a key responsibility, Mars energizes your mind and helps you focus. This is a powerhouse month for planetary activity, with a number of shifts occurring.

Relationships
The Solar Eclipse conjunct Venus on the 25th in Scorpio and your solar fifth house heightens romantic feelings. Enjoy quality time with your love partner and share intimate moments. Schedule lunch dates with friends on the 12th. Single Cancers meet prospects at happy hours and sporting events.

Success and Money
Despite Mercury-driven mix-ups and staffing shortages, you get the job done and your efforts net an increase in your paycheck. Showcase commitment to the mission and vision and compete for new opportunities that fit your skill set. Set aside extra cash for savings and holiday spending. Put a larger portion into retirement funding.

Pitfalls and Potential Problems
Planetary stations occur all month. Mercury goes direct in Virgo on the 2nd, followed by Pluto in Capricorn on the 8th and Saturn in Aquarius on the 23rd. Curtail travel and think through details of pending decisions on these dates. Mars turns retrograde on the 30th in Gemini and your solar twelfth house and could mean that you edit or rethink the flow of material you've been writing.

Rewarding Days
4, 12, 14, 25

Challenging Days
1, 3, 9, 22

Cancer | November

Overall Theme

The last Lunar Eclipse of 2022 occurs on November 8 in Taurus and your solar eleventh house of goals, plans, dreams, and friendships, tempting you to book holiday travel, purchase festive decorations for your home, and tackle your ever-expanding gift list. Meet spending goals with restraint.

Relationships

Family members located at a distance propose a holiday gathering that requires considerable coordination. Make sure someone takes charge to avoid disappointments. Your home could be the center of the festivities, with guests arriving as early as the 20th. Extend warm and loving wishes to those who are ill or fearful of travel. Arrange a Zoom session that includes relatives in diverse locations.

Success and Money

Problem-solving skills put you at the top of your game on the 23rd, the day of the Sagittarius New Moon, which coincides with Jupiter going direct in your solar sixth house. Travel works well for you on the 4th and could include entertainment and errands. You'll see exceptional value for your purchases on the 14th.

Pitfalls and Potential Problems

Carefully plan and monitor spending on the 1st and 16th, when attractive sales put pressure on your wallet and can lead to impulsive spending. Do comparison shopping to be sure you don't overpay when purchasing electronic equipment. Accommodating guests and cleaning up after significant meal preparation could make people at home base testy on the 27th, when departures are imminent.

Rewarding Days

4, 14, 20, 23

Challenging Days

1, 8, 16, 27

Cancer | December

Overall Theme
Everything is smelling like roses in your work environment. If only the feeling of euphoria would last all year, as a festive mood hangs in the air, strengthening bonds with staff. Thank the stellium of Sagittarius planets hanging out in your solar sixth house for the celebratory mood. Wrap up pending contracts for the coming year by the 15th.

Relationships
Renew ties with family and issue invitations to siblings, cousins, and neighbors to spread the holiday spirit. Cherish these bonds. Gatherings early in the month compliments of company officials could include one or more celebrations. Enjoy getting to know the families of executives and coworkers.

Success and Money
Neptune in Pisces goes direct in your solar ninth house on the 3rd and gives the greenlight to pending travel plans. Get the terms of travel discounts in writing before committing to a trip. Grab the mistletoe and take off with your significant other for a late December vacation.

Pitfalls and Potential Problems
The 6th shows mixed results for anticipated interactions with professional memberships, yet someone new appears on the scene and adds a note of spontaneity to the gathering. Table nonthreatening medical exams or procedures until after the 1st of the year. Avoid them on December 7 and 22. The 11th works well for flu shots.

Rewarding Days
4, 11, 15, 23

Challenging Days
2, 7, 18, 22

Cancer Action Table

These dates reflect the best—but not the only—times for success and ease in these activities, according to your Sun sign.

	JAN	FEB	MAR	APR	MAY	JUN	JUL	AUG	SEP	OCT	NOV	DEC
Move	7		4					14			4	
Romance	14				16		7		6	25		23
Seek counseling/coaching		27				8			17		23	
Ask for a raise			28		26		2			12		
Vacation		3		27								15
Get a loan				22		23		12				

Leo

The Lion
July 22 to August 22

♌

Element: Fire

Quality: Fixed

Polarity: Yang/masculine

Planetary Ruler: The Sun

Meditation: I trust in the strength of my soul

Gemstone: Ruby

Power Stones: Topaz, sardonyx

Key Phrase: I will

Glyph: Lion's tail

Anatomy: Heart, upper back

Colors: Gold, scarlet

Animals: Lions, large cats

Myths/Legends: Apollo, Isis, Helios

House: Fifth

Opposite Sign: Aquarius

Flowers: Marigold, sunflower

Keyword: Magnetic

The Leo Personality

Strengths, Talents, and the Creative Spark

Your Sun sign has an affinity for royalty and favors purple tones, magentas, and rich blues in your color scheme. Your personality sparkles with drama and daring while you bring good vibrations to your family, friends, and associates. The Sun rules your sign and the fifth house of adventure, fun, games, social life, children, lovers, dating experiences, freelancing, sports, exercise, romantic interludes, speculation, risk-taking, and entrepreneurial enterprises. You have a flair for individualism, and what you express complements your magnetic personality in displaying the qualities most affiliated with Leo. Those attributes include a can-do attitude, pride of accomplishment, entertaining and socializing skills, cherishing your love interests, leadership, loyalty, recreational pursuits, and a fascination with the big picture. Many of you present a dramatic picture to the world, wearing expensive, fashionable clothing, plus elegant hair and jewelry that makes a statement to complete your look.

The planets you have in your fifth house describe the range of emotions and the diverse creative and recreational activities that interest you. Many Leos are hard-core sports fans and may be either an active participant or a spectator. For others, the world of entertainment and showmanship drives your passion. You are a creature of habit—if you dance, it is a hot pursuit. Yours is the second fixed sign and the second fire sign of the zodiac. Your magnanimous spirit attracts others who are impressed by your enthusiasm. Leos come in two distinct personality styles: exuberant Lions who want their share of the limelight and the more reserved yet equally powerful Cats who bask in glory in a more subtle way. If a parent, you are supportive and enthusiastic about your children's interests and enjoy sharing their accomplishments with others.

Intimacy and Personal Relationships

Finding the right partner is worth every bit of the effort you expend in your search. Once you find "the one," you bubble over with enthusiasm to tell your family and friends you're in love. Every moment spent with the object of your affection prompts you to care more about your partner and look for ways to say "I love you." Romantic gestures are your specialty: passionate love notes, intimate candlelit dinners, getaway weekends, and movie dates to see romantic films. Leos typically get along well with Aries, Gemini, Libra, Sagittarius, and your opposite sign, Aquarius. Another Leo may be suitable too, as long as you establish that your partnership is about sharing and not fighting over who rules the roost. Bossiness can be overpowering at times and leads to conflict and wasted words. Say it with flowers instead!

Values and Resources

The gift of generosity you possess attracts many friends and colleagues charmed by your display of enthusiasm. You believe in achieving life balance by including work and play in your daily routine. That often includes fitness and exercise programs. Leos love their children and spend hours reading to them, playing games with them, and teaching, coaching, or entertaining them. Vacations are one of your favorite ways to give your children the happiness they deserve. You know how to make each trip a memorable experience by focusing on favorite activities and encouraging participation. You are a loyal friend and place loyalty at the top of the list in your quest for compatible companions. A natural leader, you show those in your sphere of influence how much you value their commitment and work contributions by extending party invitations in your home to employees and collaborators. Your home reflects your taste for elegance, with creature comforts designed to give everyone a place to relax, including guests. Not surprisingly, you want the same ambience present in your work space, and give it a decorative makeover conducive to compatible work conditions.

Blind Spots and Blockages

Your sign rules the back, blood, circulatory system, heart, spine, and metabolism. Illness often results when your emotions are blocked or you don't know how to release your anger. You feel the wounds deeply when someone rejects you or bashes your ego. Leo often holds lengthy grudges and stops speaking to the perpetrator indefinitely. Even if you don't react outwardly, you feel the pain and may hold on to sadness and disappointment for a long time, especially with a broken romantic relationship. Cheerful, sunny Leo takes a detour from sociability and tends to emotional wounds behind the scenes. After the pain passes and your heart regains its spark, you go on to find new connections. Critics say you have a big ego. When overconfidence in the form of stubbornness gets in your way, you fail to see shortcomings connected with people and career aspirations. You can fall for promises of advancement and work long hours to prove your worth by earning the offered raises and promotions only to find you believed empty words that were not backed up with action. Of significant importance is that you seek work that suits your talents best, rather than accepting the highest starting salary you can find and then realizing that the challenges you were seeking are not available. Unfulfilling work leads to boredom, overeating, and sometimes drinking too much to escape the reality that your choice was a mistake.

Goals and Success

A job that gives you a chance to lead and display your entrepreneurial side fits your idea of the perfect career. You seek recognition for accomplishments through your innovative management style and ability to direct the mission and vision of the organization. Part of your strategy is to coach subordinates to reach the pinnacle of success through outstanding performance and goal achievement. Even if you are not the top dog, you value working in an environment that offers autonomy, with a trusting attitude toward and confidence in employees. You are a high-energy doer who is often the cheerleader for team spirit and energizes the group, if you manage it, with creative work breaks and rewards such as catered lunches, parties, field trips, or sporting events. Task diversity keeps you motivated. Dramatic self-expression via talks, speeches, and presentations reflects your communication style. Share information updates with the team frequently and delegate accountability and authority so that subordinates gain experience that qualifies them for moving up the ladder. Provide encouragement and watch your popularity grow.

Leo Keywords for 2022

Effervescence, encouragement, enthusiasm

The Year Ahead for Leo

As you embark on your journey through 2022, you enthusiastically leave the disruptions resulting from coronavirus-enforced social distancing behind you. Normally, you're not easily suppressed, but in the past two years, this painful COVID-19 pandemic descended like no other on important facets of your life, affecting relationships, routine activities, schedules, and plans. You enter 2022 with an abundance of coping mechanisms that will aid you in decision-making and managing your workload. Life will not be dull. Your solar seventh house of partners highlights the responsibilities that accompany personal and professional unions, with Saturn in Aquarius transiting this collaborative sphere. Competing for attention, Uranus, another fixed-sign planet, begins the year in retrograde motion in Taurus and your solar tenth house of career. For certain Leos that spells disruption and sets up a pattern called a *T-square* with your Leo-ruled solar first house, your solar seventh house of relationships, and your ambitious solar tenth house. There are challenges ahead in terms of use of skills, compatibility in relationships, and recovery of emotional and financial stability.

As the new year begins, four planets occupy Capricorn and your solar sixth house of work—but only one will stick around all year, Pluto, which has been in residence since 2008 and urges you to examine stuck patterns in your work world to release what no longer matches your goals. Jupiter moves into Pisces in 2022 and occupies your solar eighth house, initiating new opportunities to pay down joint debt and build savings. Transiting Neptune continues its journey, which began in 2011, in Pisces and your solar eighth house of partnership assets and money you owe, investments, estates, regeneration, and psychological depth. You may experience powerful psychic breakthroughs and insight about others through meditation and visualization practices. All four eclipses in 2022 fall in the fixed signs of Taurus and Scorpio and generate activity in your solar chart's action-oriented first, seventh, tenth, and fourth houses. Enjoy the teachable moments that accompany awakenings in your personal and business life. Embrace growth enthusiastically.

Jupiter

In 2022 Jupiter occupies Pisces and your solar eighth house for most of the year. This transit puts the spotlight on partnership funds, money from new or dual sources, joint ventures, and investments in property, stocks, and bonds. It may be time to update your will or increase the contributions in your retirement account. Seek advice from a family or estate attorney if you have questions about legal procedures. In the first half of April, this Jupiter transit joins transiting Neptune in Pisces and stimulates an interest in mystical experiences, dreams, and spiritual studies and may reveal hidden information that has been buried in your psyche. Leos born between August 15 and 17 may benefit the most from the insight that evolves during this cycle. On July 28, Jupiter will turn retrograde in Aries and your solar ninth house, leading to delays in plans, business and personal trips, vacations, and educational pursuits. Jupiter in Aries most benefits Leos born between July 23 and August 1. Jupiter moves back into Pisces and your solar eighth house on October 28 and goes direct in motion on November 23, before moving back into Aries for good on December 20 for a yearlong journey.

Saturn

After having spent last year with Saturn in Aquarius transiting your solar seventh house of personal and business partners, you're aware that relationship dealings can be tension-filled, even those that are long-term and considered stable. If you have a feeling that a dispute is imminent, it could be a Saturn lesson moving in to remind you to communicate clearly and listen more. You can better determine what you do or don't want in terms of partners. Investing in an assessment of the qualities each of you brings to the relationship gives you a clear picture about the commitments you've made. Saturn in this house either strengthens existing bonds or creates painful conditions that leave you searching for greener pastures, whether in a business or a personal setting. What do you want your future to look like? For some Leos, Saturn in the seventh house brings a marriage, often a long-lasting one, or a renewal of your loving feelings or a proposal to expand business agreements. At the other end of the spectrum, Saturn in a fixed sign like Aquarius can make you stubborn and reluctant to acknowledge your own shortfalls or those of a partnership. Restrictiveness smothers creative enterprise. Clear up doubt and enjoy the fruits of your investment in a meaningful partnership. This year Saturn's retrograde period occurs from June 4 through October 23. Those of you born between August 2 and 19 see the most activity from Saturn in 2022. Venus and Mars in Aquarius line up in your solar seventh house for most of March and part of April, bringing effervescence to your close relationships and highlighting love. You can count on Saturn to bring you a mature vision.

Uranus

Imagine waking up about four years ago and finding out that you have a guest who has taken up residence in your solar tenth house of career, authority figures, ambition, organizational conditions, family, and the status quo. Uranus, the planet associated with sudden blow-ups, shake-ups, and chaotic behavior, has been in stable, usually grounded Taurus since May 2018, making everything in your career environment sit up and take notice as it completes a seven-year odyssey that delivered a number of shocks to your professional equilibrium. Leo, you are one of the signs that may have had your entire work world disrupted by the arrival of the coronavirus pandemic that began in 2020. A variety of disruptions occurred: businesses closed, employees were laid off or fired, employees received reassignments to other work units, unemployment claims broke records, and employees were ordered to work from home and had to scramble to find ways to care for their children since schools and daycare centers closed for months on end. In 2022 you are in a recovery year, making adjustments in how you perform your work or starting a new job. The planet of chaos is not finished yet with his tour of your solar tenth house and moves into retrograde motion on August 24, going direct on January 22, 2023. Leos born between August 1 and 12 will feel the most significant pressure from the erratic Uranus cycle this year.

Neptune

Neptune, the watery planet of compassion, healing, psychological health, and secrets, has made a home in your solar eighth house in Pisces. This house represents finances belonging to you and your partner, transformation, deep thinking and perception, psychological influences, detective skills, inner analysis and healing, debts, karma, mortgages, loans, credit cards, estates, insurance, and surgery, as well as birth, sex, death, and regeneration. When Neptune transits the solar eighth house, it may leave you feeling confused and shaky about your decisions and uncertain about your deepest feelings. Emotional encounters are often very intense and draining. You and a partner may be stuck in how you handle unresolved issues between you. You may cope by overeating. If you get to the heart of the matter, you'll shed the unwanted pounds that represent the baggage you want to unload. You'll benefit most from open and straightforward discussion to clear the air. Neptune moves only four to five degrees each year. In 2022 it most affects Leos born between August 12 and 19. The retrograde period for mystical Neptune will be from June 28 to December 3 this year.

Pluto

Pluto in Capricorn in your solar sixth house of work-related matters, health, pets, and nutrition connects most strongly this year with Leos born between August 17 and 22, when it makes a stressful inconjunct aspect to your Sun through your entire birthday cycle, suggesting that you pause and look closely at your work scene, resume, and your activity schedule. Since Pluto first showed up here in 2008, it is logical to think that you have had ample time to release stuck patterns and give serious thought to how you want to fulfill your work goals. Your inner knower recognizes the truth. While you admire your colleagues, you could be disappointed in what you perceive to be a lax management style, contributing to your lack of job satisfaction. This transit could also indicate health issues, suggesting that you make time for a thorough medical exam and take on an exercise program that reduces stress. In 2022 Pluto in Capricorn goes retrograde on April 29 and moves direct on October 8, giving you time to retool plans, give serious consideration to a job change, or break out of a rut, especially if you have had your fill of restrictive work conditions.

How Will This Year's Eclipses Affect You?

Two other fixed signs, Taurus and Scorpio, feature prominently in the eclipses of 2022. A total of four eclipses occur this year, two solar (New Moon) and two lunar (Full Moon), bringing intense periods that begin manifesting about two months before they actually occur. All four eclipses take place in two of your solar chart's angular houses, the tenth and the fourth, representing your career, employer, and prevailing home and family conditions. Your solar first and seventh houses may receive strong vibrations from these eclipses, putting the spotlight on action from you or from personal and business partnerships. These houses also have fixed-sign rulers, Leo and Aquarius. Eclipses manifest in cycles involving all twelve signs of the zodiac and usually occur in pairs about two weeks apart. Never fear eclipses—think of them as welcome opportunities that allow you to face old, outworn patterns and release them. Eclipses often have six months to a year to show their effect on certain houses in your chart. Their presence may trigger unexpected revelations, surprises, and windfalls. The closer an eclipse is to a planet or point in your chart, the greater the importance it plays in your life. Those of you born with a planet at the same degree as an eclipse are likely to see a high level of activity and a major change in the house where the eclipse occurs.

The first Solar Eclipse of 2022 occurs on April 30 in Taurus and your solar tenth house of career, authority figures, ambition, recognition for achievements, and organizational and affiliated conditions.

With a tenth-house eclipse, the pressure is on, pushing you to keep goal commitment and promises on track. You have to put your money where your mouth is and deliver the work you said you would accomplish and make sure it is on time. No one but you is accountable for making adjustments to your work and forming healthy habits that give you time to play, ensuring that you achieve life balance. If your physical appearance and health have been problematic, this eclipse will remind you to seek solutions and get counsel from medical specialists, dieticians, and behavioral consultants.

Two weeks later, the first Lunar Eclipse of the year occurs on May 16 in Scorpio and your solar fourth house of home and foundation, family (especially parents), occupants of your home, the physical structure of and conditions in your home, and features of the home such as the garden, kitchen, family room, and dining quarters. If you have planets located in this house, expect revelations of any problem areas associated with principal residents to come to light. If relationships are positive, you'll benefit from strengthening bonds and fulfilling goals. Should you be experiencing challenges, any rough spots could hit with possible shock value and call for discussion with a focus on workable solutions. A child's divorce could lead to temporary residence with you. Be sure you and your spouse are on the same page with the new arrangements.

On October 25, the second Solar Eclipse of 2022 takes place in Scorpio and your solar fourth house of home and foundation, family (especially parents), occupants of your home, the physical structure of and conditions in your home, and features of the home such as the garden, kitchen, family room, and dining quarters. When this eclipse hits after months of examining what you found regarding relationships back in May, you will know whether remedial action taken had the desired positive results or whether the relationships or affiliated issues are headed for trouble. Seek only peaceful solutions.

The year's final eclipse is a Lunar Eclipse on November 8 in Taurus and your solar tenth house of career, authority figures, ambition, recognition for achievements, and organizational and affiliated conditions. Close to this degree is transiting Uranus in Taurus, so if your birthday occurs between August 8 and 10, this eclipse makes an action-oriented square aspect. Expect a change in direction in career matters. Consider the bright side of liberating moves.

Leo | January

Overall Theme

The new year begins with an emphasis on interactions with partners and a close look at your financial picture. Mercury goes retrograde in your solar seventh house on the 14th, affecting matters related to partners that need a closer look before taking action. Uranus in Taurus moves direct in your solar tenth house on the 18th, highlighting work conditions that affected productivity last summer and are ready for action.

Relationships

Communication with your significant other takes on a serious tone, especially if the topic is spending versus saving money. Get opinions from estate planners and lenders who offer solutions to help you build a secure future. Children or romantic partners could be argumentative early in the month but chill after Venus goes direct on the 29th.

Success and Money

Good credit makes you eligible for the best loan rates if you are buying a home or auto or refinancing your residence. You may have more equity than you realized and make plans to fund a remodeling project. Economic turnaround brings you a much anticipated raise late in the month.

Pitfalls and Potential Problems

A planned trip the week of the 10th is likely to be canceled due to the arrival of unexpected visitors. Don't rush to reschedule the travel after company leaves. Instead, look at the gift offered by the Full Moon in Cancer on the 17th: a chance to chill and regroup after feeling drained from intense discussions with others.

Rewarding Days

5, 7, 20, 21

Challenging Days

1, 10, 12, 17

Leo | February

Overall Theme

The relationship theme continues when the Aquarius New Moon on the 1st puts the spotlight on your personal and business partners in your solar seventh house. Use the lunar energy to romance your significant other with a special dinner. Then build goodwill with work cooperators and show your boss how well your workplace is recovering after the setbacks related to COVID-19.

Relationships

You and your significant other are feeling renewed closeness and relief after you made key decisions to bolster financial security. Celebrate Valentine's Day with your spouse and children. Work authorities are cordial and supportive of collaborative efforts to carry out planned goals. Parents report renewed good health.

Success and Money

Networking through your workplace contacts helps you identify potential collaborators and teammates suitable for work on new initiatives. Set up meetings to discuss skills and roles and exchange resumes after Mercury goes direct on the 3rd. A windfall around the 18th brings unexpected cash. Put lottery tickets in Valentine cards to surprise loved ones.

Pitfalls and Potential Problems

You're wise to table important meetings on the 16th, when the Full Moon in Leo creates opposition energy for productive discussions. Meetings with professional associates are cut short on the 10th, when key members don't show up and the planned agenda falls flat. Check the tone at home base on the 23rd and listen to unexpected complaints without judgment.

Rewarding Days

1, 3, 8, 18

Challenging Days

5, 10, 16, 23

Leo | March

Overall Theme

No doubt you're learning much about partnerships in the early months of 2022 and the need for clear communication. Convey feelings of support and trust to special people in your personal or work life. Your attention to detail paves the way for better relationships as those in your circle adjust to changing family and work demands after a couple of years of uncertainty.

Relationships

You'll hear from siblings and cousins this month. Expect them to trade notes about coping mechanisms and hear news about shifting work norms or job changes. Your significant other plays a strong role in showing cooperation with goals and gives you a boost of confidence. Children enjoy special events with you around the 24th.

Success and Money

Contracts and agreements look favorable and show how your excellent assessment of terms leads to successful payoffs. Building a good relationship in your community may lead to a request for your services in a leadership role. Get estimates for home improvements on the 3rd and compare costs for materials and labor.

Pitfalls and Potential Problems

Your solar second house shows challenging aspects from the Virgo Full Moon on the 18th, when Jupiter, Saturn, and Neptune interfere with smooth execution of a home improvement contract or a proposed outlay of cash for a vacation. Don't go over budget when buying gifts for family and friends. Egos at your workplace clash over assignments on the 7th.

Rewarding Days

1, 2, 19, 24

Challenging Days

7, 10, 15, 18

Leo | April

Overall Theme

A New Moon occurs twice in your chart this month: in your solar ninth house in Aries on the 1st and in your solar tenth house of career matters in Taurus (the year's first Solar Eclipse) on the 30th. The Full Moon in Libra on the 16th occurs in your solar third house, generating lively discussions in your neighborhood. Electronic media is a possible hot topic due to implementation of innovative upgrades.

Relationships

In-laws, people at a distance, and family members are in the spotlight this month. You can take that much desired getaway now to meet up with them. You'll have better success in scheduling lunches with friends or planning a special event with them receiving excellent support from Mercury, Venus, Mars, and Saturn. Quality time with family opens up on the 18th.

Success and Money

An infusion of cash helps with planned organizational expansion, alerting you to upcoming announcements about available positions. Be sure to apply if the opportunities are a good match for your skill set. Look for action after the Solar Eclipse in Taurus on the 30th.

Pitfalls and Potential Problems

Don't get caught up in workplace gossip on the 4th, when the Moon in Taurus lands in your solar tenth house. Defuse rumors related to candidate selections if you know that no announcements have been made. You and spouse deal with tense discussions on the 25th over unpleasant topics. "I'm sorry" is a powerful healer. Use it.

Rewarding Days

1, 7, 18, 30

Challenging Days

10, 16, 20

Leo | May

Overall Theme

Confidential matters steal the limelight this month, starting with candidate selections your boss shares with you privately as the month begins. You may be asked to evaluate candidates' qualifications and will probably take work home over the weekend of May 7 to 8. You'll feel pulled in two directions with children's sports schedules and entertainment requests from your spouse.

Relationships

Your boss and workmates play a role in claiming your attention due to demands for meeting timeline deadlines before mid-month. Next, your children or those you teach or coach step up to compete for your attention at competitive sports or contests. When the Moon in Aquarius moves into your solar seventh house of partnerships on the 20th, your spouse looks for the go-ahead to initiate a decorating project that adds value to your home.

Success and Money

Satisfaction comes from seeing your blueprints come to life, whether you are building a home or remodeling your kitchen. Begin your household projects by May 2 to make sure they are underway before Mercury turns retrograde on the 10th. Take delight in the perk your contractor offers to add value to the job.

Pitfalls and Potential Problems

Nobody saw it coming when a professional contact stretches the truth around the 4th or confuses issues by stating "facts" without providing sufficient research to back them up. Don't make a spending decision on the 18th, when project costs escalate considerably over original estimates. Shipping costs and foreign manufacturing firms could be blamed for construction delays.

Rewarding Days

1, 7, 18, 21

Challenging Days

4, 9, 16, 29

Leo | June

Overall Theme

Shifting planetary activity this month starts with Mercury resuming direct motion in Taurus on the 3rd, giving you an opportunity to catch up on work so you can spend more time with loved ones. Accept incoming social invitations. Your spouse and immediate family, as well as loved ones near and far, benefit from quality bonding time and a change of pace.

Relationships

The spotlight is on your romantic partner, children, or young ones you teach or coach. Plan outings that include sporting events, perhaps cheering for your child's team or obtaining tickets to games or amusements the whole family enjoys. Children respond lovingly to the special attention you shower on them. Surprise your sweetheart.

Success and Money

You're able to snag a travel bargain late in the month and take the trip you've been postponing either for business or to see loved ones in faraway places. Mercury, Venus, and Uranus unite in your solar tenth house this month, generating productive collaborative opportunities for critical projects.

Pitfalls and Potential Problems

Don't start a new household project on the 4th, when Saturn turns retrograde in Aquarius and you find that materials you need are unavailable. Home base matters intensify on the 12th, potentially leading to heated verbal exchanges. Neptune in Pisces turns retrograde on the 28th in your solar eighth house, creating confusion over wording in pending financial transactions.

Rewarding Days

3, 8, 16, 21

Challenging Days

6, 12, 23, 28

July | Leo

Overall Theme

After a couple of years of social restrictions, party gatherings take on new meaning. Everyone on your holiday guest list takes a cue from you to unwind as you feast, dance, play games, and share news with seldom-seen visitors. Toast guests with your magnanimous Leo spirit and treat them to an eye-popping fireworks display.

Relationships

Those of you ready to list your home for sale or get estimates for remodeling work usher in a parade of appraisers, decorators, realtors, and home stagers. Your Leo charm works overtime in establishing rapport with potential business contacts. You and your spouse opt for personal bonding and a night out around the 16th.

Success and Money

A low-risk business investment pays a bigger dividend than you anticipated, leaving you with extra cash to treat your partner to a night out. Debt reduction puts a smile on your face when you use the remaining cash to pay off a credit card or other expense. Organizational meetings exude high energy on the 22nd, leaving team members in a celebratory mood for the weekend.

Pitfalls and Potential Problems

Regroup on the 1st to check materials and to verify that your product is error-free. A business lunch could get expensive for you on the 5th, when the bulk of the bill falls on your shoulders. Teammates argue over key practices, showing conflicting attitudes on the Full Moon in Capricorn on the 13th.

Rewarding Days

3, 16, 18, 22

Challenging Days

1, 5, 13, 26

Leo | August

Overall Theme

With Mars occupying your solar tenth house from the 1st through the 20th, work demands escalate and get downright tense as Uranus applies extra pressure on August 1 and 2. Spend money at sales to pick up supplies and clothing for the family vacation that starts around the 15th.

Relationships

Now that your remodeling project is complete, plan a family dinner on the 6th to invite parents and siblings to share the feast and see the fruits of your redesign. In-laws join the tour and weigh in on the fine points of your finished work. Treat young children to an ice cream bar and let them create their own sundaes with favorite toppings.

Success and Money

Bonus money arrives early in the month, just in time to fund the family vacation you booked for the middle of August. If you or a family member applied for specialized training or classes, you'll receive good news about acceptance around the 15th. Details about purchasing books and materials arrive by the 27th, with classes beginning the following week.

Pitfalls and Potential Problems

Arguments over parking issues could crop up in your neighborhood around the 4th. The Aquarius Full Moon on the 11th in your solar seventh house of partnerships brings out the beast that disrupts domestic tranquility. The disagreement revolves around choices of amusement and recreational options for your upcoming getaway. Children start weighing in on the 8th with diverse requests that need a resolution before the bags are packed.

Rewarding Days

1, 15, 20, 27

Challenging Days

3, 7, 11, 23

Leo | September

Overall Theme

Most of the positive activity in your chart this month takes place in the zone of intimacy—solar houses five, six, and seven—with a strong nod to your solar tenth house of authority and career. Mercury turns retrograde on the 9th in your solar third house of communication, so stay flexible with plans and accomplishment deadlines.

Relationships

Social networking gets a boost during the Labor Day holiday weekend when you make stimulating connections that inspire you to join new groups. Teamwork is in the spotlight around the 6th, and collaboration moves the goals forward. You and your partner enjoy a harmonious connection on the 8th and discuss fall plans.

Success and Money

You get star billing for your leadership skills in finding a solution to a long-reaching annoyance that has hindered productivity. A raise could be on its way to your bank account by the 15th, although you'll have to contend with a couple of green-eyed monsters who take a few jabs at your ideas from the 17th to the 29th. Is there a promotion in your future?

Pitfalls and Potential Problems

The New Moon in Libra on the 25th opposes transiting Jupiter in Aries in your solar ninth house of travel, making this a good day to avoid air travel and testy conversations. Weekend confusion materializes when the Full Moon in Pisces on the 10th crosses paths with Mars in Gemini. Taxi or Uber drivers may lose their sense of direction. Don't eat the extra charges.

Rewarding Days

4, 6, 8, 15

Challenging Days

2, 10, 17, 29

Leo | October

Overall Theme

October is a breakthrough month when several planets shift course starting on the 2nd, when Mercury goes direct in Virgo in your solar second house. Pluto shifts to direct motion on the 8th in Capricorn and your solar sixth house, and Saturn turns direct in Aquarius on the 23rd in your solar seventh house of partners.

Relationships

Workmates steal the limelight, playing a key role in getting the job done. All hands are on deck for most of the month. You may be seeing medical practitioners, bodyworkers and dentists, and changing your approach to caring for your health. The Solar Eclipse in Scorpio conjunct Venus on the 25th occurs at home base and creates a welcoming romantic tone for you and your partner.

Success and Money

Making money makes you very happy. When the redirection of key planets lifts restrictions, you soar to attention to demonstrate the depth of motivation. The value of collaboration brings the success you desire. Even with disruptive Uranus in your solar tenth house all year, you manage to outperform most of your colleagues. Your boss recognizes your superior performance.

Pitfalls and Potential Problems

For dating Leos, romance goes awry on the 2nd when communication breaks down. The Full Moon in Aries on the 9th could bring disappointing news regarding advanced education. Mars in conversation-oriented Gemini makes a retrograde station in your solar eleventh house on the 30th and affects friendships and the flow of goal achievement.

Rewarding Days

5, 14, 19, 25

Challenging Days

2, 8, 12, 27

Leo | November

Overall Theme

Although you enjoy hosting dinners and parties, you'll have a personal matter to settle with your partner around the 1st and a few fires to put out at your job site when the Taurus Lunar Eclipse conjunct Uranus implodes on the 8th. Mix-ups and misunderstanding are part of life and won't stop you from getting into the holiday spirit.

Relationships

Right around the time that Jupiter goes retrograde on the 23rd in Pisces and the New Moon occurs in Sagittarius, single Leos could meet a romantic prospect while traveling home for the Thanksgiving holiday. Other celebrations include siblings who accept plans to attend your feast. The neighborhood hosts a special gathering for those undergoing economic hardships.

Success and Money

Taking inventory of your growing retirement fund puts a smile on your face. You're all set for holiday shopping after you receive a nice bonus on the 4th that allows you to raise the cap on your gift-giving budget. Venus transiting your solar fourth house promises a warm and loving holiday get-together.

Pitfalls and Potential Problems

The last Lunar Eclipse of the year falls on the 8th in Taurus and your solar tenth house, making harsh aspects to Mercury, Venus, Saturn, and Uranus. Keep a low profile if you can manage to stifle the disruption that is likely to shake up your work environment. Leave work early and head for the gym. Look into a more reliable security system at home base.

Rewarding Days

4, 14, 20, 23

Challenging Days

1, 8, 16, 27

Leo | December

Overall Theme

Enthusiasm and holiday cheer capture your exuberant spirit. You're in the mood to party and welcome others to join you for a cocktail, a celebratory lunch, or a party. Venus and Mercury line up cheerfully in your solar fifth house in early December, creating an opportunity for a mini vacation from the 3rd to the 5th. Invite your sweetheart to join you for relaxation and fun.

Relationships

Relatives at a distance finalize plans for a visit to participate in holiday festivities. Spread cheer and boost the spirit of those in your workplace who are ill or have family members whose struggles with medical care put a damper on spending for holiday festivities. Bosses host special gatherings to honor employees. Pamper your significant other late in the month.

Success and Money

The 15th is a perfect date to complete holiday gift buying. With an assist from Uranus, you find an amazing bargain for a coveted present that is going to wow a family member. Saturn transiting your solar seventh house all year stabilized relationships with personal and business partners. Enjoy the banquet.

Pitfalls and Potential Problems

Neptune stations to move direct on the 3rd, redirecting a transfer of funds that has been on hold since late June. Forgetful friends put a crimp in your entertaining style on the 7th when they overlook lunch reservation plans. Don't start a trip on the 29th, when Mercury goes retrograde in Capricorn.

Rewarding Days

4, 6, 15, 26

Challenging Days

1, 7, 18, 28

Leo Action Table

These dates reflect the best—but not the only—times for success and ease in these activities, according to your Sun sign.

	JAN	FEB	MAR	APR	MAY	JUN	JUL	AUG	SEP	OCT	NOV	DEC
Move			19	2				15				
Romance		3			5				4		23	26
Seek counseling/coaching	20			7		17		21		6		
Ask for a raise		8	24		1		3		6			
Vacation						22				19		4
Get a loan	21						18				4	

Virgo

The Virgin
August 22 to September 22

♍

Element: Earth

Glyph: Greek symbol
for containment

Quality: Mutable

Anatomy: Abdomen,
gallbladder, intestines

Polarity: Yin/feminine

Colors: Taupe, gray, navy blue

Planetary Ruler: Mercury

Animals: Domesticated animals

Meditation: I can allow
time for myself

Myths/Legends: Demeter,
Astraea, Hygeia

Gemstone: Sapphire

House: Sixth

Power Stones: Peridot,
amazonite, rhodochrosite

Opposite Sign: Pisces

Flower: Pansy

Key Phrase: I analyze

Keyword: Discriminating

The Virgo Personality

Strengths, Talents, and the Creative Spark

Your intelligent Sun sign presides over the sixth house of work, daily environments and routines, health, pets, colleagues, alternative medicine, workouts, nutrition, certain medications, herbs, spices, your kitchen's utility, pets the size of dogs or smaller, vitamins, efficiency of output, bodyworkers, and assimilation. Mercury rules your mentally driven sign, and many of you seek employment in communication-oriented careers, fact-finding, libraries, patient advocacy, publications, massage, editing, and problem-solving or administrative roles. Virgos take a hands-on approach to whatever needs attention and thrive on systems that keep them organized and cross-referenced. Many Virgos make good space organizers or feng shui consultants, while others prefer the healing fields, massage, and veterinary medicine. Those of you who love to cook like state-of-the art equipment and may excel as the top toque in your place of employment or at home. Yours is a sign that moves through processes and does it well. Virgo rules the bowels and intestines; digestion problems bother some of you, while others display signs of hypochondria, vitamin overdose, or germ phobia, as well as the extreme end of the spectrum of messiness. Recent health care advice on managing the COVID-19 pandemic was right up your alley.

Virgo is the second of three earth signs, the others being Taurus and Capricorn. One of your strengths is that you notice all the details, much like Gemini, the other mutable sign that shares rulership with Mercury. Very little escapes your sharp mind, allowing all of the parts to come together to form the big picture. Organization is one of your talents. You like to make lists and develop a plan to get your work environment in tip-top shape, allowing you to navigate your assignments smoothly and efficiently. Business management comes naturally to you, allowing you to analyze practices, procedures, and systems to keep operations running with continuous improvement. You excel at communication of all types, making you an attractive candidate for positions in large or small organizations and in careers that give you the lead in preparing correspondence, proofreading material for publishing, and writing reports. Virgos enjoy taking charge and looking for whatever needs attention, using systems that keep them on top of work and social scheduling.

Intimacy and Personal Relationships

You're not the type of partner who wants to play the field by keeping a collection of lovers. You're much more comfortable exploring one relationship at a time, preferably on a quest to find your true love, your soulmate. Potential partners had better be on the lookout for your critical eye, with your knack for spotting the rough edges in others. When you see the potential in a partner, you're not judging their flaws even if you see them. Instead, you look for ways that you can help them be a better person and stand ready to assist them when problems come up. Sentimental and romantic, you treasure special shared events, family memories, and dining out. Signs that make good matches are Taurus, Cancer, Scorpio, and Capricorn or someone with a Virgo Ascendant who thinks about you all the time and makes you feel safe and secure. After you meet your mate and marry, you prefer to entertain in your home and bond with friends and family at dinners and holiday events. You treat bosses and coworkers like family, along with special friends, educators, and pets. As your family expands and you have children who play on teams, you become friends with the parents of team members and treasure the connections long after the children grow up and marry.

Values and Resources

Ingrained in you is the notion that you have to do everything that lands in your lap as well as meet the demands of others. When someone mentions a task that has to be done not necessarily by you, you often take it upon yourself to follow through and get the job done. You're proud of your high standards, and they are admirable, yet being a workhorse could leave you exhausted mentally and physically. You enjoy taking charge and looking for whatever needs attention. Mercury drives your mental state, attracting you to employment in communication-oriented careers, fact-finding and research firms, libraries, and think tanks. Virgos often prefer the healing modalities (like bodywork), health-related fields, massage, nursing, and veterinary medicine. A plus is that your sign understands planning processes and thrives on using them for daily balance. Many Virgos are self-taught cooks, often learning this skill after they turn thirty to provide their family with healthy meals. Whether creating light fare or a full banquet, you can cook with the best of them without sacrificing the nutritional value of food.

Blind Spots and Blockages

Being detail-oriented can be both a blessing and a curse. You can be very picky about select life conditions and won't budge much even if you know you are wrong. Sometimes you fixate on excessive information and lose time in muddling through the trivia instead of seeing the broad view. In forming close relationships, you're quick to notice the negative traits yet feel your influence may diminish the warts and awkward parts in time if you just stick with the person. It doesn't always occur to you that if there is so much to complain about, you may be with the wrong partner. Although known for preferring an orderly environment, certain Virgos have no interest in domestic chores and let the cleaning and scrubbing pile up, along with the guilt-driven stress, until company is coming. Give yourself a break and hire a cleaning service.

Goals and Success

Your idea of nirvana in the work world is loving your job, enjoying harmonious relationships with employees, making sure the operation goes smoothly, and getting recognition for the efficient contributions you make to ensure the organization's success. Service-oriented professions attract your attention, especially those where you have a good deal of leverage to run the show and see the positive effect your work has on satisfied clients, patients, and support staff. If coronavirus has disrupted your work schedule or decreased billable hours this year, search for part-time work that uses other skills you have perfected, such as bookkeeping, accounting, or payroll solutions. The demand for remote services from writers and editors has grown, giving you yet another option to enjoy fulfilling work. The initiative to seek supplemental income has the potential to launch a lucrative business venture. Throw your hat in the ring and take a well-calculated risk.

Virgo Keywords for 2022
Details, direction, discrimination

The Year Ahead for Virgo

With Uranus in Taurus starting out the year retrograde in your solar ninth house, where it turns direct on January 18, you may get the green light to resume matters that were put on hold in late summer, such as business or personal travel, visits from in-laws that were canceled due to the pandemic, enrollment in classes or degree programs, business or personal travel, or publication of articles, books, or user manuals. As the year begins, Venus is retrograde in Capricorn and your solar fifth house of romance, socializing, vacations, and children. If you're single, you may put out feelers to begin dating again. You have dealt with several Capricorn planets in this house in recent years and now have only Pluto in the late degrees of Capricorn left to help you release any karmic conditions associated with love and romance.

Mercury, the planet of communication, becomes the first planet to turn retrograde this year in Aquarius on January 14th, occupying your solar sixth house of daily environment, work, health, and nutrition. The signal to move ahead with anticipated work plans will not be as strong as you would like. This feeling will be exacerbated by the presence of transiting Saturn in Aquarius while it occupies your routine-driven solar sixth house. Saturn, the taskmaster, comes with a set of fiscal restrictions that impede the organizational recovery from economic and staffing shortages resulting from the pandemic's toll on the planet. In case your job is on the line, start searching for new employment opportunities as you broaden your field of expertise.

Jupiter

Jupiter, the planet of expansion, occupies Pisces and your solar seventh house for most of the year (with the exception of a retrograde and a sign-change period), until it moves into Aries for good on December 20. What a good place to be if you're making plans with your significant other to marry, start a business, celebrate a milestone anniversary, or attract publicity for accomplishments that catch the public eye. Investors may catch the wave and line up to sign a cooperative agreement for services with you. Collaborators in your professional world show enthusiasm about taking on a joint project. Enjoy recognition from authority figures for past efforts, even if the nature of the work is changing. A change of focus in your work challenges you to seek different employment options, including starting a business or engaging in independent consulting, even part-time assignments that help you pay the bills, especially if COVID-19 cutbacks led to directed reassignment of duties and schedule changes. Jupiter travels rapidly through Pisces until May 10, when it moves into Aries and your solar eighth house of partnership funds and debt and generates a long teaser period in that sign. On July 28, Jupiter will turn retrograde in Aries and your solar eighth house, moving back into Pisces and your solar seventh house on October 28, until it goes direct again on November 23 through the end of the year. Virgos born between August 24 and September 3 feel the most impact from the inconjunct aspect made to their Sun when Jupiter is in Aries. Note that Jupiter in Pisces connects with transiting Neptune in Pisces in April, an asset that favors an interest in or creation of mystical or spiritual materials.

Saturn

In December 2020, Saturn entered Aquarius and your solar sixth house of work, daily routine and environment, coworkers, health, nutrition, and pets. Planets in Aquarius often clash with Virgo placements, creating a stressful inconjunct aspect that adds pressure, demands discipline, and can call overly analytical attention to the work you manage. That's like "picky" meeting "pickier" and putting a choke hold on creativity. No doubt you've noticed the tension over the last few years. Now you're being asked to take a close look at operational problems, skills matches, compatibility issues among coworkers, and possible health matters connected with the social impact of living through a pandemic. Conditions imposed by COVID-19 threats have repositioned where you perform work, whether you have face-to-face contact with workmates, and how you monitor productivity to meet deadlines. Depending on the financial health of your organization, it is possible that some employees will lose their job, undergo temporary layoffs, be reassigned to other duties, or receive notice that the company will close. Stress affects job performance and tests the strength of our health and welfare systems. Although restrictions may be imposed on your schedule due to safety and budgetary mandates, some of you will discover that revamping an existing structure creates a better product and a stronger organization. Pitch in, share your knowledge, and offer solutions that improve productivity. This year Saturn touches the lives of Virgos born between September 3 and 18 most intensely. Saturn's retrograde period in 2022 occurs from June 4 through October 23.

Uranus

What is your plan for hosting transiting Uranus for another year in your solar ninth house of the higher mind, education, foreign countries and cultures, in-laws, philosophy, religion, publishing, and long-distance travel? The planet of chaos disrupted many of the goals you visualized in these designated areas and doesn't get along that well with transiting Saturn in Aquarius. Natal planets in Taurus, while friendly to Virgo, clash with quirky Saturn in Aquarius, the character that has put your solar sixth house of work in quarantine since 2020. Get your spirit back, Virgo, and trust the feelings you have about the philosophical mindset, political stands, and stale thought processes that you're ditching to reclaim your charisma and spirit. Welcome the erratic liberator. With two eclipses in Taurus in 2022 in your solar ninth house, sudden events shake up your schedule. If you planned to travel, go back to school, study metaphysics, or write a book, Uranus and the constraints of COVID-19 will keep you busy but grounded. If you were born between September 2 and 12, the planet of unexpected events has the strongest impact on your everyday routines. Touch base with your network to connect with others in your field who have leads to emerging positions. Uranus moves into retrograde motion on August 24 and goes direct on January 22, 2023. Be ready for a breakthrough and run to the nearest office pod to develop your business plan.

Neptune

Planets in ethereal Pisces tend to clash with pragmatic, health-conscious Virgo planets, sending confusing messages and engaging in excessive daydreaming instead of focusing on the timeline that discriminating Virgo monitors to assess progress. Neptune's residence since April 2011 in Pisces and your solar seventh house of personal and business partners brought you opportunities to cross paths with creative, inspiring people, among them advisors, consultants, cooperators, dreamers, lovers, psychics, and legal and medical professionals. In 2022 Neptune opposes the Sun of Virgos who were born between September 12 and 19, generating the most challenging activity. Single Virgos can meet new partners during this transit, which brings love and romance but not necessarily the permanent commitment you desire. When the attraction fades, you discover the person you brought into your life was not what you thought but a glamorous illusion that fooled you for a while. A similar condition applies to forming new business alliances under the opposition energy. If a proposal sounds too good to be true, examine it closely and let the Neptune fog clear away. If you meet new medical professionals, don't schedule cosmetic surgery while Neptune opposes your Sun. Work with Neptune to stimulate ideas and create a compatible vision with your significant other. In selecting work partners, recognize collaborators whose talents are more suited to promotional work than to content analysis. Neptune greatly enhances intuition, so listen to it when your Sun makes contact. Use positive Neptune insight to help others through a crisis and let your compassionate side shine.

Pluto

In 2008 Pluto, the karma cleaner of the zodiac, made its first appearance in Capricorn and your solar fifth house of children, romance, social life, vacations, speculation, and sports. During this long transit, Pluto in Capricorn touches themes that may be on the front burner and need clarification. How is Pluto stifling your life now? Understand your fear of commitment, for example, and just let go. Without the excess baggage, you're able to embrace personal freedom. Will 2022 be the year you get engaged or marry? Has fear of intimacy driven the urge to criticize potential partners by pushing good prospects away? Pluto can help you grow confident and empower you to be more adventurous, expressive, or entrepreneurial. What about children? Have you postponed having them because you lack confidence in your parenting skills? Replace that fear with a vision of love and contentment that bonds your whole family together. Pluto has a reputation for creating very intense situations in relationships that show up as power struggles and can make a potential partner seem intimidating, even though the truth lies in your own hesitation about walking down the aisle. Pluto is occupying the final degrees of Capricorn as it wraps up this long transit in 2025. The planet of rebirth forms an empowering trine aspect to your Sun this year if you were born between September 17 and 22. Jupiter and Neptune in Pisces favorably aspect Pluto this year and give you the spark you need to take a chance on love and life. Acknowledge the depth of your feelings and take a chance on love.

How Will This Year's Eclipses Affect You?

A total of four eclipses occur in 2022. Two eclipses are solar (New Moon) and two are lunar (Full Moon), which create intense periods that begin to manifest a few months before their actual occurrence. All four of these eclipses occur in two of the cadent houses in your solar chart, the ninth and third houses. Eclipses unfold in cycles involving all twelve signs of the zodiac and usually occur in pairs about two weeks apart. Eclipses are opportunities to release patterns and conditions that have outlived their usefulness. Never fear them, since they may bring you unexpected surprises and windfalls. The closer an eclipse is to a degree or point in your chart, the greater its importance. If you were born with a planet at the same degree as an eclipse, you are likely to see a high level of activity in the house where the eclipse occurs, and its impact may last six months or more.

The first Solar Eclipse of 2022 occurs on April 30 in Taurus and your solar ninth house of the higher mind, education, foreign countries and cultures, in-laws, philosophy, religion, publishing, and long-distance travel. You could be struggling with emotional setbacks that prevented you from moving for job advancement, pursuing a degree program at a university, or recovering from a pandemic-related career dilemma that affected job security. Contact with relatives at a distance continues to be limited, especially travel, until pandemic restrictions subside. Network online for income options.

On May 16, the first Lunar Eclipse of the year takes place in Scorpio and your solar third house of communication, education, local travel, neighbors, siblings, and transportation. Activity in this house increases when assignments you perform from home become the new norm. Online courses attract your attention to learn new skills applicable to changing work conditions. Expect an increased workload if you take on independent consulting assignments.

The year's second Solar Eclipse takes place on October 25 in Scorpio and your solar third house of communication, education, local travel, neighbors, siblings, and transportation. By this time, your entire work routine will have changed, as well as that of the coworkers who collaborate with you on assigned projects. The pace picks up and the incentive to meet deadlines increases. Virgos who opted for a job change may be working in a neighborhood business easily accessible by car. Volunteering at a neighborhood food bank is a choice many Virgos make to support community needs.

The year's final eclipse on November 8 is a Lunar Eclipse, again in Taurus and your solar ninth house of the higher mind, education, foreign countries and cultures, in-laws, publishing, and long-distance travel. If you're thinking of relocating for work, you may find the perfect opportunity now. Make choices compatible with family goals. Visits to family members at a distance resume, and perhaps travel out of the country as well. When the dust settles, write about this life-changing pandemic and how it affected your world. You want closure, Virgo, and a clear path. Follow the direction of your discriminating intellect.

Virgo | January

Overall Theme

Your solar fifth house of romance gets a boost with Venus and Pluto in Capricorn stoking the fires of intimacy and creating magical moments for you and your partner. An after-holiday getaway on the 2nd gives you the perfect bonding vehicle. Mars in Sagittarius welcomes the new year with an energetic blast in your solar fourth house of home and family. Fire up your organized mind for demanding projects.

Relationships

The focus right now is on your significant other, romantic partners, and children. Plan events for your children that include safe indoor activities like movies and games early in the month. Add outdoor tours in sparsely populated areas during the first two weekends. Authorities at work make encouraging announcements mid-month.

Success and Money

Super sales around the 22nd offer an extra incentive for purchasing household goods. Cash flow is good as long as you don't splurge on a whim for your partner on the 7th. Jupiter in your solar seventh house of partnerships yields increased income and the extra cash for an appliance. Protect assets while Venus is retrograde through January 29.

Pitfalls and Potential Problems

Mercury, your ruling planet, turns retrograde on January 14 in Aquarius and your solar sixth house of work while the Moon is in your solar tenth house—not a good day for making a commitment or signing a contract. After months of mobility restrictions, erratic Uranus goes direct on the 18th in your solar ninth house of travel and people at a distance.

Rewarding Days

2, 7, 14, 22

Challenging Days

1, 10, 12, 17

Virgo | February

Overall Theme

The New Moon in Aquarius on February 1 creates optimism in your workplace, giving hope to employees that stability is on the horizon after painful adjustments to the pandemic constraints. Celebrate small victories while the plans unfold to reveal productive goals. Submit your resume for a job opening after Mercury goes direct on the 3rd.

Relationships

Get ready to enjoy an especially loving Valentine's Day, with Jupiter in Pisces in your solar seventh house of partnerships pointing to a happy celebration with your significant other. Siblings reach out to bond and share family news around the 23rd. Enjoy the camaraderie.

Success and Money

The fixer in you wants to get involved in a power struggle that surfaces on the job around the 11th. Use discrimination in staying neutral, because an authority figure is observing your behavior while sizing you up for a future promotion. Your top-notch communication skills are about to star in the negotiations of terms for a lucrative business alliance.

Pitfalls and Potential Problems

An unexpected conflict with a friend surfaces on the Full Moon in Leo on February 16 and reveals hidden resentment and jealousy. An attempt to get to the bottom of the conflict fizzles on the 25th. Don't push the issue. Confusion over household plans and expenses creates friction on the 25th, leading to a disappointing, laborious discussion.

Rewarding Days

3, 8, 18, 23

Challenging Days

5, 11, 14, 25

Virgo | March

Overall Theme

Enjoy the optimistic shine that the New Moon in Pisces on the 2nd beams on you and your spouse in your solar seventh house of personal and business partners. Plan a special dinner date before work schedules intensify. Business travel sends you abroad to scope out options for working with a new client.

Relationships

What a good month for scoring points with your spouse for attentiveness and loving gestures. Both business contacts and relatives at a distance weigh in on your eye for detail. Venus and Mars in Aquarius bring harmonious vibes to your work environment, uplifting spirits and motivating teams. Single Virgos meet new prospects at local happy hours on the 21st.

Success and Money

Diplomacy stars in serious discussions where differences of opinion need resolution. Jupiter in Pisces in your solar seventh house comes to the rescue in bringing hidden details to light through your insightful mediation techniques. Your grateful boss responds by giving you more responsibility and a much deserved raise.

Pitfalls and Potential Problems

You could be more tired than usual when the Full Moon in Virgo on the 18th seems to zap you of energy. An early bedtime is your best cure. Forget about applying for a loan on the 6th. The loan officer you hoped to speak to is unavailable and the person you ultimately reach seems inexperienced. Mixed vibrations resonate at home base on the 24th. Misinformation is shared, yet rumors are quickly dispelled by alert observers.

Rewarding Days

2, 8, 20, 21

Challenging Days

6, 10, 18, 24

Virgo | April

Overall Theme

Are you ready to travel? Two New Moons appear this month, the first on April 1 in Aries and your solar eighth house of joint income and the second (the first Solar Eclipse of the year) on the 30th in Taurus and your solar ninth house, accenting travel and education. Make both a part of your life by attending an out-of-town conference or exploring a vacation destination.

Relationships

The New Moon in Aries on the 1st connects you to loan officers and estate planners whose products match your current needs. Your supervisor gives you a plum assignment, communicating confidence in your abilities. Give your children a weekend treat on the 22nd, choosing a favorite destination to enjoy bonding as a family and with nature.

Success and Money

A favorable asset report received on the 1st validates the choices you made to increase joint savings in January. An accounting error in your health savings account frees up extra money for dental work. Invest some seed money in a start-up fund to get your dream business off the ground.

Pitfalls and Potential Problems

Pluto in Capricorn goes retrograde for six months on the 29th, interrupting the flow of an entrepreneurial venture you've been working on since last November. You hit a few snags on the 4th in discussing strategies with out-of-state business contacts and set up an all-access conference for the 13th, when more stakeholders are available.

Rewarding Days

1, 7, 13, 22

Challenging Days

4, 12, 16, 18

Virgo | May

Overall Theme

The intensity of the action from the Solar Eclipse in Taurus on April 30 near transiting Uranus in your solar ninth house and the Lunar Eclipse on the 16th in Scorpio and your solar third house leads to a sudden regrouping in your communication, education, and transportation houses to minimize disruptions in plans and test the strength of cybersecurity. Upgrade equipment mid-month.

Relationships

Relatives and business contacts at a distance express gratitude for your thoughtfulness and sensitive handling of problems. Friends or members of community organizations invite you to lunch on the 7th and pick your brain for fundraising ideas. The Lunar Eclipse in Scorpio on the 16th brings neighbors together to lobby for community improvements. You and your boss reach an agreement on a proposal to expand your responsibilities.

Success and Money

When Jupiter moves into Aries and your solar eighth house on the 10th, you'll have more money available via a raise your spouse receives. You'll be making decisions on a new benefits package from your employer, especially if you've returned to work after a long period of reduced hours or pay.

Pitfalls and Potential Problems

Your ruling planet, Mercury, is about to go retrograde in Gemini on the 10th and affects organization plans, the timing for new hires, and the implementation of a revised timeline for completing an ongoing project. Say no to a request for the purchase of home goods on the 17th until you have done a market comparison on price.

Rewarding Days

2, 7, 16, 30

Challenging Days

4, 10, 13, 17

Virgo | June

Overall Theme

Diverse relationships dominate activity this month, along with planetary stations. The Moon appears in Cancer twice this month, on the 1st and then again on the 28th, when the New Moon occurs in your solar eleventh house. Jupiter is in Aries and your solar eighth house for the next few months, giving you a preview of what is in store for you financially in 2023.

Relationships

Friends meet after work on the 3rd for a socially distant night out to catch up on news. Children want to spend quality time with you in recreational activities. Single Virgos pursue dating clubs or accept a blind date on the 16th. Around the 27th your work team gets well-deserved recognition from the boss for handling sensitive situations discreetly and avoiding misunderstandings.

Success and Money

Your expertise in accounting alerts you to some funny numbers that won't work for the allocated budget. You clarify findings with financial managers and avert release of inaccurate data. Jupiter in Aries in your solar eighth house shows that your money picture is secure and indicates promising income increases.

Pitfalls and Potential Problems

Mercury goes direct on the 3rd, while taskmaster Saturn in Aquarius and your solar sixth house slips into retrograde motion on the 4th, interfering with work schedules that will need modification. On the 28th, Neptune in Pisces turns retrograde in your solar seventh house until December 3 and calls for resolution of confusing relationship attitudes.

Rewarding Days

3, 8, 16, 27

Challenging Days

6, 14, 18, 20

Virgo | July

Overall Theme
A critical deadline comes up right before the 4th of July holiday and influences your decision to keep the celebrations low-key and local. Loved ones with compromised immune systems continue to practice social distancing and talk to you online. The Moon in Virgo on the holiday treats you to a happy celebration. Savor the downtime.

Relationships
Cookouts with siblings and neighbors and sharing amusement park outings with your spouse and children could be part of your summer outdoor recreation break. Include favorite sports venues and backyard games in the mix to provide entertaining memories for your guests. Cousins and their families may join you for a mini reunion.

Success and Money
You have money set aside to take a vacation with your family, yet work obligations limit the length of time you can be away. Jupiter turns retrograde on the 28th in Aries and your solar eighth house of financial dealings, alerting you to keep savings allocations current and discouraging you from making risky stock purchases.

Pitfalls and Potential Problems
When the Full Moon in Capricorn and your solar fifth houses opposes Mercury in Cancer in your solar eleventh house on the 13th, tension mounts as you attempt to spend time with your friends and keep your significant other happy, too. Invite friends to your home for a party on the 10th, a more compatible date for a gathering.

Rewarding Days
10, 13, 16, 28

Challenging Days
1, 5, 7, 21

Virgo | August

Overall Theme

Start off the month with one big romantic blast. A major theme is intimacy. On the 1st, the Moon in devoted Virgo trines transiting Mars and Uranus in sexy Taurus and sextiles emotional Venus in Cancer, favoring loving moments. That combination exudes a romantic tone. Bring out the candles, chill a bottle of fine wine, and dine decadently at home.

Relationships

Your interest in starting your own business introduces you to an exciting seminar with entrepreneurs on the weekend of the 10th, confirming your perceptions about being your own boss. You gain insight from this new network and commit to working on your business plan. Invitations for fun and games thrill your children.

Success and Money

The wheels turn as you examine the asset column in your financial picture. Your pile of cash is growing and tempting you to invest what you'll need to start a business. True to your cautious nature, you're making a list of the pros and cons before taking the plunge. Oh how you love the idea of being your own boss!

Pitfalls and Potential Problems

Lightning-bolt energy strikes when Uranus in Taurus goes retrograde on August 24 in your solar ninth house until January 22, 2023. Aspects to transiting Venus in Leo could indicate hurtful relationship discoveries. Depending on planetary placements in your natal chart, some Virgos may break up with a partner or receive news of the death or illness of someone close in a distant location.

Rewarding Days

1, 10, 15, 25

Challenging Days

3, 6, 19, 23

Virgo | September

Overall Theme

Look before you leap and do your homework first. Four planets are retrograde this month, with Mercury in Libra about to join them on September 9 in your solar second house of assets, income, money you spend, resources, and self-development. Clean up what you've already started and table new initiatives until after Mercury, the communication planet, goes direct next month.

Relationships

The Labor Day weekend provides perfect family bonding time in your own backyard or at a park with long tables and space for your grill and delicious eats. Bring outdoor games for the children. Phone calls with good friends increase this month, prompting an invitation to visit. On the 19th, attend a meeting hosted by a special interest group.

Success and Money

If you need legal advice related to pending contracts and commitments, schedule an appointment with your attorney on the 12th to make sure obligations are in line with your goals. The 13th works for finalizing loan papers or revising your will to accommodate changing circumstances. Come prepared with questions.

Pitfalls and Potential Problems

Too much confusion hits the wall at once on the 2nd as you attempt to get pending assignments wrapped up before the long holiday weekend. Handle the most urgent tasks and line up help with colleagues on the 8th to resolve issues. Your business partners seem testy on the 10th, when the Full Moon in Pisces tests patience.

Rewarding Days

4, 7, 12, 19

Challenging Days

2, 8, 10, 22

Virgo | October

Overall Theme

Several planets claim the limelight this month, bringing a huge dose of optimism when they go direct. The final Solar Eclipse of 2022 occurs in Scorpio and your solar third house on October 25. You could be dealing with a neighborhood mystery or a just-revealed building project that affects local traffic. Mentally, you shift into multitasking mode to juggle new work assignments.

Relationships

You form harmonious alliances with people at work and feel grateful for their professionalism and commitment to goals. Treat children to a pizza night on the 4th and invite them to open up about their concerns about disruptions to their schedule related to COVID-19 restrictions.

Success and Money

You find many unique products online to tempt you to part with your hard-earned cash. Look for deals on state-of-the art electronics and the latest smartphone upgrades to fulfill your desire to be ultra-ready in the age of cyber power.

Pitfalls and Potential Problems

Relief hits this month when three planets rush to finish their retrograde periods: Mercury moves direct in Virgo on the 2nd, Pluto in Capricorn stations direct on the 8th, and Saturn goes direct on the 23rd in Aquarius. Mars in Gemini goes retrograde on the 30th until January 12, 2023, in your solar tenth house, possibly leading to some blockages and frustration at work.

Rewarding Days

4, 9, 14, 25

Challenging Days

2, 8, 16, 23

Virgo | November

Overall Theme

The Lunar Eclipse on the 8th falls in Taurus and your solar ninth house, reminding you to make reservations for planned out-of-town holiday travel or to schedule festive dinners with relatives who visit you. If hosting events creates inner conflicts for you, alleviate mental overload with yoga or meditation techniques on this date when the Moon and Uranus are conjunct.

Relationships

The highlight of your interactions with others centers on your multicultural and multigenerational guests comprised of friends, coworkers whose own families live at a distance, neighbors, and your own revered family members who delight in sitting at your holiday table.

Success and Money

Early in the month your work leader shows appreciation for your contributions by giving you a generous incentive bonus. Wise saving habits and performance awards supply you with the money to shop for cherished gifts, surprise children, and mail packages early.

Pitfalls and Potential Problems

Review work documents or financial statements carefully on the 1st, when oversights create complex errors that delay delivery of finished products. On the 23rd, the same date as the New Moon in Sagittarius and your solar fourth house, Jupiter in Pisces goes direct as you prepare to welcome out-of-town visitors and prepare your Thanksgiving feast. Avoid arguments over menu items and holiday decorations on the 19th.

Rewarding Days

3, 11, 14, 20

Challenging Days

1, 8, 16, 19

Virgo | December

Overall Theme

Fill this holiday season with special days and cherished memories the whole family can enjoy. Neptune, the planet most associated with charities and compassion, goes direct on the 3rd in Pisces and your solar seventh house and shows your heart the way to contribute generously. Share your spirit with those less fortunate by inviting your children to participate in meal preparation or donation of food at soup kitchens or homeless shelters.

Relationships

This month reflects a deep desire to bond with your "family" at work to show how you value their outstanding service. Sing carols with school groups, call seldom-seen cousins, and meet a sibling at a holiday concert. Planets line up joyfully to help you celebrate the holiday with your significant other and children, who enjoy the ambience you create with special meals and favorite treats.

Success and Money

Jupiter occupies your solar seventh house until the 20th, giving you reason to gratefully reflect on the prosperity that blessed you and your partner during this transitional year. Earnings and savings are up and the debt load down, manifesting a goal you placed at the top of your list early in the year.

Pitfalls and Potential Problems

The year's final Full Moon occurs in your solar tenth house of career on December 7 conjunct retrograde Mars in Gemini, a time of possible frustration at work. Mercury goes retrograde in Capricorn on the 29th in your solar fifth house, reminding you to watch the habits of drivers on the road.

Rewarding Days

4, 7, 20, 25

Challenging Days

2, 9, 13, 26

Virgo Action Table

These dates reflect the best—but not the only—times for success and ease in these activities, according to your Sun sign.

	JAN	FEB	MAR	APR	MAY	JUN	JUL	AUG	SEP	OCT	NOV	DEC
Move		8			2				4			
Romance			20			16		15			7	
Seek counseling/ coaching	7				7		13			14		20
Ask for a raise		3		7		27			12		20	
Vacation	2		8					10				25
Get a loan				1			10			9		

Libra

The Scales
September 22 to October 23

Element: Air

Quality: Cardinal

Polarity: Yang/masculine

Planetary Ruler: Venus

Meditation: I balance
conflicting desires

Gemstone: Opal

Power Stones: Tourmaline,
kunzite, blue lace agate

Key Phrase: I balance

Glyph: Scales of justice,
setting sun

Anatomy: Kidneys, lower back,
appendix

Colors: Blue, pink

Animals: Brightly plumed birds

Myths/Legends: Venus,
Cinderella, Hera

House: Seventh

Opposite Sign: Aries

Flower: Rose

Keyword: Harmony

The Libra Personality

Strengths, Talents, and the Creative Spark

What you know about relationships could become the subject matter of many books if you are interested in writing. You juggle a variety of social interests that demand your time while simultaneously energizing you and helping you stay balanced. Libra is the second air sign in the zodiac, with love goddess Venus as your ruling planet. You are partnership-oriented and strongly identify with the seventh house of romantic, business, and professional connections, as well as roommates, the public in general, advisors, counselors, diplomats, doctors, attorneys, recruiters, collaborators, and your shadow self. Suitable careers that play to your strengths include those that put your social and diplomatic skills to work while providing courteous and thoughtful service to clients and customers. Creativity is a strong trait for Libras, many of whom enjoy the artistic pursuits that involve the use of the hands. This preference opens up many paths to a successful career in the beauty industry, which includes hair, fashion consulting, makeup, bodywork (such as massage), reiki, Pilates, or makeovers that improve the appearance of clients.

Although Libra is an air sign, a number of you avoid most types of web communications and social networking. You'd rather grab the phone. The COVID-19 restrictions imposed in 2020 that changed the structure of your work day may have helped you realize the importance of being tech-savvy by staying current with the latest equipment, especially if the location of your work shifted. The rest of you spend a big chunk of time on the internet and learn much from information exchanges, relishing time-saving devices. You're good at problem-solving and put your advising and consulting skills to work in fields that may involve coaching, industrial psychology, sales, teaching, and therapy.

Intimacy and Personal Relationships

With a Sun sign that rules the solar seventh house of intimate partners, you prefer to have a spouse or significant other in your life. If divorce occurs, no matter how painful, you'll pick yourself up and get back in the dating market before too much time elapses. You're a joiner and will ultimately link up with a dating service, a dance class, or a group that caters to single parents to meet eligible prospects. Libras aren't loners, and most of you get energy from being with other people. You tend to put a priority on how your date likes to spend downtime, even if it's not your first choice. Just be sure you don't get bogged down in someone else's preferences and lose yourself catering to another's needs. Then friends and family will rarely see you if you have fallen in love again and can't live a day without your honey. Libras find other air signs (Gemini and Aquarius) to be attractive partners who love to talk in person or on the phone. You may also date Leo, who loves to be the center of attention and would be thrilled at the thought of being the object of your persistent love and devotion, or Sagittarius, who never tires of planning adventures, demonstrates a sense of humor, and finds comedic humor a blast. You could have problems with Cancer, Capricorn, and your opposite sign, Aries, yet sometimes you fall for them and get used to the squabbles and stylish earplugs.

Values and Resources

With Venus as the ruling planet of your sign, you seek careers that give you the freedom to put your diplomatic skills to work. You have a way with words that brings opportunities to provide service to clients and customers. Your knack for organizing social functions attracts requests to chair committees for charities, community causes, and fundraisers. Tech-savvy Libras enjoy spending time on social media, along with other professional networks where you're active in initiatives that claim your attention. The internet is your jam, along with the need to have a highly sophisticated cell phone so you can swap photos and stay in touch with contacts in both family and business spheres. You have a strong need to communicate and be heard, yet you sometimes forget to take a breath and listen to what others have to say. Partnership ventures and cooperation appeal to you, and sometimes your business partner is your spouse.

Blind Spots and Blockages

When someone lobs a message at you that you don't care for, especially when the tone grates on you, you will tune it out and block the unpleasantness with a distraction, such as a crossword puzzle, a TV program with the volume turned up, or a headset to listen to music or use your phone. You don't care for tense situations and chaos and are able to relax more by engaging in a well-structured exercise program to work out the stress. Libra rules the kidneys, pancreas, lower back, and urethra, suggesting you would benefit from drinking more water to avoid dehydration and muscle cramps, although you don't always carry a water bottle. Creative avoidance or procrastination are downfalls, yet they may be minimized by the presence of a practical Moon or strong Mercury in your natal chart. A frequent criticism is that you are wishy-washy and leave contacts scratching their head because they can't figure out where you stand on issues. Others label you indecisive because you don't like to be pushed into making choices too quickly.

Goals and Success

Many Libras have a highly developed artistic gene and make use of their hands in artistic or construction projects, taking great pride in the finished product. Mediation appeals to a significant number of Libras, who either incorporate the talent into everyday life or seek out these services when troubleshooting problem areas on the job or with personal connections. You naturally look for ways to compromise and find balance when it is out of bounds, seldom resting until you reconcile ideology stalemates and restore balance to turbulent conditions. With a flair for negotiating contracts and identifying what a project needs to succeed, you excel in an environment that makes use of your consulting expertise, which includes resolution of personnel problems and opportunities to encourage competition, and keeps you abreast of any legal issues. You have no interest in going to court, preferring to go to arbitration to resolve differences. A career in law may appeal to you to satisfy your interest in people, what makes them tick, and how you can help them get a fair shake in life.

Libra Keywords for 2022
Participation, peace, poise

The Year Ahead for Libra

As you optimistically embrace 2022, you shift expectations toward attracting challenging opportunities to demonstrate your talent and let go of the dreaded restrictions imposed by the COVID-19 pandemic. The year starts out with Venus in Capricorn retrograde in your solar fourth house of home and family, reminding you that you have emotional baggage to clear away at your base of operations before the love planet goes direct on January 29. Take the initiative to address any lingering misgivings you have about relationships and open the door to meaningful discussion. Pluto in late Capricorn and your solar fourth house since 2008 remains a force to be reckoned with in terms of letting go of anger, resentment, or blocks to progress that keep you from acknowledging others' feelings and calling a truce if you are rehashing family history that includes hurtful incidents. On January 14, Mercury makes its first retrograde station of the year in Aquarius and your solar fifth house of romance, children, and social life. Be on the lookout for mixed messages regarding dates, travel, and plans with your children's school or sports plans, which are subject to change with little notice. Remaining in your solar fifth house this year is Jupiter, the planet of expansion, travel, and adventure, in Aquarius.

Uranus in Taurus has been retrograde since August 19, 2021, and turns direct in your solar eighth house of joint income, debt, and estate matters on January 18. Wouldn't it be great if this shift leads to unexpected monetary windfalls, a promotion, or the completion of investment transactions that have been on hold? Neptune in Pisces occupies your solar sixth house of daily routines, health, and nutrition, reminding you to be vigilant of any shifts in how you are feeling and schedule timely medical appointments. Minimize workplace stress by addressing matters that come up rather than burying them and letting the consequences fester. Apply your powerful skills of people management and tact in 2022 as you step into a world of unlimited possibilities.

Jupiter

With the exception of a retrograde and a sign-change period in 2022, Jupiter occupies your solar sixth house in Pisces until December 20, when it moves into Aries for a yearlong adventure in 2023. Each member of your sign is going to benefit from Jupiter's presence in this ultrabusy house as you examine the strengths and shortcomings of coworkers, organize your personal and work space, adapt to organizational changes, and meet newcomers to your networks. As you contemplate goals, Jupiter stimulates activity related to them and supports the successful ventures you desire related to collaboration, health improvement, and weight management. Jupiter stimulates hanging on to unwanted pounds, if you forget to monitor your diet and cut back on eating rich foods, especially sugar. Add new exercise programs to meet this challenge. On July 28 Jupiter will turn retrograde in Aries and your solar seventh house of partners, moving back into Pisces and your solar sixth house on October 28. Those of you born between September 22 and October 3 see the most activity from Jupiter while it is in Aries and occupies your solar seventh house. You'll enjoy harmonious relationships with existing partners and may begin a new connection if you are without a significant other. While in Pisces, Jupiter gives you insight into how to improve your daily environment, enhance work relationships, and heal physically and emotionally. Visualize the outcome you desire and internalize it.

Saturn

Since December 2020, Saturn in Aquarius has occupied your solar fifth house of children, entertainment, risk-taking, romance, and social life. Demands on your time seem to pop up so frequently that even you, the ultimate socialite, have trouble keeping up with the hectic schedule. You could be wearing more than one hat—managing your job and coaching a team or teaching your students during the day while offering fitness classes at night. If you made a job change or were recently promoted, the orientation process puts you in touch with new contacts and steps up activity with your professional network. The entrepreneurial among you may have started a business after weighing the pros and cons of remaining in your employing organization prior to the pandemic. A Saturn transit in the solar fifth house alerts you to any processes that need improvement or any resources you may lack to succeed in this new venture. A number of Libras may be examining romantic relationships to assess the quality of communication and mutual goals, especially if there are signs of distraction that seem to be pulling you apart. Those of you born between October 4 and 19 experience the most pressure and activity from this Saturn transit in 2022. Saturn's retrograde period occurs from June 4 through October 23. Cover the bases of issues related to this house that are currently dominating your life, including matters related to your children and their education, your love life or a pending engagement, the world of entertainment or vacation destinations, sports venues, and business ventures that increase your responsibility and may require an investment of funds and physical resources. Staying healthy and in balance generates wisdom and leads you to the wealth you desire. Stay poised and dream big.

Uranus

What do you think of the condition of your solar eighth house of mutual funds, debt, other income sources, retirement assets, sex, birth, death, wills, and estates? Since the planet of chaos first showed up here in Taurus in May 2018 to begin a seven-year passage through this sign, have you noticed improvement or additional angst over the state of your financial affairs or matters connected to this house? What impact did the coronavirus have on your security? How are you handling fears that you have buried deep in your psyche? The eighth house is a repository for them, and the passage of Uranus is the perfect force for helping you confront and shed them once and for all. In 2022 Uranus turns direct on January 18, opening up options for reducing debt, paying off loans, securing favorable loan rates, and adding to savings accounts that benefit you and your partner. This shift in motion has you seeking advice from financial advisors and medical or marriage counselors, especially if you have issues on your mind and are willing to confront them. Be ready to act on excellent advice that comes your way and participate fully in solutions for greater peace of mind. Those of you born between October 3 and 13 experience the most activity from Uranus this year, with a stress-inducing inconjunct aspect that shakes up any stagnation existing in these important areas.

Neptune

Neptune, the watery, slow-moving planet, advances only four to five degrees a year and has occupied Pisces and your solar sixth house of health and daily routines since April 2011. Your work environment has been the hub of Neptune's influence for a lengthy period, sending confusing messages, generating unreliable information about people and circumstances, possibly changing the physical location of work, and causing you to wade through the haze to make sense of unfolding conditions. That is the operational style of Neptune—it looks good, but you had better look beneath the surface to see the details. Although the chaos is more subtle than the type Uranus emits, Neptune is foggy and inconsistent and easily keeps you going around in circles. Using a daily mantra to ground you, such as "I remain calm and poised under stressful circumstances," helps you focus on essential business, guard against negative energies, and accommodate the shift in responsibilities that has emerged over the last few years for you and coworkers. Trust your instincts that major changes are in the works related to practices and procedures. If you're single, don't be surprised if you meet a romantic prospect through your work under the influence of Neptune's matchmaking spell. Those of you born between October 13 and 20 will experience the most Neptunian action during 2022. The planet of illusion will be retrograde from June 28 to December 3.

Pluto

Since January 2008, Pluto, the planet of transformation and rebirth, has been deeply planted in Capricorn and your solar fourth house of home, base of operations, family, and foundation, reminding you that housekeeping is an ongoing process and you have more to do to rid your environment of unwanted possessions and emotional baggage. Call the charities, Libra—they'll be glad to help you pack the boxes and load up the truck with treasures you've accumulated over the years and still find hard to give away. With this long passage of Pluto, you've probably gifted several charities or given relatives who are furnishing a home some linens, lamps, and appliances to get them started. Make peace with relatives living with you or moving out to eliminate karma that interferes with the peace and serenity you desire at home base. Those of you born between October 18 and 22 see the most activity in manifesting healthy relationships after acknowledging the challenges to your Sun from the irritant-inducing square aspect from Pluto that brought arguments and disappointing conversations to the domestic scene.

How Will This Year's Eclipses Affect You?

The signs Taurus and Scorpio dominate the eclipse cycles of 2022. A total of four eclipses occur: two solar (New Moon) and two lunar (Full Moon), which bring intense periods that start to manifest about two months before they actually occur. All four eclipses take place in two of your solar chart's money houses, the second and the eighth, putting the spotlight on activities associated with money you earn, how you spend it, assets you possess, and how you use resources aimed at self-development, as well as money from joint income, savings, or retirement plans, the debt load shared by you and your partner, and wills and estates. Eclipses manifest in cycles involving all twelve signs of the zodiac, usually occurring in pairs about two weeks apart. Never fear eclipses—think of them as golden opportunities that allow you to face old, outworn patterns and release them. Eclipses trigger unexpected revelations, surprises, and windfalls. The closer an eclipse is to a planet in your chart, the greater the importance it plays in your life. Those of you born with a planet at the same degree as an eclipse may see a high level of activity in the house where the eclipse occurs.

The first Solar Eclipse of 2022 occurs on April 30 in Taurus and your solar eighth house of joint income, resources and debt, savings and reduction of money you owe, psychological depth, secrets, and the estates of the dead, wills, and inheritances. Those of you born between October 3 and 5 experience the strongest vibes from this eclipse. You feel the pressure to keep goals on track, balance work with activities that increase your holdings, and reduce any debts or financial burdens. Transiting Uranus in Taurus is also present in your solar eighth house to keep you alert to unexpected changes or chaotic conditions.

Two weeks later, the first Lunar Eclipse of the year occurs on May 16 in Scorpio and your solar second house of assets, personal income, planned purchases, financial plans, and what you value in life. If you have planets located in this house, expect revelations regarding problem areas connected to these matters to come to light. Other people may have a hand in outcomes, so do what you can to make sure connections are positive. You'll benefit from strengthening bonds and establishing a solid budget to secure a stable financial base. If you are experiencing challenges, any rough spots will hit hard and call for analysis and workable solutions. Balance your time so that you work fewer hours, get proper rest, and have more time for fun and games. Be health-conscious by exercising and adding an extra hour of sleep a night to your schedule. Unwind with comedy, movies, spectator or contact sports, and a night where you do nothing but relax, have fun, and enjoy life.

On October 25, the second Solar Eclipse of 2022 takes place in Scorpio and your solar second house of self-development, money, resources, how you spend your money, and what you value. When this eclipse hits after months of working on your financial security back in May, you'll see whether the interim actions you took netted the desired results. If you landed a new job, you are sitting pretty and enjoying a delightful raise for your effort. Earning new credentials expanded your qualifications and self-worth in the evolving job market.

The year's final eclipse is a Lunar Eclipse on November 8 in Taurus and your solar eighth house of joint savings and income, debt, karmic conditions, psychological matters, mental depth, and executing duties tied to other people's money. In close proximity to this degree is transiting Uranus in Taurus, so be sure to take stock of interest rates on loans, debt ratios, and insurance premiums and shop for the best terms. New income streams for you or a partner generate solid gains in your financial security. Congratulate yourself for implementing a long-desired partnership goal.

Libra | January

Overall Theme

Connecting with family near and far looks good this month as long as you don't travel too far. The rapport you share generates a feel-good state that sets the tone for 2022. Get ready for planetary stations from Mercury, Uranus, and Venus before the month is out. The New Moon in Capricorn on the 2nd stimulates lively discussion in a relaxing environment.

Relationships

Invite distant relatives to visit for a post New Year's gathering, some of whom will probably be traveling for the first time in a couple of years due to lingering COVID-19 restrictions. Show your sentimental side to your significant other on the 9th. Cherish the intimacy and strengthen bonds of love. Acknowledge valuable professional alliances when you return to work after the 9th.

Success and Money

Outstanding communication shines on the 13th when you report on the status quo and give credit to the contributions of others. Double-check budget figures and review terms of agreements before Mercury goes retrograde in Aquarius on the 14th in your solar fifth house. Uranus goes direct on the 18th in your solar eighth house in sync with well-planned financial activity.

Pitfalls and Potential Problems

The Full Moon in Cancer on the 17th does not favor holding a spontaneous meeting with your work group due to a hostile undercurrent that stems from misunderstandings about the scope of new work projects. Clarify concerns first.

Rewarding Days

2, 9, 13, 22

Challenging Days

5, 12, 17, 20

Libra | February

Overall Theme

Work vibes are rewarding and showcase solid teamwork. A coworker organizes a holiday lunch to reflect Cupid's playful side. The gathering sends a personal reminder your way. Participate and schedule a Valentine's Day celebration to show that special someone how much you care. A prominent charity clothing drive nets outstanding results.

Relationships

Siblings make frequent contact this month hoping for a reunion of relatives. Colleagues at your work site hold a successful meeting on the 3rd that focuses on 2022 initiatives and sets timelines for work completions. Make plans with neighbors or school groups on the 24th.

Success and Money

Extra money in your bank account lets you repay bills faster than you thought and entertain plans for a weekend getaway in March. Mercury goes direct on the 3rd, clearing up communication and reversing the tension in personal relationships that have been uneasy for the last month with a lineup of Capricorn planets affecting serenity in your solar fourth house of home and family.

Pitfalls and Potential Problems

The presence of abundant Capricorn planets this month creates challenges for you in keeping schedules, completing assignments, and participating in smooth business discussions. Mixed messages on the 8th and 14th require a revision of approaches to problem-solving. Partners are cranky on the 5th, so steer clear of awkward arguments over money and entertainment spending.

Rewarding Days

1, 3, 21, 24

Challenging Days

5, 8, 14, 27

Libra | March

Overall Theme

With the New Moon on March 2 in Pisces and your solar sixth house, your focus is on workplace projects and getting to know your teammates' assets and communication styles. Neptune transiting this house prompts questions about how best to use the available skills. Schedule health checkups or routine dental visits early in the month.

Relationships

This month, the most prominent relationships revolve around business associates and coworkers who interact productively and hit the mark on meeting deadlines. You benefit from advice from key medical professionals around the New Moon on the 2nd. Meanwhile excellent Mars-Venus connections showcase your romantic closeness with a special person around the 28th.

Success and Money

Business travel leads to new contracts and builds solid relationships in untapped markets around the 8th. Outcomes set the agenda for salary increases in the coming months and include prominent members of the work group. Enjoy a short getaway before mid-month to spend some quality downtime.

Pitfalls and Potential Problems

Don't beat your gums to death discussing financial woes and debt or your partner will tune you out on the 8th. You could have words with your boss over raises or bonuses on the 11th, especially if you disagree over who deserves the increase on your team. The Full Moon in Virgo on the 18th could leave you feeling exhausted. Avoid sticky discussions until you have more information on the 21st.

Rewarding Days

2, 8, 19, 28

Challenging Days

6, 11, 18, 21

Libra | April

Overall Theme

The New Moon in your opposite sign of Aries on the 1st creates harmonious aspects with Mercury in Aries and Venus, Mars, and Saturn in Aquarius, boosting the energy you are pouring into your solar seventh house of romantic and business partnerships.

Relationships

Plan an unexpected treat for your family for the weekend starting on the 22nd by adding fun and games to the mix. Moods improve and so does romance. The bonds you share result in better understanding of the minds and hearts of loved ones. The hierarchy at work responds to your stellar performance and invites you to lunch to pick your brain for options that meet goals.

Success and Money

The first Solar Eclipse of 2022 occurs on April 30 in Taurus and your solar eighth house of joint holdings, mortgages, investments, and debt, calling attention to strategies for reducing debt. A raise could come your way by the middle of the month.

Pitfalls and Potential Problems

Expect disagreements over money early in the month when the Moon transits your solar eighth house on the 4th. Members of groups hold grudges over decisions they oppose on the 11th, and could withdraw support for leadership or a role you play in implementing change. It's stress all day for you on the 15th, so don't sign contracts for another week, when the planets align favorably in your solar fourth house.

Rewarding Days

1, 8, 18, 22

Challenging Days

4, 11, 15, 24

Libra | May

Overall Theme

Take a mini vacation during the first few days of the month to get you primed for what follows in May. Although the month starts out with several Pisces planets in compatible aspect in your solar sixth house of work, they soon move to your opposite sign of Aries and bring a large dose of angst to your romantic and business partnerships. Work demands present challenges.

Relationships

Relatives at a distance claim your time during the early part of May and could include your mother (if she is alive) to share her nurturing spirit. Authority figures at work show their respect for your contributions on the 6th. Family members enjoy spontaneous outings with you around the 19th while creating new memories. Host a reunion lunch with colleagues or old friends.

Success and Money

Savor the praise that comes your way and honors you and your coworkers on the 24th for outstanding contributions to professional goals. Someone shares advance information about the prospect of a promotion opportunity that will open up soon. Prepare your resume to be ready for the competition. Security lifts your spirits.

Pitfalls and Potential Problems

Mercury goes retrograde on the 10th in Gemini and could delay business travel or the start of a career-enhancing training program. Breathe deeply. The Lunar Eclipse on the 16th occurs in Scorpio and your solar second house of income and assets and makes you reluctant to discuss finances with your partner.

Rewarding Days

2, 6, 19, 24

Challenging Days

4, 9, 16, 27

Libra | June

Overall Theme

Your most memorable days this month revolve around successful encounters at the workplace, interaction with your boss, and team performance. For some Libras, the spotlight is on education, communication, increased local travel, and neighborhood events. Stay flexible to accommodate sudden news about a child as Mercury stations to move direct in Taurus on the 3rd, and Saturn goes retrograde in Aquarius on the 4th.

Relationships

With Venus in Taurus and your solar eighth house for most of the month, you and your significant other share intimacy and lovingly touch each other's hearts and souls. Mars in Aries and your solar seventh house brings passionate encounters to the mix. Siblings contact you frequently and touch base to share family news or make summer plans. Participate joyfully.

Success and Money

Nothing is better than challenging work assignments to get your passion flowing, with the prospect of successful accomplishments. From the beginning to the end of June, your work environment shines with possibilities, including a focus on collaboration. Work quality boosts morale. New contracts replace outmoded practices with winning solutions.

Pitfalls and Potential Problems

Between June 15 and 18, tension and arguments affect household relationships, including harmony with children who have unreasonable expectations about parental responsibilities. You may be forced to cancel plans to travel on the 28th due to work priorities, leading to family disappointments. Discuss the situation with affected parties and ask for understanding.

Rewarding Days

3, 13, 20

Challenging Days

5, 15, 18, 28

Libra | July

Overall Theme

Jupiter in Aries moves forward this month in your solar seventh house of partners and looks fondly on anticipated travel plans involving you and your family. The best times to get away are on the 4th for a local trip and the 23rd for an all-inclusive resort experience or cruise. Celebrate the 4th of July with your family and friends. Complete assignments by the 20th so you're free to travel.

Relationships

Children are raring to go by the 17th, and plans for unusual experiences fill their active minds. You have work to wrap up or delegate to team members by the 20th. Look over recreation and amusement options and coordinate events with relatives and contacts at a distance whom you'll meet after the 23rd.

Success and Money

Your best bargains revolve around travel discounts including airfare, car rentals, and amusement park fees. Maximize purchasing power when negotiating for perks. Don't book cruises too early if hints of COVID-19 surface. Lighten your heart as you prepare for some much deserved relaxation.

Pitfalls and Potential Problems

It's touch and go with friends early in the month, especially on the 2nd, when those in your circle are not on the same page in planning a 4th of July celebration. Let it go and celebrate with family. Friction from the 28th to the 30th festers among members of a professional group when Jupiter turns retrograde in Aries on July 28, the date of the Leo New Moon.

Rewarding Days

4, 10, 17, 23

Challenging Days

2, 5, 11, 30

Libra | August

Overall Theme

Ready, set, let go! Give yourself a break! A day trip or short outing on the 7th piques your interest to attend a concert or take in a special museum collection. The Full Moon on the 11th in Aquarius and your solar fifth house stimulates fun and games with the kids, favorite pals, or a current love interest.

Relationships

Invite a love interest to join you for brunch. Savor the valuable life connections this month that include your siblings and neighbors. Enjoy satisfying interactions with bosses and coworkers whose complementary styles showcase your original ideas. Demonstrate your love and affection for your significant other by sharing secret plans.

Success and Money

It was so worth it to hole up in private on the 1st to put final touches on project details that you're ready to unveil. Early completion of timelines grabs the attention of workplace hierarchy, who laud the efficiency and impressive cost savings. Recommendations are likely to include bonuses or salary increases for key contributors.

Pitfalls and Potential Problems

Avoid showdowns with children or those you teach or coach on the 11th, when considerable tension is in the air after a hostile exchange. Mars and Uranus are in hard aspect to the Full Moon, suggesting that time is better spent on lighter fare. Stay safe while handling money when Uranus goes retrograde in Taurus on the 24th.

Rewarding Days

1, 7, 15, 23

Challenging Days

3, 9, 11, 18

Libra | September

Overall Theme

Your cup runneth over early in the month when a mix of social gatherings dominates the landscape that includes parties, short vacations, and visits with relatives or old friends. Execute your plans before Mercury goes retrograde in your solar first house on the 9th. Ignore rumors you hear through the workplace grapevine on the 10th, as information proves false by the 15th.

Relationships

What a month for counting your blessings with family relationships, including rapport with children and parents. Forge inspiring alliances with teachers, coaches, and children's friends as the academic year gets underway. Bankers share good news about assets, while your boss announces a raise by the 20th.

Success and Money

Successful networking produces exciting leads to new work ventures around the 7th. The Libra New Moon on the 25th creates an opportunity to bond romantically and spiritually with your significant other. Funding for loans comes from an unexpected source around the 15th, with unbeatable terms that favor your budget.

Pitfalls and Potential Problems

The phone rings off the hook with demands for your time on the 2nd, canceling your wish to leave early to get a jump start on holiday plans. When you return, you have a pile of details to sort through just as Mercury turns retrograde on the 9th. Contacts in distant locations seem a bit edgy on the 17th over communication misunderstandings.

Rewarding Days

6, 7, 15, 20

Challenging Days

2, 9, 17, 22

Libra | October

Overall Theme

The Solar Eclipse in Scorpio on the 25th highlights income streams and assets. Educational matters dominate your personal space. Mars in the intellectual sign of Gemini highlights your interest in distance learning, credentials for new career opportunities, or an advanced degree. Help a child with complex subject matter and celebrate new enthusiasm for learning.

Relationships

Spend a conversation-filled night with your love partner on the 14th, acknowledging the passion and nurturing you feel in your partner's company. Discuss plans for a future getaway. If you are an unattached Libra, you may be unexpectedly attracted to a person you meet through work on the 17th.

Success and Money

The value of your home is a topic of importance on the 3rd, when you have a serious discussion about refinancing or remodeling it. You and your partner delight in the extra cash that shows up in your paycheck, which you use to pay off credit cards or other bills. Kudos to you for using your funds wisely.

Pitfalls and Potential Problems

Multiple planetary shifts occur this month. Mercury moves direct in Virgo on the 2nd, followed by Pluto in Capricorn on the 8th and Saturn in Aquarius on the 23rd. Table travel and postpone making sudden decisions on these dates. Mars turns retrograde in Gemini on the 30th in your solar ninth house and could delay the start date for classes, travel, contracts, or furniture deliveries.

Rewarding Days

3, 4, 14, 17

Challenging Days

1, 9, 12, 25

Libra | November

Overall Theme

With a Lunar Eclipse in Taurus on November 8 in your solar eighth house of joint income, debts, and savings, you'll be poised to pay cash for holiday gifts to beat the rush. Decorating is your jam. You have big plans to showcase your home's assets with striking lights and greenery. Strategic shopping trips allow you to monitor sales.

Relationships

The 3rd favors creative gatherings with workmates to monitor progress and chart accomplishments. Celebration on the 13th involves an invitation from your boss. Enjoy a special outing on the 6th with your partner. Family and friends gather early for Thanksgiving on November 23rd amid love, gratitude, and cordiality. Call loved ones at a distance on the 23rd and 24th.

Success and Money

Do your research, then shop online for the best prices, including free shipping. Negotiate for free gift-wrapping and have merchandise sent directly to recipients' addresses. Jupiter goes direct on the 23rd, the day of the Sagittarius New Moon, and favors plans for holiday travel. Shopping works well at this time, with the exception of November 25.

Pitfalls and Potential Problems

The last Lunar Eclipse of the year occurs on November 8 in Taurus, a date on which to curb spending until you have assessed your debt load. Friends or members of professional groups show strain at meetings on the 15th. Don't take it personally, but don't expect much in the way of agreement either. Conserve energy on the 25th.

Rewarding Days

3, 6, 13, 23

Challenging Days

8, 15, 22, 25

Libra | December

Overall Theme

Aren't you pleased that your Libra Sun is compatible with transiting Sun, Mercury, and Venus in Sagittarius as they congregate playfully in early December to give your month a jovial start? These planets get support from compatible Saturn in Aquarius too, giving you an opportunity to get away with your love interest on the 3rd for a relaxing time at a favorite resort.

Relationships

Connections with family, children, and work staff dominate the last week of the month. Invitations roll in and you'll have a busy calendar. Attend as many gatherings as possible with your favorite partner. The Full Moon on the 7th could bring phone calls and messages from relatives at a distance who have a lot on their mind regarding upcoming travel and health concerns.

Success and Money

Neptune in Pisces goes direct in your solar sixth house on the 3rd and clears up ambiguity over puzzling health issues that have lingered since May. Colleagues express positive attitudes as the new year wanes. Schedule personal medical exams on the 28th.

Pitfalls and Potential Problems

Health matters emerge for a relative on the 7th, leading to discussions with medical professionals. Avoid this date for scheduling personal medical procedures. Work efficiently to complete assignments before holiday leave begins. Mercury goes retrograde in Capricorn on the 29th, creating delays in the flow of activity.

Rewarding Days

3, 24, 25, 28

Challenging Days

1, 7, 13, 26

Libra Action Table

These dates reflect the best—but not the only—times for success and ease in these activities, according to your Sun sign.

	JAN	FEB	MAR	APR	MAY	JUN	JUL	AUG	SEP	OCT	NOV	DEC
Move	13				2			7		14		
Romance		1	28	7				15	7		6	
Seek counseling/ coaching	9											3
Ask for a raise				18		3			15			
Vacation			8		19		9			4		25
Get a loan		21					10				3	

Scorpio

The Scorpion
October 23 to November 22

♏

Element: Water

Quality: Fixed

Polarity: Yin/feminine

Planetary Ruler: Pluto (Mars)

Meditation: I let go of the need to control

Gemstone: Topaz

Power Stones: Obsidian, garnet

Key Phrase: I create

Glyph: Scorpion's tail

Anatomy: Reproductive system

Colors: Burgundy, black

Animals: Reptiles, scorpions, birds of prey

Myths/Legends: The Phoenix, Hades and Persephone, Shiva

House: Eighth

Opposite Sign: Taurus

Flower: Chrysanthemum

Keyword: Intensity

The Scorpio Personality

Strengths, Talents, and the Creative Spark

You have a profound interest in motivations deep within your psyche, including the need to control others' feelings through demands on their emotional or material resources. Often you are not even aware of the pressure you exert until another strong personality resists and pushes back, probably another with dominant fixed-sign planets. The detective within you picks up on every scrap of evidence that inclines you toward understanding what makes others tick. Those who surround you have most likely stated that they never noticed something you point out so effortlessly. Then comes the statement that you must be psychic—and some of you are. In reality, you often become obsessed with people and conditions that interest you. Individuals who know you well or would like to get closer think they can change you. They are in for an exhausting ride. Little do they know that you seldom reverse a decision. It's not your fault that you stated your position early in the game and they weren't paying attention.

When you are ready to tackle a goal, you take determination to new heights, working relentlessly to bring it to completion. You have Class A willpower, with a serious approach to life that tends to pick up on subtle nuances that others emit, capturing your interest and adding to your personal data file. Your magnetic personality draws people from many different fields your way who are curious about your views and what makes you so intriguing. You don't say much at times when you are absorbing new information and controlling facial expressions, not wanting to reveal your position before you're ready to state your opinion. Adept at research, keeping secrets, and solving problems, you offer employers an intriguing portfolio of options for earning income.

Intimacy and Personal Relationships

While you sometimes show a cool façade, you take love very seriously. You wait cautiously when you meet a kindred spirit to see how well the sparks fly before demonstrating the signs of your commitment. You're a bit afraid of letting your vulnerability show and losing ground in controlling important facets of the relationship. Underneath the poker face you wear, your heart may be beating wildly and longingly when the object of your attraction comes into view. As a passionate water sign, you look carefully for signs that the chemistry is there before making your sexy moves. You want to find your soulmate, and when you do, you release a floodgate of love, loyalty, and adoration. You make an excellent partner for another Scorpio, Cancer, or Pisces, whose water-sign understanding of emotions meshes with your own. Taurus, your opposite sign, is another excellent romantic catch. As a friend, you attract others who share your interests and tell you their secrets. Strangers seem to sense your understanding and integrity as well, divulging personal details at initial meetings. A number of relatives maintain close connections with you and confide in you, yet show jealous tendencies over your material acquisitions.

Values and Resources

The meaning of life and its mysteries drives the state of curiosity submerged deep in your psyche. This quest has a deep impact on your choice of career and what you value. With your innate analytical skills that span several fields of expertise, you might select a career in consulting, marriage counseling, or business psychology. A government career appeals to many Scorpios, who revere with patriotic pride the opportunity to serve their country in a civilian or military capacity. Another option covers a full range of medical services, from doctors to insurance providers. Life experiences often become the basis of studies and the work you choose as a means of support. You expect security needs to be met generously, with significant benefits that follow you into retirement. Married Scorpios prefer that spouses hold steady positions with excellent pension plans so that as a couple you have your financial future on solid ground. As the sign that rules the eighth house, you opt for solid investments, a continuously growing retirement plan, and savings that cover emergencies, college funds, and major purchases. A major goal is living debt free, with a plan to pay off the mortgage early and wisely keep credit card debt at bay.

Blind Spots and Blockages

Since you often run on pure emotion in personal relationships, you overlook areas that are badly in need of change, including intimate connections. You stubbornly cling to people, routines, and old habits that have long outlived their usefulness. No wonder Pluto, the built-in eradicator, rules your sign. You have baggage to unload, yet fear keeps you in a state of paralysis over taking an unknown path that could mean a release to a better life. To get there you have to be willing to remove psychological blocks that keep you in dead relationships or in positions that keep you stuck materially (same job you have hated for twenty years) and emotionally (maybe I did something in my last life that brought this toxic person to me and now I have to pay back the karma by staying in this painful marriage). No, you don't, but you do have to acknowledge the lesson behind the situation. Many Scorpios won't budge, becoming martyrs or skeptics. Critics say you keep too much inside and have to learn to lighten up with meditation, relaxation techniques, and yoga. You benefit greatly from uplifting experiences while you heal internally.

Goals and Success

You have a passionate spirit, can be very intense about keeping commitments, and take obligations seriously. A call from deep in your soul awakens you to embrace the career of your dreams, finding work that is a pleasure to embrace and that gives you passion and energy. As a water sign, the second in the zodiac, you have powerful intuition that draws you to situations where you are called on to ferret out the truth using your investigative powers to put all the puzzle pieces together. Even when huge setbacks occur, like the COVID-19 pandemic, you have been known to rise out of the ashes like the phoenix via rebirth and a positive attitude. A position that provides private time to unwind, recharge your batteries, and find time to play or travel is an excellent fit. You feel most successful when you have a challenging, mentally stimulating calling that inspires you to work joyfully in your field every day and recognizes your contributions.

Scorpio Keywords for 2022
Adjustment, amendment, analysis

The Year Ahead for Scorpio

Key solar houses that come to life this year, with planets and eclipses occupying them in fixed signs, will feature intensified activity. Saturn in Aquarius continues its journey through your solar fourth house of home and family, where it affected the daily routine of those in your household whose plans were greatly disrupted by the worldwide COVID-19 pandemic. You and family members may have caught the virus or cared for those who fell ill. Children's classrooms became home-based and virtual until a combination of learning accommodations allowed them to return to school again, at least part of the time. Work as you know it, for those who were able to keep their jobs, has undergone major overhauls and continues to reflect a shift to working from home and retraining employees in safer work and health protective practices. On January 14, Mercury makes its first retrograde station of the year in Aquarius and your solar fourth house, sidelining plans you had for starting home projects or purchasing furniture. Anticipated funds may be temporarily unavailable.

Uranus, the planet of chaos, is opposing your Sun this year in Taurus from your solar seventh house of personal and business partners. What unsettling circumstances are affecting relationships now? Did they creep up on you, or did you know they were around for a long time? Uranus starts 2022 in retrograde motion in this house and moves direct on January 18, giving you a chance to address unexpected marital conditions and figuring out why you're engaging in more arguments than usual, especially if you feel emotionally restless. You could be meeting a number of new connections at public gatherings.

Jupiter

For most of 2022, Jupiter makes a home in Pisces and your solar fifth house of recreation, socializing, sports, children, entertainment, romance, creativity, risk-taking, entrepreneurial ventures, and vacations. You enjoy going places with partners, children, and special friends rather than exploring alone. Travel and amusements appeal to your sense of adventure. With the exception of both a retrograde and a sign-change period, Jupiter occupies this space until December 20, when it moves into Aries for a challenging assignment in your solar sixth house in 2023. Compatible Jupiter in Pisces makes a positive aspect to each degree of your sign during this cycle, opening up opportunities to enjoy a few of your favorite pastimes, like drama, musical extravaganzas, and comedic entertainment. On May 10, the benevolent planet enters Aries for a teaser stretch in this sign. On July 28, Jupiter will turn retrograde in Aries and your solar sixth house, moving back into Pisces and your solar fifth house on October 28, until it goes direct again on November 23 through the end of the year. Step up your goals to spend quality time with your children that includes school activities, sports, and park visits. Add a unique adventure that has long been on your bucket list and savor the experience. Single Scorpios may attract a new love interest at a social event and begin a new dating routine.

Saturn

As 2022 begins, Saturn in Aquarius occupies your solar fourth house of home, foundation, family, parents, domestic undertakings, relatives in residence, redecorating or remodeling, landscape design, real estate matters (including sales, purchases, exchanges, and rentals), and the end of matters. Saturn's role is always to remind you of responsibilities and any restrictions that affect conditions in your home and the people who live with you. In recent years you have dealt with COVID-19 limitations that left many of you working from home for a very long stretch after places of business closed and many lost their jobs or were laid off indefinitely until safer conditions returned, some of which is happening this year. If you are part of a large core family, children or other relatives may have come home to live with you temporarily. Perhaps you have been a caregiver for family or friends who contracted coronavirus, or you took on the role of purchasing groceries or supplies for those who could not leave their homes. If you thought about relocating or selling your home, this is a good year to get it in top shape to list it as the real estate industry looks for ways to meet the supply and demand of housing that slowed but is surging now. Continue to protect your immune system and get more sleep and nutritious food to sustain the high level of Scorpio energy you desire. Those of you born between November 4 and 20 see the most action at various times during 2022. Saturn's retrograde period occurs from June 4 through October 23. Venus and Mars in Aquarius line up here for most of March and part of April, making for lively interplay in your home, with much hustle and bustle if someone is moving in or out or you decide to sell your home and buyers invade your space daily. Be sure to oversee the quality of any work projects that are underway in your home, and take safety precautions to keep everyone healthy. Ramp up the household mood with cheerful optimism.

Uranus

The new year begins with Uranus, the planet associated with sudden blow-ups, chaotic behavior, and shake-ups, remaining in residence in Taurus and your solar seventh house of personal and business partners and the public. Life connected with these themes may be unpredictable, as well as with matters affecting collaborators, cooperators, advisors, consultants and those related to the legal or medical profession. Interactions with many of these affiliates may have been severely disrupted by the arrival of the coronavirus pandemic in 2020. In 2022 you are in a recovery year, making adjustments in your personal relationships as well as business dealings and hoping to tone down the volume of any stress-related arguments and shouting matches. Uranus started 2022 in retrograde motion and went direct on January 18 but is not yet finished with its provocative journey through your solar seventh house. The icy planet moves into retrograde motion on August 24 until January 22, 2023. Scorpios born between November 3 and 13 feel acute pressure from this provocative planet to maintain their cool.

Neptune

Although you are driven to complete assignments on time and stick to your word, you too need a break from the erratic work patterns you have dealt with lately and could use a change of momentum. Here comes Neptune in Pisces to the rescue, one of the current occupants of your solar fifth house of love and romance, children and their interests, vacations, amusement, sports, teaching, and risk-taking. Since this planet with the mystical aura has been traveling through this house since April 2011, you are aware of the spiritual allure it brings to attracting relationships, enjoying favorite adventures, and savoring relaxing getaways. Neptune expects you to take a sabbatical from pressure-filled norms without shirking responsibilities or taking sick days from work to escape what bores you. Or is that true? Watery Neptune has been known to hide behind allure and glamorous trappings to get you to let down your guard and ignore your survival instincts. Just because Neptune is compatible in Pisces with your Scorpio Sun does not mean you can ditch obligations indefinitely, but while it is in your solar fifth house, enjoy the playful moments with treasured companions. Invite others who need a break along for a healing interlude. Note that Neptune moves only four to five degrees each year. In 2022 it most affects those of you born between November 13 and 20. The retrograde period for Neptune will be from June 28 to December 3.

Pluto

Way back in 2008, Pluto entered Capricorn and your solar third house with the intention of transforming your mind by helping you let go of rigid thinking patterns and the self-talk that sabotages communication. Over the past fourteen years, you are fortunate to have had a wealth of information fertilizing your brain in the form of expanding your educational options, taking classes, earning degrees, and learning from the school of hard knocks. You have formed strong bonds with relatives (especially siblings and cousins), connected with neighbors and community groups, gained a new respect for the art of purchasing a vehicle, and met contractual obligations fully and on time. Many Scorpios, perhaps once loath to work with sophisticated electronic equipment, have become the experts in the family. Those who know you well comment now on how much you have dropped your guard in keeping them at bay when they ask questions or want to help you solve a problem or reach a decision. Thank Pluto for being the wind beneath your wings as you venture into new territory. Expect changes this year in third-house matters if your birthday occurs between November 18 and 22. In 2022 Pluto in Capricorn goes retrograde on April 29 and moves direct on October 8.

How Will This Year's Eclipses Affect You?

Your sign, Scorpio, features prominently in the eclipses of 2022. A total of four eclipses occur this year: two solar (New Moon) and two lunar (Full Moon), which bring intense periods that start to manifest about two months before they actually occur. All four of them take place in two of your solar chart's angular houses, the first and the seventh, putting the spotlight on action from you and from partnerships. Eclipses always manifest in cycles involving all twelve signs of the zodiac and usually occur in pairs about two weeks apart. Never be fearful of eclipses—think of them as welcome opportunities that allow you to face old, outworn patterns, develop a plan for addressing them, and release them. Eclipses generally trigger unexpected revelations, surprises, and windfalls. The closer an eclipse is to a planet or point in your chart, the greater the importance it plays in your life. Those of you born with a planet at the same degree as an eclipse are likely to see a high level of activity in the house where the eclipse occurs.

The first Solar Eclipse of 2022 occurs on April 30 in Taurus and your solar seventh house of relationships, which includes partners, spouses, business collaborators, roommates, advisors, consultants, legal or medical professionals, open enemies, and the public. If you have planets (natal or progressed) located in this house, expect to encounter revelations of any problems with principal players to come to light. If current connections are positive, you'll benefit from strengthening bonds and fulfilling goals. Should you be experiencing challenges with others in partnerships, any difficulties will manifest openly and call for discussion with an eye on workable solutions. Any previous awareness of contentious behavior could mean you're on the path to separate from your intimate partner or dissolve the affiliation you have with a business partner.

Two weeks later, the first Lunar Eclipse of the year occurs on May 16 in Scorpio and your solar first house of appearance, assertiveness, character, enterprise, image, individuality, self-development, and personality. The pressure is on to keep your goals and promises on track by delivering what you said you would accomplish on time and making any adjustments to your work and play habits that will contribute to achieving life balance. If you have neglected your physical appearance or your health has been problematic, the eclipse will remind you to seek solutions and get counsel from medical specialists, dieticians, and behavioral consultants who provide assistance in managing these critical areas of your life.

On October 25, the second Solar Eclipse of 2022 takes place in Scorpio and your solar first house of action, assertiveness, passion, and self-interest. How well have you managed your intended goals for improving your health and appearance, made adjustments to grooming and fitness habits, or established sound nutrition habits?

The year's final eclipse is a Lunar Eclipse on November 8 in your opposite sign of Taurus and your solar seventh house of business and personal partners. Hanging out close to this degree is transiting Uranus in Taurus, so if your birthday is between November 8 and 10, this eclipse falls opposite your Sun—so stay safe, keep your emotions in check, and understand what you learned after thoroughly examining troubling relationships in May. If remedial action had the desired results, then take the necessary actions, seeking peaceful solutions while nurturing your body, mind, and spirit.

Scorpio | January

Overall Theme

People make your world go round this month, paying attention to every little thing you do and showering you with compliments and invitations. What a way to start the year! Uranus in Taurus goes direct in your solar seventh house on the 18th, increasing contact with individuals you haven't seen since last summer, including proposals for collaborative work.

Relationships

The New Moon in Capricorn on January 2 stimulates communication with siblings and neighbors ready for a replay of holiday festivities. A much-desired date night fulfills romantic leanings on the 7th, a day that you might also find appropriate to bond with children at a favorite event. Ring in the new year with business colleagues on the 12th, or take your partner dancing for a delightful change of pace.

Success and Money

By the middle of the month you see an increase in your paycheck and a vote of confidence from management that economic conditions are stabilizing. Goals that were put on hold during the COVID-19 pandemic are cited for implementation over the next two months. Love partners are ready for serious talks after Venus goes direct on the 29th.

Pitfalls and Potential Problems

A night of family fun is derailed on the 4th when conflicting schedules and bad moods squelch enthusiasm. Avoid erratic financial negotiating on the 14th, when Mercury goes retrograde and key components of the transaction are missing and you discover legal constraints. The 21st brings clarity.

Rewarding Days

2, 7, 12, 21

Challenging Days

4, 14, 17, 25

Scorpio | February

Overall Theme

February 1 is the start of the Lunar Year of the Water Tiger. It is also the day of the Aquarius New Moon that puts the spotlight on your family life in your solar fourth house. Why not celebrate the blessings you're enjoying with a festive meal and create positive chi with delicious treats and a colorful party decor?

Relationships

The month features a family bonding opportunity to discuss needed changes that will be unfolding in your home. Someone ill may require extra help with chores and errands. The planets favor February 7 as a good day for an early Valentine's Day party. Invite friends and family for some lighthearted fun. Save the 26th for a casual dinner with neighbors.

Success and Money

If you are in search of a new job, the 26th favors interviewing and distributing resumes. Make phone calls to key people and follow up on networking leads between the 22nd and 26th. An unexpected proposal from a business collaborator whets your appetite for a unique assignment on the 7th.

Pitfalls and Potential Problems

The 10th is dangerous for impulse spending, so be sure to plan purchases carefully. The Full Moon in Leo on the 16th contributes to a tense work environment, conflicts with the boss, and calls for an attitude adjustment. You and a partner want different accommodations on a planned trip, which prevents a firm decision.

Rewarding Days

4, 7, 18, 23

Challenging Days

1, 11, 16, 21

Scorpio | March

Overall Theme

The New Moon in Pisces on the 2nd in your solar fifth house joins Jupiter and aspects Uranus in Taurus, creating excitement and an adrenaline rush that makes it memorable and launches a compatible month for your social undertakings. Neptune in this house adds an aura of glamour to new relationships. It's okay to flirt.

Relationships

March is a busy month for accelerating the flow of social connections. Single Scorpios meet new prospects or plan fun events with romantic partners on the 5th, while the 7th gives you private time with your significant other or a business colleague. Communication with siblings leads to an agreeable adjustment of plans on the 26th.

Success and Money

Take the time mid-month to go over financial statements and estimated taxes owed so that you're prepared to apply for loans or file early. Make sure needed forms are available and follow up with your tax accountant if you have earned more money and should change your withholding amount.

Pitfalls and Potential Problems

The Virgo Full Moon on the 18th in your solar eleventh house of goals and friendships opposes transiting Mercury, Jupiter, and Neptune in Pisces in your solar fifth house, tempting you to spend lavishly on gifts or entertainment venues. Tension with authority figures over approaches to work escalates on the 14th. Home base could have an icy tone on the 28th.

Rewarding Days

2, 7, 12, 26

Challenging Days

6, 14, 20, 28

Scorpio | April

Overall Theme

Lunar activity is high this month when you experience the New Moon in your chart twice: first in Aries on the 1st in your solar sixth house of daily routines and second on April 30, when a Solar Eclipse occurs in Taurus. This eclipse receives a hard aspect from Uranus and falls in your solar seventh house of personal and business partners. Revelations bring multiple questions.

Relationships

Learning opportunities for you or your children put the attention on interactions with instructors, teachers, and educators this month. Set goals for obtaining desired credentials that improve job prospects. Spend quality time with children, hire a tutor if they are struggling, and stay active in the PTA.

Success and Money

Good news about business expansion occurs around the 1st. You and colleagues discuss what the changes will mean for assignments and teamwork. If you have been applying for a new job, you get a response around the 30th. Pursue a research-oriented work project.

Pitfalls and Potential Problems

Avoid making stinging comments to your partner around the 4th, when impatience surfaces. The Full Moon in Libra on April 16 highlights sensitive subjects that you walked away from on the 10th. Your instincts were accurate. Stay away from controversy by analyzing facts and minimizing stressful encounters. The tendency to be a "fixer" in this dilemma could backfire because the issue is someone else's to resolve.

Rewarding Days

1, 7, 22, 27

Challenging Days

4, 10, 16, 24

Scorpio | May

Overall Theme

You're able to finalize the use of funds for home improvement projects on the 2nd and spend most of the month approving plans and overseeing the work of contractors. Choose bold designs and striking colors to pick up the energy in strategic places in your home. Efficiency in the undertaking gives you the time to take a well-deserved vacation around the 24th.

Relationships

Redecorating delights family members, especially your children, who take pride in new bedroom accommodations and excitedly select options for making a statement with new furniture and accessories. Sharing a family project strengthens bonds, making each of you a stakeholder in your home's appearance. Be sure to consider feng shui conventions.

Success and Money

As long as you start your projects before Mercury goes retrograde in Gemini on the 10th, you'll savor the enthusiasm that comes from seeing your efforts come to life. Goodwill and festive touches flourish when you attend a company-sponsored holiday event on the 7th with your significant other.

Pitfalls and Potential Problems

An unanticipated setback occurs on the 5th when you hear from a relative at a distance. Phone calls follow with suggestions for pending action as facts unfold. The Lunar Eclipse in Scorpio on the 16th falls in your solar first house, bringing critical information to light and affecting travel decisions. Watch spending on the 18th, especially if building costs are subject to increases.

Rewarding Days

2, 6, 7, 24

Challenging Days

5, 9, 15, 18

Scorpio | June

Overall Theme

Venus is in your opposite sign of Taurus right now, prompting you to pay greater attention to the love of your life. Shower your significant other with tender loving care. Plan a dinner for the 7th. Single Scorpios looking for a partner could meet a prospect on the 20th. Mercury goes direct on the 3rd, and plans resume. Saturn in Aquarius and Neptune in Pisces make retrograde stations on the 4th and the 28th, respectively.

Relationships

Connections with friends and group members strengthen and lead to memorable social and organizational experiences. Heartfelt talks with loved ones bring stability and appreciation of each other's cherished traits, which puts you in the mood for intimacy and spending quality time together. Pamper children on the 20th.

Success and Money

Your paycheck includes a raise or bonus that you put to good use to save for holiday expenses and summer vacations. Camaraderie with your work team soars on the 21st, when a breakthrough solution clarifies puzzling situations. Mercury, Venus, and Uranus unite in your solar seventh house this month, strengthening collaborative undertakings.

Pitfalls and Potential Problems

Avoid acquiring battle scars at home base on the 4th, when Saturn turns retrograde in Aquarius and verbal exchanges turn hostile. Neptune in Pisces clashes with the Moon in Gemini as it turns retrograde on the 28th, putting a damper on getaway plans and stifling spending splurges.

Rewarding Days

7, 13, 20, 21

Challenging Days

1, 5, 15, 18

Scorpio | July

Overall Theme

Excitement and a holiday mood prevail as the nation gets ready to celebrate the 4th of July. Invite close friends to stay with you this week. Throw a party. With sociable Venus and Mercury in Gemini bonding with passionate Mars and Jupiter in Aries, you talk about old times, eat delicious food, and marvel over the fireworks display.

Relationships

Friends warm your heart this month as you fill your home with laughter and happy hugs and kisses. Children of friends bond with your children, engaging in playful banter and favorite games. When you've had your fill of recent news, dig in to a tasty barbecue and sumptuous sides to complement the uplifting air. Schedule a park visit on the 5th.

Success and Money

The week of the 17th brings welcome announcements about business expansion and higher salary caps. You'll be singing the praises of management decisions that strengthen your bargaining power. Around the 23rd you learn details of new work alliances. Schedule a celebratory lunch to cheer successful initiatives.

Pitfalls and Potential Problems

Written materials look sketchy to you on the 6th, and you take work home to review details. Don't sign loan papers or contracts on the 13th, the date of the Capricorn Full Moon. The 23rd is more advantageous for successful outcomes. Jupiter turns retrograde on the 28th, which is also the date of the Leo New Moon in your solar tenth house.

Rewarding Days

4, 10, 17, 23

Challenging Days

2, 6, 13, 28

Scorpio | August

Overall Theme
Your financial picture looks healthy this month, with deals falling into place, mortgage loans approved, and extra cash, compliments of a performance bonus. Service workers who count on tips to supplement income see more generous compensation after a long dry spell.

Relationships
Friends gather to toast a birthday celebrant on the 1st and suggest a weekend getaway for the group in September. An engagement could be in the cards for single Scorpios. Form intimate bonds with your significant other on the 20th, when you take time for a romantic escape. The New Moon in Virgo on August 27 opens the door to new friendships.

Success and Money
Find a sweet deal on a beautiful ring around the 20th. Be sure the style is in line with your beloved's taste if you're purchasing it without them. A good part of the month revolves around discharging debt or consolidating payments, a refinance, paying off college loans, or making a child's tuition payment for the upcoming school year.

Pitfalls and Potential Problems
The green-eyed monster is around on the 5th when the Moon is in Scorpio. A struggle for power seems to be the culprit. Too many negative comments surface at a meeting on the 9th, leaving you trying to rationalize why the meeting was scheduled when no agenda was set. The Full Moon in Aquarius on the 11th exacerbates simmering home-based tension.

Rewarding Days
1, 7, 16, 20

Challenging Days
5, 9, 11, 27

Scorpio | September

Overall Theme

Neighborhood goals to improve the community image are successful thanks to your impressive analysis of plans and relentless determination to implement them. The 6th through the 15th largely favor family and partnership gatherings and much deserved breaks in routine. Suggest holding a meeting in an outdoor setting to discuss upcoming projects.

Relationships

Siblings and cousins take an interest in subjects you're studying and want to sign up too. Entertain at home on the 7th, serving a unique menu and setting up a variety of games. Invite close neighbors to participate. Spend quality time with your significant other on the 15th, showing your love with romantic affection and a gourmet meal.

Success and Money

If you are considering a fall vacation, the 30th works best for landing travel bargains and negotiating for additional perks. This date also favors the purchase of jewelry or quality furniture for your home at a reduced cost. Refinish the deck and trim landscape around the 7th. Confer with your financial advisor to review asset allocation and increase retirement savings.

Pitfalls and Potential Problems

When Mercury turns retrograde in Libra on the 9th in your solar twelfth house of seclusion and healing, you'll be grateful it falls on a weekend, after two preview days of stressful communication. Unfriendly vibes dominate partnership exchanges, some quite harsh, on the 16th. Confusion over goal alignment surfaces in the workplace on the 22nd.

Rewarding Days

6, 7, 15, 30

Challenging Days

2, 5, 16, 22

Scorpio | October

Overall Theme

Delays related to completion of work, scheduling medical tests, and vacation starts are about to end. Significant planetary activity drives momentum, starting with Mercury going direct on the 2nd in Virgo, Pluto moving direct on the 8th in Capricorn, and Saturn turning direct in Aquarius on the 23rd. Implement those household plans.

Relationships

Harmony prevails and trust emerges among siblings on the 3rd. Heartfelt exchanges put you in sync with the mindset of others. The management team seems highly attuned to performance accomplishments and effective use of subordinates' talents. Energy gets a boost from the Solar Eclipse in Scorpio on the 25th.

Success and Money

You pay down debt via consolidation on the 8th and put extra cash into savings accounts. Validate the easy collaboration that drives your interest in a new project despite a few testy moves from Uranus in your solar seventh house. Members of your team learn of upward adjustments to bonuses and raises.

Pitfalls and Potential Problems

Balance your checkbook before energetic Mars in Gemini makes a retrograde station in your solar eighth house of joint income and debt on the 30th. Coworkers express opposition on the 9th to proposed shifts in direction that are better addressed on the 18th, after considerable research has been completed. Expect some concessions.

Rewarding Days

4, 14, 18, 27

Challenging Days

1, 9, 17, 20

Scorpio | November

Overall Theme
On the 3rd your social life gets a boost in the romance department or with children's interests and amusements. When the Lunar Eclipse in Taurus settles in your solar seventh house on the 8th, it can zap your energy while influencing travel decisions. If you're ready for a beach vacation, the 13th is perfect, as the Moon in Cancer forms a compatible trine to Neptune in Pisces.

Relationships
Special bonding takes place with a child connected to a sports program. If you coach or teach, your reputation for using spot-on strategies to motivate others shines. Venus in your sign makes compatible aspects to the Moon, Mercury, Jupiter, and Neptune on the 13th. How do you spell romance with these vibes? Go for it!

Success and Money
Right before Thanksgiving, you get good news about financial stability and a cash gift when the Moon, Mercury, and Venus get together in your solar second house of income just as Jupiter moves direct in Pisces. Make adjustments for visitors who extend their stay through the 28th.

Pitfalls and Potential Problems
Maintain your cool with members of your household on the 1st, when lunar vibes rattle sensitivities. Let the involved members work out their differences. Weather disrupts sightseeing plans on the 25th, so bring out the games and select movies to keep guests entertained. Leftover Thanksgiving turkey is a godsend for the sandwich crowd.

Rewarding Days
3, 13, 23, 28

Challenging Days
1, 8, 11, 25

Scorpio | December

Overall Theme

Prosperity comes your way when Venus and Mercury line up in your solar second house of income as you get ready to celebrate year-end festivities. Neptune in Pisces moves direct on the 3rd, sending a celebratory vibe to your solar fifth house and leading the way with glamour and glitz to make your holidays sparkle.

Relationships

Bond with those you love over the holidays. Start with work connections as you finish problematic assignments from the 1st through the 8th. Invite relatives and neighbors for a Christmas Eve buffet. Embrace family on the 25th, sharing sentiments of love and caring. Help out at a soup kitchen in the morning to show holiday spirit to others.

Success and Money

With Saturn in Aquarius transiting your solar fourth house all year, you're ready to delegate responsibilities among family members. Ask for volunteers to cover routine chores, and rotate responsibilities. You received much deserved rewards for work contributions. Enjoy them as you plan the perfect holiday for your appreciative family.

Pitfalls and Potential Problems

Friends have more on their minds than a Friday holiday lunch on the 16th, when the Moon opposes Jupiter. Someone dwells on old grudges. Be sure waitstaff or sales associates return your credit cards when you pay for food or goods on the 21st. Mercury goes retrograde on the 29th in Capricorn in your solar third house, delaying local travel or the arrival of guests.

Rewarding Days

3, 24, 25, 28

Challenging Days

1, 6, 16, 21

Scorpio Action Table

These dates reflect the best–but not the only–times for success and ease in these activities, according to your Sun sign.

	JAN	FEB	MAR	APR	MAY	JUN	JUL	AUG	SEP	OCT	NOV	DEC
Move	2			7			17				9	
Romance		7			24	20			15			28
Seek counseling/ coaching	21		12				4					
Ask for a raise			2	1				16		18		3
Vacation									6		5	
Get a loan		26			2	13		20		14		

Sagittarius

The Archer
November 22 to December 21

Element: Fire

Quality: Mutable

Polarity: Yang/masculine

Planetary Ruler: Jupiter

Meditation: I can take time to explore my soul

Gemstone: Turquoise

Power Stones: Lapis lazuli, azurite, sodalite

Key Phrase: I understand

Glyph: Archer's arrow

Anatomy: Hips, thighs, sciatic nerve

Colors: Royal blue, purple

Animals: Fleet-footed animals

Myths/Legends: Athena, Chiron

House: Ninth

Opposite Sign: Gemini

Flower: Narcissus

Keyword: Optimism

The Sagittarius Personality

Strengths, Talents, and the Creative Spark

Discovery becomes you, Sagittarius. You're known for experimenting with life by seeking out and unearthing new experiences that take you far beyond your current boundaries. Your symbol is the Centaur, the sign of the Archer, a mutable fire member of the zodiac and the natural ruler of the ninth house of the higher mind, religion, spirituality, the clergy, advanced education, law, publishing, in-laws, foreigners and their cultures, and travel to distant locations. Lucky you! Jupiter rules your sign and leads the way in attracting you to explore new worlds through your feelings and diverse ways of thinking. You want to hear the stories of strangers, their philosophies, and what influenced their move to a place far from birth. Expanding your mind to learn new things is a priority you desire and acquire through travel and formal education and by becoming a perpetual student who always has a slot in a mesmerizing workshop. Your sign studies a variety of religions to seek out different viewpoints and determine which concepts unify the people of the world.

A connection with the ninth house aids you in acquiring a fascinating array of subjects beyond religion that include the law and rules of the legal system, justice (criminal and civil), the courts, and judges who render decisions. Civil rights and employment law attract you as well, and may influence a career choice. Early in your employment history you gravitated toward jobs that let you learn as you go, like internships, temporary or part-time work, or assignments that were intermittent and gave you the latitude to travel and assimilate the vibes of challenging environments. You deeply care what others think and enjoy shaping the minds of coworkers, students, or children through your writing, teaching, or publishing. Your serious side emerges when you talk about the problems of the world that revolve around religion, education, health, and politics. You speak up when you see abusive behavior directed at those with no power from authorities who know better and should be protecting the interests of others. Sagittarius is a sign that profits from being skilled in more than one career, valuing deeply what you learn in each experience. Options for visiting unknown territory have been limited in recent years due to the interference of the COVID-19 pandemic. In 2022, let the exploration resume.

Intimacy and Personal Relationships

Optimism becomes you, attracting you to others who invest in happiness by displaying a solid sense of humor and enjoying a good joke. As a sign that either marries late or has trouble staying in a relationship, you rarely race to the altar. Personal freedom is deeply important to you. You've had a few nightmares to tell over being with the wrong person. When you do find true love, your loyalty is profound and there is little you wouldn't do to please your mate. A friend often becomes your long-term partner, such as Gemini, your opposite sign, who is playful, restless, curious like you, and never boring. You would drop a dullard in a heartbeat. A mate who loves to travel suits your avid desire to explore the world, eat exotic food, and be willing to internalize a different culture as part of your shared life experience. Fire signs Aries and Leo also catch your eye and star at the center of fascinating adventures and passionate dates. You're one of the signs who stays in touch with old friends, and you're often instrumental in getting the gang together for reunions or vacations. Friends from different parts of the world fascinate you with their unique occupations, interesting accents, and love of learning. Find a partner with wanderlust and book that trip!

Values and Resources

In the aftermath of the pandemic, you became painfully aware of how administration of health care benefits affected treatment of the coronavirus among different groups of citizens. Many did not survive. After the vaccines arrived, it was too late to save many ailing people in a world that is still recovering economically and socially from the pain. You prefer opportunities to expand your consciousness in line with the attributes of your ruling planet, Jupiter. Bigger is better in your eyes, and you want to take in every vision you can through travel, networking, studies, and outreach. A career that offers travel opportunities is tailor-made for your goals. Surround yourself with beautiful architecture and a preference for rich fabrics and colors such as dark blues, browns, purple, and dark green shades. Stately trees such as birch, elm, and mighty oak resonate with your sign. As a perpetual truth seeker, you honor your mission to discover a deeper passion for life.

Blind Spots and Blockages

A criticism of those who know you is that you completely lose track of time—you're late for appointments, dinners, and meeting deadlines.

Some say you'll be late for your own funeral. You're adept at writing speeches, putting tremendous passion into delivering them, yet you don't know when to quit and ramble on with complete disregard for the rest of the program. Periodically you forget to acknowledge others who played key roles in the enterprise or supported the team, forgetting to have them take a bow when it's time for introductions. A good support team helps you stay on track, but only if you give them a chance to communicate the next steps of the task and identify the missing pieces. You can get easily bored by routines and have trouble hiding your disinterest. If it leads to leaving work early or phoning in sick, it's time to look for the next challenging assignment, something many Sagittarians will be doing in 2022.

Goals and Success

Members of your sign make excellent instructors, teachers, professors, environmentalists, sociologists, or anthropologists. You excel as cruise directors, salespeople, travel agents, and tour guides. Since you enjoy temporary work, you might be up for taking a sabbatical to earn a law or medical degree while you hit the books and plan for a dream career. If writing or journalism is a passion, look for options that allow you to tell your story or use your masterful skills as an editor in this highly demanding field. Find the space to spread out to do the necessary research for telling an inspiring story. Regardless of the size of the company you work for, you prefer autonomy and considerable latitude to manage your daily work. That's why many of you prefer to be independent consultants and freelance writers. Hire an accountant to keep the books. If you're in the market to collaborate this year, look for a compatible Gemini and write a bestseller addressing the psychology of healing from the effects of the pandemic.

Sagittarius Keywords for 2022
Academia, adventure, amplification

The Year Ahead for Sagittarius

As you enter 2022, you leave behind a year of disruptions and recovery from the COVID-19 pandemic that affected routines affiliated with home, family, workplace, and education, and, most importantly, your health. Now you're ready to pursue your next steps. There will be a challenge to employment pursuits since unpredictable Uranus in Taurus starts the year in retrograde motion in your solar sixth house of work and daily environment, turning direct on January 18 and creating discomfort that suggests the status quo just won't cut it anymore. Temporary arrangements may become more permanent. Two eclipses land here in Taurus and your solar sixth house to highlight the state of your health and your employment stability. Love planet Venus is retrograde in Capricorn in your solar second house of income and resources as the year begins, suggesting that a shift may have occurred in December 2021 to affect the state of your finances. If money is tight, work on a strategy to correct the issue before Venus goes direct on January 29. After dealing with several Capricorn planets in your solar second house in recent years, the lone occupant there now is Pluto in Capricorn in late degrees, urging you to let go of any karma that stands in the way of prosperity.

This year the planet of communication, Mercury, becomes the first planet to turn retrograde in Aquarius on January 14 in your solar third house of mental outlook, neighborhood, siblings, and transportation. You'll be networking with many colleagues who are currently performing work from home or at a central shared location that requires limited physical contact and maintains social-distancing practices. Be sure you have an IT specialist on speed dial to maximize use of upgraded systems, purchases of electronic equipment, and installation of high-tech business collaboration tools.

Jupiter

With the exception of both a retrograde and a sign-change period, Jupiter occupies Pisces and your solar fourth house for most of the year, until December 20, when it moves into Aries for a challenging assignment in your solar fifth house in 2023. Each member of your sign benefits from this yearlong transit that provides insight into how to handle stressful conditions at home base, including major cleaning and decluttering tasks that have been on hold and replacement of big-ticket items like an HVAC, a new roof, or a kitchen makeover. When Jupiter goes into Aries and your solar fifth house, you learn a thing or two about your children's needs and help them become better students, athletes, or friends. You could meet a new travel buddy or two during this period and resume planning for a trip postponed due to coronavirus restrictions. Unexpected money is available to pay for the trip. On July 28 Jupiter will turn retrograde in Aries and your solar fifth house, moving back into Pisces and your solar fourth house on October 28 until it goes direct on November 23 for the remainder of the calendar year. Those of you born between November 22 and 30 see the most action from Jupiter while it is in Aries and occupies your solar fifth house. You'll find clues on how to expand important areas of your world, fulfill your entrepreneurial dreams, and experience exciting adventures. While Jupiter is in Pisces, research costs of home improvement goods and services and negotiate a fair price for contracted work. Note that Jupiter connects with transiting Neptune in Pisces in mid-April, creating a romantic vibe in your home.

Saturn

On December 17, 2020, Saturn entered Aquarius and your solar third house of advertising, communication, contracting, education, electronics, mental outlook, community and neighborhood activity, transportation (including vehicles), machinery, and relationships with siblings, cousins, and neighbors. Saturn wants you to get serious about studies you initiate, agreements you enter into, and relationships you would like to improve with family and business networks. Work responsibility seems to increase, along with demands for your services. If you are in the writing field and learned a thing or two about surviving a pandemic, consider developing a book or articles that discuss how the phenomenon affected the health and outlook of world citizens, the economy, and the way we do business now and how social distancing affected personal relationships. If mediation skills are your forte, you might find lucrative work soothing the anxieties of employees in companies that had to regroup, realign skills, and find funding for initiatives designed to provide jobs in a changing world. Recruit teams to study emerging conditions and develop solutions that benefit recovering companies. Network with foreign enterprises—you may even receive a grant and some travel money to see how others are rebuilding their resources. This year Saturn touches the lives most intensely of Sagittarians born between December 2 and 18. Saturn's retrograde period in 2022 occurs from June 4 through October 23. Tune out any lingering frustration and focus on your assets in this year of unfolding adventure.

Uranus

How do you think your solar sixth house of coworkers and work life, including colleagues, daily routines, fitness, health, healing, nutritional choices, organizational style, and pets, is holding up after another year of hosting unpredictable Uranus in Taurus? If you have any natal planets in Taurus, you understand that they are not particularly friendly with transiting Saturn in Aquarius, putting your solar third house of communication, mental outlook, and local travel in a standstill situation since the end of 2020 and blocking your spirit of independence and enthusiasm. Depression is not your jam, and you need an exit strategy from erratic Uranus, which has been making unexpected and inconsistent demands when all you want to do is get back to the world that lets you mix and mingle with others to do your best work. Two eclipses in Taurus and your solar sixth house in 2022 may help you beat the odds of staying confined for another year. If you were born between December 1 and 11, the planet of chaos and disruption has the greatest impact on your experimental mind and currently unfulfilled routine. Staying with your company is fine as long as you have a hand in revitalizing the environment. Otherwise, it is time to connect with your professional networks and scope out employment opportunities that match your unique skills. The planet of the unexpected will move into retrograde motion on August 24 and go direct on January 22, 2023. Be ready for a shake-up offer from academia or the foreign service and put your restless brain to the test.

Neptune

Although you find amusement in watching the action of those with planets in dreamy Pisces, you're aware that they tend to clash with consciousness-expanding Sagittarius planets, sending confusing messages that conflict with your vastly different viewpoints. At times during this cycle, puzzling dynamics have created time-wasting scenarios in your home, dragging out decisions and adding frustration to the mix. No doubt you're familiar with these situations since Neptune has been in Pisces and your solar fourth house of home, family, and domestic affairs since April 2011. With this long transit in place, you may be spending more time than usual sorting out hazy conditions for needy family members and listening to a litany of complaints, one of which might be unemployment woes tied to the coronavirus. Your spontaneous gift of gab heals troubled waters as the perfect words come easily to you, convincing others that misunderstandings are not fatal. Be prepared to send night owls to bed when they're watching TV all night or feeding their pain through drinking or overeating. On the other hand, joyful milestones may be in the works, such as engagements, weddings, childbirth, and retirement, giving you reason to celebrate and spread optimism. Neptune in this house of stable foundations entices you to daydream or distracts you from efficiently addressing issues when internal strife is present. Work with Neptune to stimulate resolutions that create peace and better communication. Amplify your goals and set new directions for meaningful change in the year ahead.

Pluto

Compensation has been erratic for many Sagittarians during this lengthy transit of Pluto, which began its Capricorn journey in 2008 in your solar second house of assets, income, money you earn, how you spend money, and self-development plans that tie in with long-term career goals. Pluto is slipping into the final degrees of this long transit, which wraps up in 2025. Its presence here exposed you to numerous visits from planets and eclipses in recent years that brought eye-opening challenges, creating an impact on the timing of financial goals and implementation of plans. Give your budget a hard look this year, especially if your salary or employment has been deeply affected by pandemic-related idle periods since 2020. You may have been forced to change jobs, experienced termination, or had your work hours reduced, which affected your bottom line and ability to pay bills on time—and you were not alone. If you changed careers, you are in a rebirth period, learning the ropes in a new venture and finding passion again. Now your spirit feels refreshed and you're ready for action. Recovery periods mesh with stimulating your cash flow if you were born between December 16 and 21, the birth dates most affected by this transit. Make a toast to sunny days and initiate an adventurous career journey.

How Will This Year's Eclipses Affect You?

In 2022 a total of four eclipses occur. Two eclipses are solar (New Moon) and two are lunar (Full Moon), which create intense periods that may begin to manifest a few months before their actual occurrence. All four of these eclipses occur in cadent houses in your chart's solar sixth and twelfth houses. Eclipses unfold in cycles involving all twelve signs of the zodiac, usually occurring in pairs about two weeks apart. Eclipses represent opportunities to release old patterns and conditions that have outlived their usefulness. Don't fear them, since they may surprise you with unexpected windfalls. The closer an eclipse is to a degree or point in your chart, the greater its importance is likely to be in your life. If you were born with a planet at the same degree as an eclipse, you could see a high level of activity in the house where the eclipse occurs. An eclipse's impact may last six months to a year or more.

The first Solar Eclipse of 2022 occurs on April 30 in Taurus and your solar sixth house of daily routines, fitness, health, organization, nutrition, pets, and teamwork. Stimulating activity in this house increases your workload when management assignments require your sharp communication skills that include delivering presentations, problem-solving, editing, and writing. Inspiration comes to you out of the blue with Uranus in this house—could your next project involve surviving a pandemic? Make appointments for medical and dental checkups and review current medications with your physician for efficacy.

On May 16 the first Lunar Eclipse of the year takes place in Scorpio and your solar twelfth house of healing, private matters, hospital visiting, meditation, hidden enemies, psychic insight and charities. After coping with unanticipated career or relationship setbacks, you could be healing from emotional dilemmas and taking steps to stabilize and reclaim your power. Sudden changes in direction left you exhausted and force new employment patterns, leaving you overworked and anxious. Wrap up old business, seek preferred assignments, and find the employment satisfaction you deserve.

The year's second Solar Eclipse takes place on October 25 in Scorpio and your solar twelfth house of recovery, regrouping, healing, hospital visiting, metaphysics, enemies, psychic insight, secrets, and charities. Matters connected with this house are timely and a writer's dream to develop human interest stories, write about medical cures, provide insight into the pandemic and how it affected the world, or share details of metaphysical and spiritual topics. Now that you've had time to clear the air, you can seek out reliable networks and pursue appealing job prospects. As a true Sagittarius, you'll consider at least two options and compare their merits. Put your preference for discovery at the top of the list.

The year's final eclipse is a Lunar Eclipse on November 8, again in Taurus and your solar sixth house. Adjustments to your entire work routine are ongoing, along with the addition of new collaborators who share project assignments with you. If you chose a position that includes travel opportunities, you have met your desire to expand your connections in distant locations. The volume of contracts picks up again. Get plenty of sleep, exercise, and use meditation techniques to cope with stress. Welcome each day with a grateful heart.

Sagittarius | January

Overall Theme

Money and contractual matters are on your mind this month with Venus and Pluto in Capricorn and your solar second house calling for an assessment of your financial picture. Work on it before you return to your job. Mars in your sign through the 24th urges you to get the new year off to an enthusiastic start. Savor the passion.

Relationships

Focus on the interests of your children, scheduling bonding time and planning favorite outings and entertainment venues with them. If you work with students or coach children's sports, the calendar fills up with project assignments and scheduled games. Initiatives that support teachers' needs inspire you to host an event to help fund the cost of supplies. Ask parents to join you in honoring educators.

Success and Money

You start and end the month with excellent money vibes and abundant ideas on how to spend it and share it with deserving individuals and groups. Budget for planned household maintenance. Purchasing power works favorably for you on the New Moon in Capricorn on January 2. Make large purchases after Venus goes direct on January 29.

Pitfalls and Potential Problems

Get travel booked and documents signed before Mercury turns retrograde in Aquarius on January 14, when the Moon in Gemini opposes your Sun in your solar first house, a good day for keeping a low profile. After disrupting your solar sixth house of work with chaotic moments since August, erratic Uranus goes direct on the 18th.

Rewarding Days

2, 3, 8, 29

Challenging Days

4, 9, 11, 25

Sagittarius | February

Overall Theme

Your solar second house of money and income sizzles with activity. Planets in Capricorn take up residence there, with Mercury, Venus, Mars, and Pluto lending an air of optimism after a difficult year of economic recovery. You've been vigilant the last few years in suppressing your enthusiasm. Indulge your restless spirit. Explore the emerging job market and pursue your dream job, taking action after Mercury goes direct on the 3rd.

Relationships

After the New Moon in Aquarius on February 1, the focus moves to home base, where family gathers and expresses gratitude for surviving health challenges and managing new work routines. As you reunite with returning coworkers, you trade stories of survival and begin to plan for adjusted work targets while rebuilding a team. Your boss asks for volunteers to revise the plan of work.

Success and Money

By mid-month you're talking a salary increase and a major shift in duties with management. Those considerable motivational skills you have are just what the organization needs to elevate performance levels and charge the staff's mojo. Make outreach a priority to cultivate important alliances.

Pitfalls and Potential Problems

A date with a love interest doesn't pan out on the first weekend of the month. Partners are at odds with you around the 10th and tempers flare. With little notice, an anticipated visitor cancels long-distance travel around the Full Moon in Leo on the 16th. Negotiate or you'll eat the cost of lodging and entertainment.

Rewarding Days
3, 7, 17, 26

Challenging Days
5, 10, 15, 24

Sagittarius | March

Overall Theme

The New Moon in Pisces on the 2nd highlights your solar fourth house of home and family. With Jupiter and Neptune both occupying this house, you're ready to give your home a makeover. Later on, host a party to welcome guests, share a tasty meal, and showcase the guest-friendly redecorating upgrades.

Relationships

Your sign shares compatibility with Venus and Mars in Aquarius traveling through your solar third house of communication, generating romantic opportunities this month. Relationships at home base get the greatest attention now. Shower your significant other with attention, letting your loving nature take center stage, especially around the 12th. If you're single, a new routine helps you meet eligible partners.

Success and Money

Jupiter in Pisces highlights your home and family and your plans for remodeling and buying furniture for targeted rooms. Look over proposals from vendors and ask about possible incentives if you schedule volume work. Bargains are yours for the asking. Negotiate for low upfront payments on the 12th and 26th.

Pitfalls and Potential Problems

It's bad enough that interactions with children and friends are strained on the 5th and contentious with partners on the 10th. When the Virgo Full Moon emerges on the 18th, it puts a gloomy damper on interactions with your employer. Watch out for difficult conversations and pessimistic moods. Be ready for a lengthy conversation with a troubled friend on the 20th.

Rewarding Days

2, 3, 12, 26

Challenging Days

6, 10, 17, 20

Sagittarius | April

Overall Theme

As if reading your mind to bring you something to satisfy your restless spirit, the universe delivers two New Moons this month. The first is on April 1 in Aries and your solar fifth house, and the second one is a Solar Eclipse in Taurus and your solar sixth house on April 30. How's that for a new beginning to spice up both your work and your love life?

Relationships

With the New Moon on April 1 occurring in your solar fifth house, your social life perks up, with invitations from traveling pals, school networks, and romantic connections. Control the April Fools' antics by leaving your rubber snake at home instead of shocking friends. Please the family on the 25th with a favorite takeout meal and a night of fun, games, and feasting.

Success and Money

Shop for bargains on the 22nd, a day when you could also see extra cash in your checkbook, either a refund or a job bonus. This date favors a consultation with your financial advisor if you are thinking of increasing withholdings for your retirement account. Your boss offers strategic career advice.

Pitfalls and Potential Problems

A difference in approach on the 4th creates an impasse in the work flow among team members. By the 14th, your boss balks at the points of contention, calling a meeting to reframe the timeline and move ahead with plans.

Rewarding Days

1, 6, 22, 25

Challenging Days

4, 9, 14, 20

Sagittarius | May

Overall Theme

The Solar Eclipse in Taurus on April 30 just hit transiting Uranus in your solar sixth house, revealing organizational revamping plans and highlighting personal medical issues for you or a team member. Two weeks later, a Lunar Eclipse occurs in Scorpio and your twelfth house of seclusion on the 16th, reminding you to see a doctor for a lingering ailment and schedule recommended tests.

Relationships

Loving expressions from your significant other communicate the depth of feelings you share. Their support gives you encouragement and injects your spirit with optimism. The Lunar Eclipse on the 16th could have you visiting others in the hospital and sharing concerns with close ties. Family members surprise you on the 20th with a favorite treat and compassionate gestures.

Success and Money

Your social life gets a boost on the 10th when transiting Jupiter moves into Aries and your solar fifth house. Invitations from friends increase, expanding your options for enjoying deserved leisure time. Visit the casinos when your risk-taking gene kicks in, using the extra cash you pulled in to place your bets. Money looks good for completing home improvement projects.

Pitfalls and Potential Problems

Mercury in Gemini goes retrograde on the 10th, affecting partnership plans and project scheduling. Although plans experience delays, they will materialize. Pluto turned retrograde in Capricorn in your solar second house on April 29. Avoid arguments on the 23rd, when Pluto clashes with Mars.

Rewarding Days

2, 6, 20, 23

Challenging Days

5, 9, 10, 13

Sagittarius | June

Overall Theme

The focus of activity this month in on finances. The Moon shows up in Cancer twice, on the 2nd and again on the 28th, when the New Moon occurs in your solar eighth house of joint income and debt. Inventory resources and pay down debts on the 2nd and 16th. Being debt-free is an admirable goal as long as you don't deplete your cash reserves intended for funding planned expenses.

Relationships

Relatives from local areas as well as long-distance locations visit around the 20th and late in the month, creating opportunities to bond and stage an informal reunion. Company management weighs in on one of your suggestions, nominates you for an award, or asks you to lead a meeting to introduce your proposed recommendations to team members.

Success and Money

Mostly everything you do points to success in terms of investments, salary raises, loan reduction, and increased savings. Your money picture remains solvent, while income shows promising increases as you implement thoughtful financial decisions. Transiting Jupiter in Aries favors reasoned risk-taking in your solar fifth house.

Pitfalls and Potential Problems

Venus opposes your Sun sign between June 24 and 30. Mercury goes direct in Taurus on the 3rd, while Saturn in hard aspect to Mercury moves into retrograde motion on the 4th in Aquarius and disrupts a planned family outing. Neptune turns retrograde in Pisces on the 28th in your solar fourth house, triggering frustrating episodes of confusing communication.

Rewarding Days

2, 7, 16, 20

Challenging Days

1, 11, 14, 28

Sagittarius | July

Overall Theme

You get the go-ahead to take a vacation over the 4th of July holiday to cel-ebrate with loved ones for a week of fun and games. Invite your parents to join you and extend the invitation to available siblings or close friends if logistics work. Capitalize on rare downtime by accepting invitations for family outings.

Relationships

Bonding with relatives at a distance and in local areas drives your con-nections this month. Venus is in Gemini and your solar seventh house of partners for most of the month, stimulating romantic interludes. Invite children to favorite recreation spots and amusement parks. Give guests a chance to explore new venues.

Success and Money

Gratitude envelops your heart as you savor the paid vacation that gives you time off to recharge your energy and reconnect with relatives you haven't seen in a couple of years. Meanwhile your boss has a new, chal-lenging assignment to offer you when you return. A boost of self-confi-dence arrives on the 23rd, when the Moon transits your solar seventh house of partners.

Pitfalls and Potential Problems

The Full Moon in Capricorn and your solar second house opposes Mer-cury in Cancer on the 13th and could exaggerate the seriousness of a financial matter. Don't purchase any household appliances or heirloom jewelry. Jupiter turns retrograde on the 28th in Aries and your solar fifth house of entrepreneurial investments. Steer clear of taking risky financial chances.

Rewarding Days

1, 4, 17, 23

Challenging Days

2, 5, 11, 21

Sagittarius | August

Overall Theme

Even though the month starts off with the Moon in earthy Virgo, not normally a highly compatible sign with yours, the aspects in your performance-oriented solar tenth house of career are promising. The Moon favorably aspects transiting Mars and Uranus in sensuous Taurus and sextiles emotional Venus in Cancer. That combination could bring passionate romance your way.

Relationships

Enjoy the favorable rapport in your workplace and do all you can to meet important deadlines by sharing new technology with team members. Visit an ill coworker in the hospital if safe conditions allow it. You and your spouse spend quality time together in a romantic setting on the 20th and rediscover compatibility on deeper levels.

Success and Money

Your job performance amplifies the respect you earn from peers and the observant management team. The New Moon in Virgo on the 27th draws attention to compensation for accomplishments in the form of bonuses or raises. Solve puzzling challenges on the 10th that delayed the rollout of a new product or service.

Pitfalls and Potential Problems

Like a bolt out of the blue, disruptive Uranus in Taurus goes retrograde on the 24th in your solar sixth house of daily environment, health, and work. Aspects on the 3rd put you in touch with disagreeable friends. The Full Moon in Aquarius on the 11th may put you in the middle of a neighborhood dispute. Listen, but don't take sides, since it's not your conflict.

Rewarding Days

1, 6, 10, 20

Challenging Days

3, 8, 11, 28

Sagittarius | September

Overall Theme
Take a breath and research facts before making a move. Four planets are retrograde this month, and Mercury is about to join them on September 9 in Libra and your solar eleventh house of groups, associations, friendships, and goals. Dig out the hold file and start cleaning up unfinished tasks before initiating new ones.

Relationships
Bankers, lenders, and financial experts offer advice proposing options for building cash reserves. The Full Moon in Pisces on the 10th evokes spontaneity at home and generates an impromptu getaway that pleases family members. Attend a work meeting on the 15th, even if you were thinking of skipping it due to a pressing workload. Unanticipated revelations change perceptions.

Success and Money
Sound advice from financial authorities soaks in at a seminar on the 6th. What you learn helps you cope with changing circumstances that affect a parent's money decisions and ultimately your actions as an estate executor. You score points this month in your career sector when Venus enters Virgo and your solar tenth house of ambition on the 6th.

Pitfalls and Potential Problems
Intense hustling to complete the workload leaves you fatigued and ready to chill out over a long holiday weekend. Save travel plans for later in the month, when you can enjoy a change of pace without feeling guilty. The Full Moon in Pisces on the 10th tests personal relationships.

Rewarding Days
6, 10, 15, 30

Challenging Days
2, 5, 11, 22

Sagittarius | October

Overall Theme

Your popularity rises this month with compatible Venus in Libra in your solar eleventh house. Accept invitations from professional groups and friends. The final Solar Eclipse of 2022 occurs on October 25 in Scorpio and your solar twelfth house, a fertile place to sharpen the focus of creative writing.

Relationships

Meeting new neighbors this month brings unexpected attunement and mutual interests around the 4th. You find a new best friend from academia after a long bout with social distancing. People on assignments at a distance check in with you for advice and may request your assistance on an expanding project that requires travel.

Success and Money

Outings with your significant other the weekend of the 14th exude compatibility and warmth as you explore special interests. While energetic Mars spends most of the month in Gemini and your solar seventh house, social activity increases. Meetings with cooperators and consultants on the 18th establish a firm foundation for future enterprises and commit financial support to fund proposals.

Pitfalls and Potential Problems

Pay attention to sudden shifts when three planets move direct again and the fiery planet Mars goes retrograde in Gemini on October 30. Mercury turns direct in Virgo on the 2nd, Pluto in Capricorn stations to move direct on the 8th, and Saturn goes direct on the 23rd in Aquarius. Let the energy settle before you act on matters you had on hold.

Rewarding Days

3, 4, 14, 18

Challenging Days

1, 7, 19, 25

Sagittarius | November

Overall Theme

A feeling of thankfulness and gratitude is in the air, stimulating your enjoyment for holiday shopping, festive gatherings, and lending a helping hand to those with less. Ambitious plans shortchange sleep as you participate in seasonal attractions that spell enjoyment. On the same day as the New Moon in Sagittarius, Jupiter in Pisces goes direct on the 23rd as you welcome special visitors.

Relationships

You know how to host a party. Individuals travel from distant places for a seat at your holiday table. The feast you offer is fit for those of every generation, pleasing the palates of people who prefer traditional dishes and those with a taste for the exotic. Invite guests to share Thanksgiving memories.

Success and Money

Synchronicity clicks on the 9th when a team meeting highlights major accomplishments and culminates with generous awards for performance. Enjoy the extra money, allocating a portion for holiday gifts and entertainment, along with a contribution to your savings fund. Jupiter in Pisces goes direct on the 23rd and works in your favor, making family fun affordable.

Pitfalls and Potential Problems

The Lunar Eclipse in Taurus falls in your solar sixth house on November 8 and reminds you to get plenty of rest after putting in overtime to finish important work before the holidays arrive. Review the office to-do list to avoid peer conflicts while the Moon and Uranus are conjunct.

Rewarding Days

3, 9, 13, 23

Challenging Days

1, 5, 11, 25

Sagittarius | December

Overall Theme

When mystical Neptune turns direct in Pisces and your solar fourth house on the 3rd, holiday parties start popping up on your calendar, stimulating the holiday spirit. Have a blast with friends, children, and sports aficionados whose company lightens your heart. Contribute to food banks and soup kitchens. Buy gifts for orphaned children so they celebrate the season with a cherished toy.

Relationships

Teaching your children life lessons inspires you to share insights about those less fortunate. You lead by example, showing them the way by supplying meals, buying groceries, or picking up medical supplies for those in need. Gather loved ones together to welcome the new year.

Success and Money

Embrace the new solar year with optimism driven by your ruling planet, Jupiter, who vacates your solar fourth house on the 20th, reminding you of how prosperity transformed your home all year. Electronic gifts from your wish list bring gratitude when they show up under the tree on Christmas.

Pitfalls and Potential Problems

Household arguments are center stage on the 1st, when the Pisces Moon turns maudlin. The Full Moon in Gemini occurs on December 7th conjunct retrograde Mars in your solar seventh house, a good day to avoid the company of angry people or drinkers. Don't sign purchase contracts on the 29th, when Mercury goes retrograde in your solar second house.

Rewarding Days

3, 24, 25, 28

Challenging Days

1, 10, 17, 23

Sagittarius Action Table

These dates reflect the best—but not the only—times for success and ease in these activities, according to your Sun sign.

	JAN	FEB	MAR	APR	MAY	JUN	JUL	AUG	SEP	OCT	NOV	DEC
Move				1						18		
Romance	8			6	6			20			13	
Seek counseling/ coaching	3					7	23		15			28
Ask for a raise						8	1	1		3		
Vacation			3		2		1					3
Get a loan		26	12						6		3	

Capricorn

The Goat
December 21 to January 19

♑

Element: Earth

Quality: Cardinal

Polarity: Yin/feminine

Planetary Ruler: Saturn

Meditation: I know the strength of my soul

Gemstone: Garnet

Power Stones: Peridot, onyx diamond, quartz, black obsidian

Key Phrase: I use

Glyph: Head of goat

Anatomy: Skeleton, knees, skin

Colors: Black, forest green

Animals: Goats, thick-shelled animals

Myths/Legends: Chronos, Vesta, Pan

House: Tenth

Opposite Sign: Cancer

Flower: Carnation

Keyword: Ambitious

The Capricorn Personality

Strengths, Talents, and the Creative Spark

Mastery of taking responsibility to an impeccable level is your claim to fame. If you're handed a task, you put a plan in place and make sure that every little detail is thought out and executed objectively. Your symbol is the Mountain Goat, the third earth sign and the fourth cardinal sign of the zodiac and the natural occupant of the tenth house of career, status in life, and ambition. You want your capabilities tapped and your skills used at the highest level possible to fulfill your soul's purpose. Bosses count on your pragmatic approach to problem-solving and reward your performance for saving the day, noticing the conscientious way you influence the outcome of challenging situations. Your stellar reputation comes from consistently delivering a polished and complete product, showing your quiet but firm leadership style, and tactfully delegating tasks to involve staff in the success of the mission.

Often considered a late bloomer, you spend your early years in the work world exploring options and studying the fine points of career paths that interest you. Once you figure it out, you display a highly competitive side and put what you know into landing an opportunity that allows you to climb the ladder of success and build expertise in your chosen field. Before long, recruiters are after you to apply for plum positions and you wind up holding all of the cards. The creative side of you shows up in your dry humor that you subtly deliver when tension builds and deadlines loom. Colleagues who don't know you well are pleasantly surprised to see this side of you and enjoy your lightness, since you tend to be all business most of the time.

Intimacy and Personal Relationships

When you can pull yourself away from work responsibilities, you discover that you know a lot of people who appreciate your personality, good manners, and wit. It's not unusual for a best friend to become either your business or your romantic partner. Your sphere of influence includes a wide circle of acquaintances who are socially and financially successful and prove beneficial to your career. You've been known to succumb to the charms of conservative, level-headed dating partners, choosing love connections that lack spark and hanging on to a steady, reliable person instead of moving on to find a partner who matches your passion. You have a deeply intense romantic side that comes alive when you meet the right partner.

Capricorns often make beautiful music with Cancers, your opposite sign, who share your need for emotional and financial security and want a family, home, and beautiful surroundings to complete the relationship picture. Water signs Scorpio and Pisces along with earth signs Taurus and Virgo may light up your life as well, sharing your love for people coming and going at home base at a fast pace. Although you and your ideal partner enjoy hosting many family activities, remember to find a balance instead of rushing through commitments and putting way too much time into your career. Partners need support. Parenting is a cherished commodity and you are very nurturing toward your offspring, encouraging them to cultivate creative interests. As long as you don't lay too many rules on your children, you are able to enjoy a stable home environment.

Values and Resources

Capricorns respect authority, father figures, bosses, and government. You believe that recognition of your achievements is your path to success in the world and are fiercely competitive. You know all the executives in the organization, and they get along well with you, showing appreciation for your performance excellence and outstanding work habits. Any accolades that come your way reflect the professionalism you bring to the work environment and the critical attention you give to meeting deadlines. Ageism in the work world is a turnoff. You value the wisdom of experience and seldom judge a person as inept based on accumulated years, preferring to respect life and professional knowledge as sources of important information. You'll seek out someone with the institutional memory and history of an organization and pick their brain either as a direct hire or as a consultant for your team. As an astute judge of character, you find people who share your values and become lifelong friends, yet you tend to compartmentalize them. These friends don't necessarily know one another, because they fulfill different roles in your life. You hold them in high esteem and call on them to support you through challenging times, and you have their back when they need it.

Blind Spots and Blockages

Critics, including your partners and workmates, say you don't know when to take a break from the daily grind and always seem to have your focus on tasks. Although they acknowledge your high performance standards, they wish you would chill and make some time to discuss projects and advocate options for accomplishing the work in a less demanding manner. Your show of impatience rubs others the wrong way, especially when they work at a slower pace than you do or you judge their style as faulty and sometimes criticize them in front of peers. You don't handle delays well and sometimes carry too much guilt if deadlines have to be adjusted, which can make you peevish and drives people in your circle away. When you feel that what you are contributing to life is meaningless, you show signs of depression and shut down, instead of seeking professional help in sorting through the areas that have you stumped. Take a look at where you could share the workload differently to facilitate a better outcome.

Goals and Success

One of your fondest desires is to improve yourself both mentally and physically in your quest to accomplish your dreams. It's not unusual for you to say you've been working all your life. Many of you sought employment before you hit your teens, holding jobs while going to school and loving every moment of earning spending money. The more responsibility you were given, the greater was your effort to excel. You are seldom without a goal to challenge your active mind because you equate success with piling up achievements, loading your resume with evidence of your hard work, demonstrating leadership in your field, and displaying outstanding performance. Those in charge cite your expertise and call you dependable and reliable and the go-to person for running the show and meeting deadlines. Being held in high esteem is nirvana to you and motivates you to show continuous growth in your work.

Capricorn Keywords for 2022
Goals, groundwork, growth

The Year Ahead for Capricorn

The shake-ups that occurred in your solar tenth house of career, ambition, and family status during 2021 have left you with an urgent desire to facilitate healing on inner and outer levels. The last few years may have brought relationship changes due to illnesses, marriages, breakups, employment or lack of it, death, and coping with the COVID-19 pandemic. Jupiter's entry into Pisces and your solar third house could step up communication, educational pursuits, and interaction with the community as social-distancing restrictions ease up and activity with others increases. In late May, Jupiter begins a rapid journey through Aries and interacts with members of your family and domestic affairs in your solar fourth house. Saturn in Aquarius keeps a close eye on your checkbook and all things financial in your solar second house, and brings loan officers, fiscal managers, and mortgage brokers into your circle. The presence of retrograde Uranus in Taurus in your solar fifth house of adventure, romance, and children shakes up relationships, could surprise you with an unexpected trip, and opens your eyes to the risks of speculative ventures, especially after the planet of chaos goes direct on January 18.

Neptune's sixth sense and psychic vibes leave your mind in discovery mode when the planet of deep impressions looks for hidden meanings in your solar third house, keeping company with Jupiter in Pisces until December 21. You are aware that Pluto in Capricorn is still in your solar first house of assertiveness and self-image, reminding you to discard any remaining baggage that cramps your style as you discover what you no longer need in life. On January 14, Mercury makes its first retrograde station of the year in Aquarius in your solar second house. Keep a watchful eye on cash flow and stick with your budget.

Jupiter

For most of 2022, except for a sign-change and a retrograde period, Jupiter occupies Pisces and your solar third house, until it moves into Aries on December 20 for a nearly yearlong transit in your solar fourth house. A benefit to Capricorns is improved communication with neighbors, cousins, and siblings who may contact you more often than usual, wanting to schedule events, reunions, and visits. Jupiter's presence in the solar third house means that you become more active in your community, enroll in classes, or increase the frequency of local travel. Jupiter moves rapidly through Pisces until May 10, when it launches a long teaser period in Aries until the wee hours of October 28, when it falls back into Pisces. Work on goals related to communication while Jupiter is in Pisces and focus on family and household matters while Jupiter occupies Aries. Expect a few clashes with family while Jupiter in Aries is in your solar fourth house. Use your best negotiating skills to facilitate harmony. Jupiter in Pisces is compatible with your sign and paves the way for successful communication and purchase of electronic equipment or vehicles. On July 28, Jupiter turns retrograde in Aries and your solar fourth house until it goes direct on November 23. Those of you born between December 22 and 30 experience the most action from Jupiter while it is in Aries, making you uncomfortable with the status quo in your home and whetting your appetite for initiating new rules, living conditions, and possibly redecorating projects. Develop the changes you desire, study the options, and execute your plan in 2023.

Saturn

On December 17, 2020, Saturn in Aquarius began to occupy your solar second house of earned income, assets, salary, compensation for goods and services you provide, commissions, self-development, financial resources, and people affiliated with banks, lending institutions, and investment firms. As a stickler for stable assets, Saturn has been hinting over the last few years for you to put more into savings and be on the lookout for a new environment that showcases your talents and increases earnings. Even though Saturn transiting the second house levies constraints on you, Jupiter in Pisces this year will mitigate some of the pain by opening unexpected doors of opportunity to present career options or a new job via favorite networks. Look at conditions that have limited your employment choices, including social-distancing mandates. Seek out emerging sources that open up. Those of you born between January 1 and 16 are most affected by this Saturn transit in 2022. Enjoy collaborative alliances and use headhunters or experts in your field if you feel stuck. Align your goals to experience the most success. Saturn's retrograde period occurs this year from June 4 to October 23. Examine contracts or agreements for your services to avoid disappointments in financial compensation. Check for opt-out clauses if what you agreed to is not reflected in the proposal.

Uranus

You'll have little downtime with transiting Uranus in Taurus in residence this year in your solar fifth house of children, lovers, romance, recreation, social life, speculation, sports, travel, and vacation. This passage through Taurus has brought new connections since May 2018. You hoped to strengthen bonds when Uranus laid the groundwork for increased responsibilities and responsiveness, but instead you met challenges related to relationships. The fifth house represents teaching moments and options for tapping into your creative side, which may have been stretched thin during the intensity of the COVID-19 crisis while spatial restrictions limited physical interaction with special people in your life. You likely have experienced unpredictable and erratic relationships with lovers, traveling companions, children, and investors over the past few years. If you are unmarried, you may have felt exhausted by the merry-go-round of relationships that went nowhere. That's Uranus at work, and the tumultuous planet can be a real heartbreaker. Fortunately, Jupiter in Pisces travels compatibly with Uranus this year and facilitates smoother interactions that are profitable, enjoyable, and fun. Uranus in Taurus is compatible with your Capricorn Sun. Unpredictable Uranus moves into retrograde motion on August 24 and will go direct on January 22, 2023. Expect new parameters around relationships, keep your cool in romantic trysts, be understanding of children, and avoid making rash decisions. Look at pending plans and assess whether global conditions are safe for keeping commitments. The planet of chaos has the greatest impact this year on Capricorns born between December 31 and January 9, pushing you to balance work with leisure activity that accommodates needed downtime. Find meaningful outlets for your emotional expression and creative ideas.

Neptune

Neptune, the planet of illusion, suggests that not everything is what it appears to be. No exceptions to that rule appear in 2022, when the slow-moving watery planet advances a few more degrees through Pisces and your solar third house of communication, education, your mind and how it works, your local community, neighbors, siblings, cousins, electronics, transportation, and vehicles. With interference from the coronavirus pandemic starting in 2020, you fell into dream mode often, which disrupted your plans to focus on your career and heal personal relationships. When you periodically came out of the fog, you wrote beautiful material, caught up on all your paperwork, checked in with neighbors, and even updated your resume. Now sort through the exchange of mixed messages from you to neighborhood officials, hiring authorities, and editors and lay the groundwork to volunteer, take the offered job, or write for a living instead of dabbling randomly in subjects that interest you. Land contracts, earn a steady paycheck, and use the assets you have to perform meaningful work. Goals come alive as you earn your reputation as a communicator. Although circumstances may have been beyond your control in recent years, you now have a chance to shine. You're probably proficient at telework by now and relish controlling your schedule. Consider a return to classes, learning new skills to advance career prospects, and healing relationships with relatives. Teach classes for extra income. Neptune has occupied your solar third house since April 2011, encouraging spiritual growth. Those of you born between January 9 and 16 will benefit most from Neptune's action during 2022.

Pluto

Your solar first house remains the site of transiting Pluto in Capricorn, in residence since January 2008. The planet of transformation and rebirth has been firmly planted in your action house, reminding you to push hard to rid yourself of any lingering issues, especially related to self-image, that create emotional angst. Identify the source of doubts and how fear of them is holding you back from enjoying inner freedom. You have keen insight into people and their motives and possess excellent analytical skills. Why not use them for personal growth? The solar first house is a personal hot spot that relates to adaptability, assertiveness, innovation, your physical body, and personality. You may have dealt with personal setbacks, loss of loved ones, or health issues recently. Innate resilience gives you courage to combat the unknown, so face the blocks, eliminate difficult situations, and expect better health and insight. After fourteen years of dealing with these Plutonian karma cleaners, you know what generates stress. Find useful solutions for eliminating them to manifest your goals. What are you going for this year—hanging on or healing? Those of you born between January 15 and 19 see the most activity for healing and enjoying healthy results from this Pluto transit, which challenges you to acknowledge the truth.

How Will This Year's Eclipses Affect You?

In 2022, the signs Taurus and Scorpio dominate the eclipse cycles of the year. A total of four eclipses occur: two solar (New Moon) and two lunar (Full Moon), which bring intense periods that begin to manifest about two months before they actually occur. All four eclipses take place in two of your solar chart's succedent houses, the fifth and the eleventh, putting the spotlight on activities associated with your social and romantic life, children, sports, and speculation, as well as friends, groups, and goals. Eclipses manifest in cycles involving all twelve signs of the zodiac, usually occurring in pairs about two weeks apart. Don't fear eclipses—think of them as opportunities that allow you to face old, outworn patterns and release them. Eclipses trigger unexpected revelations, surprises, and windfalls. The closer an eclipse is to a planet in your chart, the greater the importance it plays in your life. Those of you born with a planet at the same degree as an eclipse may see a high level of activity in the house where the eclipse occurs.

The first Solar Eclipse of 2022 occurs on April 30 in Taurus and your solar fifth house of children and their interests, romance, amusements, sports, and speculative ventures. If you have planets located in this house, expect revelations regarding problem areas with people connected to this house to come to light. If connections are positive, you'll benefit from strengthening bonds and fulfilling goals. Should you be experiencing challenges, any rough spots will hit hard and call for discussion and workable solutions. If you work too much, it spells trouble for your health, especially due to a lack of sleep. Relax more and enjoy life. Transiting Uranus in Taurus is also present to keep you alert to chaotic conditions.

Two weeks later, the first Lunar Eclipse of the year occurs on May 16 in Scorpio and your solar eleventh house of goals, plans, wishes, fondest dreams, associations, friendships, groups and organizations, humanitarian interests, and your employer's resources. The responsibility is on you to keep your goals on track, balance work with activities that involve memberships that serve your personal philosophy, and lead initiatives that work for the greater good.

On October 25, the second Solar Eclipse of 2022 takes place on October 25 in Scorpio and your solar eleventh house of friends, groups, and goals. Assess conditions in memberships with professional organizations and determine whether you want to continue or find a more compatible affiliation to show your support for local and global initiatives.

The year's final eclipse is a Lunar Eclipse on November 8 in Taurus and your solar fifth house of entertainment, vacations, children, coaching, teaching, romance, social life, and risk-taking. When this eclipse hits after months of working on what you learned about others last April regarding problem areas, you will know whether the action you took netted the desired results. Uranus in Taurus is hanging out in this house close to the eclipse degree, so be sure to assess your findings. You could be headed for an engagement or marriage, if single, or walking away from a challenging romance.

Capricorn | January

Overall Theme
You'll have a field day with personal connections this month and bask in the good vibes that reunions with cherished people generate. The New Moon in Capricorn on the 2nd falls in your solar first house and brings unexpected windfalls and inspiring communications. Travel is a good option after mid-January.

Relationships
Jupiter in Pisces joins the Moon on the 7th, encouraging activity with siblings and neighbors. Plan a weekend get-together with lively conversations and plenty of relaxation time. Bond with relatives at a distance around the 21st. If you plan early enough before Mercury goes retrograde on the 14th, you can enjoy a cherished vacation.

Success and Money
Interactions with friends and business associates get the green light on the 7th and 26th. Schedule lunches to renew bonds and discuss formal agreements, but don't sign them on either the 14th, when Mercury stations to move retrograde, or the 18th, when Uranus goes direct. Shop for sale items early in the month when bargains are plentiful.

Pitfalls and Potential Problems
Money could be the driver of an argument on the 4th, yet you quickly clarify a misunderstanding about an intended purchase. Children, showing a stubborn streak, are the source of tension on the 11th. Use logic to settle differences. The Full Moon in Cancer on the 17th affects partnership moods and puts a damper on romance. Revise your schedule and work on details for future outings.

Rewarding Days
2, 7, 21, 26

Challenging Days
4, 11, 14, 17

Capricorn | February

Overall Theme

You enjoy traditional celebrations and have opportunities to whoop it up twice this month. First, plan an outing on the New Moon in Aquarius on February 1, when the Lunar Year of the Water Tiger gets underway. Then coordinate a romantic event for Valentine's Day, while Capricorn energy dominates the personal planets with a boost from the Moon in passionate Leo.

Relationships

Interact with love interests for mutual enjoyment of entertainment and sports. Treat your children or other young relatives to a special event or outing around the 7th. Take a short trip out of your local area from the 16th to the 19th to bond with your significant other and get away from pressing work demands.

Success and Money

Your best money days occur on the 1st through the 7th. Luckily, Mercury goes direct on the 3rd, stabilizing the delay in transactions that has affected business since mid-January. Accept a leadership role that lands in your lap around the 26th. Listen to advice from a relative at a distance who makes a valuable suggestion around the 18th.

Pitfalls and Potential Problems

Communication at home base is confusing on the 6th and needs focused follow-up after the 7th. Workplace dynamics are off base on the 10th, leaving you frustrated over unfinished business. The Leo Full Moon on the 16th is intense and perfect for intimate encounters but drains you of mental energy and cautions you to slow down.

Rewarding Days

1, 7, 18, 26

Challenging Days

6, 10, 16, 21

Capricorn | March

Overall Theme

The quality of communication drives the monthly agenda. The New Moon in Pisces and your solar third house on the 2nd could bring you a successful networking day, when everyone you want to contact is available, appointments are set, and solutions to problems fall easily into place. Matters concerning education dominate your interests at home base and in your workplace.

Relationships

Work colleagues feature strongly in successful ventures and milestone achievements. Professional associates and members of important groups depend on you to represent their interests and provide insight into emerging initiatives. A follow-up test puts an end to a worrisome medical problem. Celebrate success.

Success and Money

Positive aspects from Jupiter and Pluto put you in line for an increase in income. Make plans to save part of the income for planned household projects and treat yourself to an item that is on your wish list. The right words spoken in an interview make you a winning candidate for a desirable job. Cherish intuition.

Pitfalls and Potential Problems

You'll wish you had stayed home on the night of the 6th if you socialize and find the dating scene a dud. Money discussions on the 14th lead to arguments and no decision. Funding for a project fizzles on the 21st, when professional connections disagree with the budget proposal during a working lunch. Revise the numbers and try again on the 26th.

Rewarding Days

2, 8, 22, 26

Challenging Days

6, 14, 21, 24

Capricorn | April

Overall Theme

Your solar fourth house is the site of a new beginning when the Aries New Moon arrives on the 1st, calling for a close assessment of planned undertakings at home base. You and your partner collaborate on projects to get your home in tip-top shape, from sculpting garden landscape to planting seedlings for spring and summer veggies to identifying household repairs.

Relationships

Family plays a prominent role early in the month, with plenty of bonding. Enjoy downtime with your partner on the weekend of the 8th with a relaxing change of pace. Include dancing to add spontaneity. A fun gathering involves your neighbors on the 27th, a day that also brings unexpected phone calls from siblings.

Success and Money

Travel bargains land you a few short getaways for spring and early summer. Good thing you had them on your wish list. The first Solar Eclipse of 2022 occurs on the 30th in Taurus and your solar fifth house of children, romance, and social affairs. Use comp tickets to schedule zoo trips and use restaurant gift cards for meals.

Pitfalls and Potential Problems

Unpleasant encounters mar plans with children or dates on the 5th. You can't get around the mixed messages and bad attitude over plans and cancel outings. Pluto goes retrograde on the 29th, followed by the Solar Eclipse on the 30th, which could generate misunderstandings over anticipated purchases. Discuss pros and cons first.

Rewarding Days

1 8, 22, 27

Challenging Days

4, 10, 14, 24

Capricorn | May

Overall Theme

A vacation bargain you snagged last month may be perfect for enjoying downtime the first four days of this month. The compatible mix of planets in Pisces and Taurus facilitates smooth communication, allowing rapport and laughter to shine. Aries steals the show when Venus moves into your solar fourth house on the 2nd, followed by Jupiter on the 10th and Mars on the 24th, adding a romantic tone to home base.

Relationships

Engagements, weddings, and recognition for the mothers in your family are strongly featured this month. Cherish traditions you shared with your mom on May 8 if she has passed on. Close out the week on the 6th by enjoying a romantic dinner with your partner, a perfect day to also make gift purchases for upcoming events.

Success and Money

Children achieve academic and sports excellence, elevating their self-esteem and adding value to the reputation of the school and teams. If you are in a teaching or coaching position, you take pride in your students' contributions and build confidence in their outlook. A promotion or raise looks promising around the 20th, after your boss acknowledges your fine performance.

Pitfalls and Potential Problems

Mercury goes retrograde in Gemini on the 10th, leaving you searching for the right words in your work environment. Just breathe. The Lunar Eclipse on the 16th occurs in Scorpio and your solar eleventh house, creating tense moments with competitive associates in a monthly meeting.

Rewarding Days

2, 6, 20, 24

Challenging Days

5, 8, 16, 31

Capricorn | June

Overall Theme

The planets are doing their thing this month adjusting energy. Mercury goes direct in Taurus and your solar fifth house on the 3rd, throwing attention on your social life, investments, and entertainment. Complete projects that may have been on hold since Mercury went retrograde last month. Saturn turns retrograde in Aquarius on the 4th, and Neptune in Pisces follows suit on the 28th.

Relationships

Venus in Taurus for most of the month favors personal relationships with family members and spouses and promises lively communication. Treat them to a special outing. Engage in discussions about your children's education and upcoming summer classes or camp. Run the numbers with your spouse to plan expenses and adjust your budget the night before the Full Moon in Sagittarius on June 14.

Success and Money

A solid windfall gives you something to smile about on the 17th and guarantees funding for a landscaping project. You get your money's worth at a furnishings sale. A nice vibe from Jupiter supports your mental health, boosts optimism, and generates enthusiasm for upcoming celebrations.

Pitfalls and Potential Problems

Tiptoe around anyone in a snit at home base when Mars in Aries clashes with the Moon on the 15th, or tension will quickly escalate. Arguments over legal matters surface on the 5th, especially over a disagreement related to settlement terms. When you criticize a younger person on the 4th, your message, especially your delivery style, may be too harsh.

Rewarding Days

3, 13, 17, 21

Challenging Days

5, 9, 14, 28

Capricorn | July

Overall Theme

Optimistic Jupiter turns retrograde on July 28 in Aries and your solar fourth house. Life has been so much more stable this year since the planet of expansion gave your goals an enthusiastic boost. Your best time to take a vacation is between the 4th and the 17th. Since you met with success in accomplishing plans, modify your goals to accommodate new circumstances.

Relationships

Long-distance travel to see relatives or take a bucket-list trip is possible on the 18th, as long as no travel or health restrictions limit options. July is a good month to strengthen family ties and include close relatives in exciting adventures. If you are home over the 4th of July, host a cookout.

Success and Money

The vacation package you negotiated takes you out of the country to a distant location where you meet up with seldom-seen relatives. Wise investments have paid dividends, increasing your savings thanks to astute money management. You were so ready to take to the skies and seek enjoyable amusements again after the long COVID-19 restrictions.

Pitfalls and Potential Problems

Corrections have to be made for cost overruns on a project and need solid discussion before spending more money on the purchase of additional materials. Confusion on the Full Moon in Capricorn on July 13 shows that principals are not on the same page and delays work production. If teammates seem confused over new assignments on the 25th, clarify roles.

Rewarding Days

4, 17, 23, 28

Challenging Days

2, 5, 13, 25

Capricorn | August

Overall Theme

Whether you've been shopping for furniture or a new vehicle, the best time to do so is around the 14th, when your solar third house has all the right vibes for negotiating contracts. Take advantage of the buying power in your healthy checkbook, especially on the 1st, 2nd, and 6th, and look for cash discounts. Work out the best terms if you plan to finance an automobile.

Relationships

Good friends get in touch with you to plan high school reunions or other celebratory events. Contact professional networks for job leads on the 6th. Surprise your significant other with a weekend treat or a short getaway around the 23rd. Treasure loving moments.

Success and Money

A recent check of credit scores nets you the best terms if you are shopping for a home or other luxury item. Start research early using all reliable sources. When you are ready to make a move, check loan term comparisons. Avoid impulsive decisions. Evaluate findings with your partner.

Pitfalls and Potential Problems

Authority figures are dealing with unpleasant financial news on the 3rd, so avoid bombarding them with details about work conflicts. Pass on a financial deal presented on the 11th that is not at all how it was represented. Control tension at home base on the 16th using humor and a lighthearted touch. Resolve differences before Uranus goes retrograde in Taurus on the 24th.

Rewarding Days

1, 6, 14, 23

Challenging Days

3, 11, 16, 27

Capricorn | September

Overall Theme

Make inroads on a work assignment early in the month to clear space for a short vacation when Venus moves into Virgo on September 5. The Pisces Full Moon on the 10th occurs right after Mercury in Libra goes retrograde on the 9th, alerting you to expect demands on your time when you return from your getaway. Work demands increase by the 14th, but you anticipate the onslaught and organize well.

Relationships

The first few days of the month, members of a professional group put pressure on you. By the 29th, you reap praise from this group for your savvy solution to a highly visible issue. Collaboration pays off and stimulates an interest in working on your team. Your significant other memorably strengthens your love bond around the 20th.

Success and Money

Partnership ventures shine this month, in both your personal and business worlds. You and your partner use unexpected resources to pay off a loan used for urgent household repairs. Work incentives lift your spirits and generate gratitude for stability in employment and trust in your talents.

Pitfalls and Potential Problems

Avoid signing important documents on the 9th, when lunar aspects to Venus and Mercury clash. The 16th brings mixed signals, possibly several meetings, and a heavy round of communication all day. Resolve differences by the 20th. Check weather conditions and table a weekend trip on the 24th.

Rewarding Days

5, 7, 20, 29

Challenging Days

2, 9, 16, 24

Capricorn | October

Overall Theme
A fully loaded month for planetary shifts occurs, starting with Mercury going direct on the 2nd. The focus for you is on your career, management team input, and accomplishment of work goals. Mars in Gemini and your solar sixth house sheds light on team productivity and the distribution of work to meet timelines. You could be writing key documents or reports to capture progress.

Relationships
Schedule lunch dates with business contacts or financial advisors on the 4th or 18th. Single Capricorns meet love prospects through these connections. The Solar Eclipse in Scorpio and your eleventh house conjunct Venus on the 25th could bring a new love interest into the picture or strengthen bonds with an existing partner.

Success and Money
Money vibes are excellent this month and shed light on lucrative investments, bonuses, and promotion potential. Put an unanticipated performance award into savings to cover upcoming holiday expenses. Compete for new job opportunities that mesh with your skill set.

Pitfalls and Potential Problems
Planetary stations occur all month. Mercury goes direct in Virgo on the 2nd, followed by Pluto in Capricorn on the 8th. Saturn in Aquarius follows on the 23rd, freeing you from spending restrictions and giving income a boost. Mars turns retrograde in Gemini on the 30th in your solar sixth house and could shift the flow of work, alter deadlines, or send you to the doctor for a health exam.

Rewarding Days
4, 14, 18, 20

Challenging Days
2, 7, 12, 25

Capricorn | November

Overall Theme

The final Lunar Eclipse of 2022 occurs on November 8 in Taurus and your solar fifth house of children, entertainment, romance, and vacations, tempting you to surprise those on your gift list with expensive holiday travel. Stay within spending limits and participate in local celebrations. Decorate elegantly.

Relationships

The Sagittarius New Moon on the 23rd occurs in your solar twelfth house, suggesting you prefer to entertain family and friends at home for Thanksgiving. You'll be issuing invitations around the 3rd. Your lovely home and festive food captivate guests. Include absent relatives via social media technology.

Success and Money

Quality communication makes it easy to convey important personal and work-related information this month, especially between the 3rd and the 13th. Shopping for gifts and running errands nets successful results on the 28th. Spend money on entertainment and food, with special offers resulting in outstanding purchasing power and value.

Pitfalls and Potential Problems

Be sure to monitor spending on the 1st and the 8th, when advertised sales tempt you to open your wallet and spend for gifts. Avoid overpaying for electronics and games. Colleagues could be antsy about finishing up work to get away for the holiday on the 21st. Jupiter goes direct on the 23rd, possibly affecting the arrival time for traveling guests.

Rewarding Days

3, 13, 23, 28

Challenging Days

1, 8, 11, 21

Capricorn | December

Overall Theme

Neptune in Pisces goes direct on the 3rd, paving the way for implementing plans that have cast doubt on feasibility since June. Keep a low profile while you work out dilemmas behind the scenes aided by a conjunction of Mercury and Venus in Sagittarius. Show concern for those less fortunate on the 3rd through the 7th by donating to a fundraiser or toy drive.

Relationships

Check in with family members around the 3rd to get their feedback on desired holiday activities and entertainment. Then grant their wishes on the 24th to the 28th, covering all the bases to spread holiday spirit equitably. Issue invitations to siblings, cousins, and neighbors around the 28th.

Success and Money

Details of upcoming contracts surface throughout the month, putting a smile on your face thanks to the careful analysis you did to produce a winning proposal. Local travel is most successful after the 25th, and expenses for entertainment venues have been covered through your careful budgeting. Enjoy a festive gathering with relatives on the 25th.

Pitfalls and Potential Problems

On the 1st, a child could bring home a report card with poor grades or suffer some other type of educational setback. The Full Moon in Gemini on the 7th puts a temporary damper on enthusiasm in the work environment when a major component of a project has to be reworked. Wait until early next year to schedule nonthreatening doctor visits.

Rewarding Days

3, 24, 25, 28

Challenging Days

1, 7, 13, 21

Capricorn Action Table

These dates reflect the best—but not the only—times for success and ease in these activities, according to your Sun sign.

	JAN	FEB	MAR	APR	MAY	JUN	JUL	AUG	SEP	OCT	NOV	DEC
Move			2				4				3	
Romance		7		8		3		23		20		24
Seek counseling/ coaching	26				2			6	29			
Ask for a raise			8				23			18		
Vacation	21			27		17						28
Get a loan		1			20				7		28	

Aquarius

The Water Bearer
January 19 to February 18

Element: Air

Quality: Fixed

Polarity: Yang/masculine

Planetary Ruler: Uranus

Meditation: I am a wellspring of creativity

Gemstone: Amethyst

Power Stones: Aquamarine, black pearl, chrysocolla

Key Phrase: I know

Glyph: Currents of energy

Anatomy: Ankles, circulatory system

Colors: Iridescent blues, violet

Animals: Exotic birds

Myths/Legends: Ninhursag, John the Baptist, Deucalion

House: Eleventh

Opposite Sign: Leo

Flower: Orchid

Keyword: Unconventional

The Aquarius Personality

Strengths, Talents, and the Creative Spark

You have the most eclectic mix of traits of any sign, showing your conventional and friendly side when it suits you and alternatively revealing your eccentric, innovative, and progressive mien. Sometimes you leave people scratching their heads because they don't know who you are. The truth is you have a very serious inner depth, and if observers would only watch you walk away after an encounter, they would note by the energy in your walk that you're all business. What a big job you've undertaken for the universe as the fixed air sign of the zodiac and keeper of the eleventh house of humanitarian endeavors, optimism, and group synergy. Uranus, the planet of the unexpected, is your ruler. Sometimes strictly for shock value, you act in accordance with the affiliated behavior of this planet by demonstrating your radical, rebellious, and outspoken side. You'll be the icebreaker, the prankster, and the one who brings up controversy for the sheer enjoyment of challenging the stodgy status quo. If you have natal planets in the eleventh house, they describe the range of interests, creative solutions, and adaptability as well as input you extract from others and use to facilitate emerging organizational changes.

Living up to the charge of your symbol, the Water Bearer, you're a master at keeping up with current events, which makes you a fascinating date, employee, and friend. With your rapid-fire mind and analytical skills, you excel in the role of change agent. Instigator Uranus answers the call to shake things up when momentum flounders and progress fizzles. That's when your lightning-quick insight kicks in by making you aware of where the company needs to be to emerge as a world leader, creator of global initiatives, and model for new trends for doing business. You'll jump at the chance to reframe current policies and procedures, giving them a fresh new look and inspiring productivity.

Intimacy and Personal Relationships

Communication is central to having a meaningful relationship in your world. You often carry on long-distance relationships and fall in love with the mind of your object of affection first. Your charismatic personality draws inspiring, intelligent partners into your life. It takes a very special type of person to keep you interested for the long haul. The person who wins your heart is competing with your strong sense of independence, which slows your path to the altar until you determine you're ready for a committed union and a family, a condition that appeals to your more traditional side. Partnership choices are many: you enjoy qualities of air signs Gemini and Libra, who share your love of communication and talking things out. Leo, your opposite sign, can be alluring with strong physical chemistry. The other fire signs, Aries and Sagittarius, match your love of travel and adventure. Fixed signs Taurus and Scorpio may clash with your freedom, especially when jealousy is a factor. If you're a parent, you strongly encourage children to develop and use their talents and strengths. Diverse acquaintances are your jam, even though you appreciate the small number of close friendships you have and connect with them frequently.

Values and Resources

Since you prefer to keep most friendships on an impersonal level, you seldom divulge much about your private life, letting others wonder what makes you tick. Information comes to you easily from diverse sources and you willingly share what you learn. With a preference for permanent employment, you will stay in the same company for years if conditions are right. If not, you set goals to attain positions in various organizations and locations in your country and abroad. Predictable positions bore you, so you may go after the most unique ones that offer travel, learning opportunities, and challenges. You are committed to protecting your organization's assets and take pride in assessing the financial strength and resources of the firm, targeting incremental outlays of cash for different phases of work. With an interest in finding the best people for the job, you keep your eye on the strength of human capital and actively recruit or make recommendations for hires. Aquarians often rent housing instead of buying to avoid the hassle of selling a property every few years. Your taste in a home stands out for its design or style, and you'll balk if your agent shows you a fixer-upper or poorly maintained property when you're house hunting.

Blind Spots and Blockages

Although problem-solving, mastery of high-tech electronic systems, and innovation are your strengths, you'll have to be flexible and open to change as conditions evolve. Release what is no longer working, whether it is an application in need of refinement or a relationship that has run its course. Never accept a permanent position in a job you don't like or with bosses whose management styles clash with your values, especially if micromanagement is an issue. You've been known to do this during the course of your career and wind up being rebellious, angry, and depressed, and these reactions upset conditions in your personal life, leaving you with many regrets. Others may not realize that when you go through binges of constant complaining, you are really blowing off steam and venting over unresolved problems that you haven't addressed. Critics say that in meetings you get up on your soapbox to drive home a point and forget to step down. Learn to check the fidgety body language of your audience, give others the floor, and wrap up.

Goals and Success

As one of the most analytical signs of the zodiac, you achieve success through your astute application of innovative problem-solving skills that affect outcomes for much needed social conditions. Your insight may have been put to the test with the recent disruption from the life-changing coronavirus pandemic that is affecting the way we do business, educate others, and live our daily lives. With the planetary lineup you'll be subject to in 2022, you could be looking for a new perspective to ignite the depth of passion for your work. Tap your network for links to emerging initiatives. Inventory your qualifications to see your career and job objectively, and decide what path creates the best options for blazing a trail that takes your support for humanitarian causes, community enterprises, and future growth for the planet to new heights.

Aquarius Keywords for 2022
Incentives, independence, intelligence

The Year Ahead for Aquarius

In 2022, with transiting Saturn in Aquarius in your solar first house, you just might be the center of attention in your circle, hoping that the unpredictable conditions imposed by the coronavirus pandemic are a welcome part of your past. As one who likes the freedom to come and go on our fast-moving planet, you're hoping the burdens of the COVID-19 slowdowns are gone. You begin the year with full knowledge of coping mechanisms that aid you in making decisions and managing your workload, whether you work from home or from the physical location of your company. Your solar first house of activity, innovation, passion, and self-image has a yearlong rendezvous with Saturn in Aquarius moving through it. In competition for attention, another fixed-sign planet, Uranus, begins the year in retrograde motion in Taurus and your solar fourth house of family, home, and foundation, stirring the pot to meddle with serenity and get family members to talk about their feelings. Your Leo-ruled solar seventh house of partnerships may add to the tension, especially if you have any Leo planets in this house or people in your life who have opinions about controlling household dynamics. In your Scorpio-ruled solar tenth house of career, authority, and ambition, you may be given a vital role in helping returning coworkers adjust to new phases of work, build on skills, develop compatible relations, and provide counsel to heal emotional and financial setbacks.

In 2022 Jupiter moves into Pisces and your solar second house, initiating new opportunities to earn more income, invest in your retirement, develop supplemental skills via targeted coursework, and build savings. In company with Jupiter, transiting Neptune continues its journey in your solar second house of income, assets, financial resources, and self-development plans. You may be on the brink of experiencing powerful psychic breakthroughs or gain insight about security and savings through your meditation and visualization practices. Outer planet Pluto in Capricorn works intently on completing a long transit in your solar twelfth house of seclusion. This transformative planet urges you to examine stuck patterns and fears in your life to release conditions that no longer match your goals. All four eclipses in 2022 fall in the fixed signs Taurus and Scorpio, generating activity in your solar chart's action-oriented fourth and tenth houses. Enjoy the eye-opening moments that accompany awareness in discoveries about your family and business life. Celebrate growth cycles.

Jupiter

In 2022 Jupiter occupies Pisces and your solar second house for most of the year. This transit puts the spotlight on diverse options for earning income through financial choices, investments, business deals, new jobs, promotions, unexpected windfalls, and contracts for your goods and services. Why not update your resume this year so you're ready to throw your hat into the ring when opportunity comes calling? Seek advice from human capital specialists if you have questions about job openings. In the first half of April, this Jupiter transit joins transiting

Neptune in Pisces and stimulates an interest in playing the lottery, mystical journeys, dreams, and revelations that bring hidden information to light. Aquarians born between February 11 and 13 may benefit the most from the insights that appear during this cycle. The benevolent planet spends a long period in Aries and your solar third house of education, mental agility, local travel, and systems equipment beginning on May 10, giving you an eye-opening preview of what it will be like to experience neighborhood adventures. On July 28, Jupiter turns retrograde for a few months in Aries and your solar third house, leading to delays in plans, purchases of electronic equipment, and signing contracts.

Saturn

Since you spent last year with Saturn in Aquarius transiting your solar first house of action, appearance, assertiveness, health, individuality, and self-discovery, you know that when Saturn hits your Sun, the cycle can be tension-filled, creating inner and outer conflict until the taskmaster planet is sure you understand the reasons behind the imposed restrictions. Instead of stewing and fretting over delays, search for missing information and listen more to others' input to put all the pieces together. Communication is the key, and you know a thing or two about that. Take advantage of opportunities to shine and look for ways to strengthen bonds, analyze plans, and review commitments. For some Aquarians, a first-house transit of Saturn brings either a marriage or a divorce. If love appears in your life, it may lead to a long-term relationship. When Saturn is in a fixed sign like Aquarius, it can bring out your stubborn side, making you unwilling to acknowledge shortfalls that you own or that surround the agreements or partnerships in which you are engaged. Embrace creative enterprise and enjoy a healthy lifestyle by eating well and getting more sleep. Those of you born between January 30 and February 15 see the most activity from Saturn in 2022. Venus and Mars in Aquarius line up in your solar first house for most of March and part of April, bringing self-love and lasting relationships and highlighting loving feelings. Let Saturn heal your doubts and bring you a joyful vision.

Uranus

Did you think only four years ago that you would wake up to find that a "guest" had moved into your home to create a flood of chaotic activity that affected the status quo in your residence, disrupted peace with your family, and interfered with household activities? Well, that's what happens when Uranus comes calling and settles into your solar fourth house for seven years. Uranus, the planet associated with sudden blow-ups, shake-ups, and bizarre behavior, has been in usually grounded Taurus since May 2018, making everything in your home environment feel a bit wobbly while it delivers a number of shocks to your family's equilibrium. Aquarius, you are used to the antics of your sign ruler, Uranus, but nonetheless you may have had your home life and entire work world disrupted by the arrival of the coronavirus pandemic in 2020. In 2022 you are in a recovery year, making adjustments in how you manage household conditions and continue to perform your work. Aquarians born between January 29 and February 8 feel the most pressure from Uranus's erratic cycle this year.

Neptune

Neptune, the watery planet of compassion, healing, psychological health, and secrets, has made a home in Pisces and your solar second house. This house represents the money you earn, how you spend it, raises and bonuses you receive, and self-development opportunities you pursue to keep your skills current and your goals for a promotion or a new job viable. When Neptune transits this house, you may have second thoughts about your salary or may have lost your job due to economic downturns or reorganizations. You could be skeptical about ideas you have for spending your hard-earned cash or be on the fence about refinancing your home. Neptune has been hanging around in this house since April 2011 and may have given you regrettable moments over purchasing goods that did not meet your standards, salary increases that were disappointing, or problems with credit or identity theft. Do your homework before making major purchases so you feel more grounded in your decisions and parting with cash is less emotional. Engage in open and straightforward discussion with partners before you spend. In 2022 Neptune most affects Aquarians born between February 8 and 15.

Pluto

Pluto in Capricorn and your solar twelfth house of charity, dreams, healing and recuperating, privacy, secrets, and work done behind the scenes most strongly affects Aquarius born between February 14 and 18 this year, creating provocative thoughts throughout your entire birthday cycle. In this low-key house, the planet of transitions suggests that you examine what worries you, how you are coping with your fears, and what you are willing to unload from your mind to enjoy a better life. Since Pluto first showed up here in 2008, it is logical to think that you have had ample time to release stuck patterns and give serious thought to how you want to meet your goals. The impersonal side of you may have become a hermit, unwilling to admit that life could be better. Your inner knower recognizes the truth and realizes that you seldom let it all out, preferring to hold grudges, never admit you made a mistake, and hang on to guilt, when all you have to do is tell the truth and make peace. Excessive secrecy or inventing the truth takes a toll on your health. Be sure to make time for a thorough medical exam and take on an exercise program that reduces stress. In 2022 Pluto in Capricorn goes retrograde on April 29 and moves direct on October 8, giving you time to rethink strategies, give serious consideration to life changes, or mend broken relationships. With your abundant altruistic qualities, wouldn't you rather attract love and caring relationships?

How Will This Year's Eclipses Affect You?

Two fixed signs, Taurus and Scorpio, feature prominently in the eclipses of 2022. A total of four eclipses occur: two solar (New Moon) and two lunar (Full Moon), bringing intense periods that start manifesting two months before they occur. All four of them take place in two of your solar chart's angular houses, the fourth and the tenth, representing home and family matters and your career, employing organization, and ambition. Your solar first and seventh houses may simultaneously receive strong vibrations from these eclipses, putting the spotlight on action from you or from personal and business partnerships.

Eclipses occur in cycles involving all twelve signs of the zodiac, in pairs, occurring two weeks apart. Never fear eclipses—consider them opportunities to release old, outworn patterns. Eclipses often have six months or more to show their effect on certain houses in your chart, triggering unexpected revelations, surprises, and windfalls. The closer an eclipse is to a planet or point in your chart, the greater the importance it plays in your life. Those of you born with a planet at the same degree as an eclipse are likely to see a high level of activity and a major change in the house where the eclipse occurs.

The first Solar Eclipse of 2022 occurs on April 30 in Taurus and your solar fourth house of home and foundation, family (especially parents), occupants of your home, your base of operations, and the physical structure, conditions, and features of your home, such as the garden, kitchen, family room, and dining quarters. If you have planets located in this house, expect any problem areas associated with principal residents to surface. If relationships are positive, you'll benefit from strengthening bonds and fulfilling goals. Should you encounter challenges, rough spots hit with possible shock value and call for discussion to work on viable solutions. A situation like the coronavirus could bring a child home temporarily to live with you. Be sure you and your spouse are on the same page with the new arrangements.

Two weeks later, the first Lunar Eclipse of the year occurs on May 16 in Scorpio and your solar tenth house of career, authority figures, ambition, recognition for achievements, organizational and affiliated conditions, family, and the status quo. With a tenth-house eclipse, the pressure is on, pushing you to keep goal commitments and promises on track. You have to manage timelines and deliver the work you're responsible for accomplishing, making sure it is of excellent quality. Form healthy work habits that give you adequate downtime to achieve life balance. If your physical appearance and health have been problematic, this eclipse will remind you to seek solutions and get counsel from medical specialists, nutritionists, and behavioral consultants.

On October 25 the second Solar Eclipse of 2022 takes place in Scorpio and your solar tenth house of career, authority figures, ambition, recognition for achievements, organizational and affiliated conditions, family, and the status quo. If your birthday occurs between January 22 and 24, this eclipse creates an action-oriented square aspect. Expect a change in direction in career matters. Consider the relief that comes from liberating moves.

The year's final eclipse is a Lunar Eclipse on November 8 in Taurus and your solar fourth house of home and foundation, family (especially parents), other occupants of your home, your base of operations, and the physical structure, conditions, and features of your home, such as the garden, kitchen, family room, and dining quarters. Transiting Uranus in Taurus is moving through this house too. When this eclipse hits after months of examining what you found regarding relationships back in May, you will have greater insight into whether remedial action brought the positive results you desired. Search for positive, loving solutions.

Aquarius | January

Overall Theme

January is a big money month for you since Jupiter in Pisces recently entered your solar second house of income. The new year begins with a close look at your financial outlook—what you are earning and spending and what you owe. Mercury goes retrograde in your solar first house on the 14th, affecting matters related to personal responsibility. Look before you leap.

Relationships

Individuals in financial, estate, and real estate fields communicate with you frequently this month. Set aside time on the 7th and 21st to work with mortgage brokers or planners and assess net worth. Communication with romantic partners improves after Venus goes direct on the 29th. Minimize arguments early in the month.

Success and Money

Good credit makes you a prime candidate for the best mortgage loan rates if you are purchasing or refinancing a home. A look at savings shows you have accumulated a significant down payment that benefits the size of your future mortgage payment. Look for a much anticipated raise after the 26th.

Pitfalls and Potential Problems

Uranus in Taurus moves direct in your solar fourth house on the 18th, highlighting conditions at home base that have experienced disruption since last summer and are ready for a decision. The Full Moon in Cancer on the 17th brings a rush of assignments and curtails plans to travel that you'll postpone due to workload escalation. Lie low this month after engaging in intense verbal discussions.

Rewarding Days
3, 7, 21, 29

Challenging Days
11, 15, 17, 19

Aquarius | February

Overall Theme

The Aquarius New Moon on the 1st casts its friendly light on relationship matters and all things fresh and unusual. The spotlight remains on financial transactions, approvals, and good vibes from transiting Jupiter in Pisces. If you're single, you might meet a potential partner with your opposite sign of Leo, and make beautiful romantic music after the 7th over a dinner date.

Relationships

After agreeing on key monetary decisions, you and your partner feel at one and appreciate the lightheartedness that comes with financial security. A Valentine's Day gathering that includes friendly neighbors and their children is a welcome treat and engages all participants. Buy art supplies so younger children can create valentines.

Success and Money

After Mercury goes direct on the 3rd, build rapport with workmates by showing your boss how effectively the workplace is recovering after COVID-19 setbacks. Plan meetings around the 22nd to facilitate networking for recruiting contacts for work projects. Collect resumes and mind-map the use of diverse skill sets to fill all critical roles. A windfall around the 2nd boosts cash flow.

Pitfalls and Potential Problems

Keep activities low-key on the 16th, when the Full Moon in Leo skews energy and dampens momentum for romantic trysts and productive work sessions. Meetings with professional associates in long-distance locations fizzle on the 21st when media equipment behaves erratically and key stakeholders are missing. Listen to ensuing complaints without judgment.

Rewarding Days

1, 2, 7, 22

Challenging Days

6, 10, 16, 20

Aquarius | March

Overall Theme

The quality of communication dominates this month's focus. Convey your trust and support for key personnel in your workplace. Help others regain confidence in their future after a few painful years of uncertainty and disruption. Attention to worker concerns and operational details wins loyalty from those in your circle.

Relationships

Connect with siblings and cousins on the 5th. Be a good listener to those who have experienced significant financial setbacks and share ideas for coping and lowering stress levels. Discuss operating policies with team-mates regarding upcoming shifts in work practices or job realignment. Go shopping with your spouse on the 3rd, when goods that mesh with your goals go on sale.

Success and Money

Work with community organizers on the 5th to suggest improvements to playgrounds, meeting facilities, and daycare centers that are overused and would benefit from makeovers. Finalize contracts and agreements on the 5th or 12th that offer competitive prices for materials and labor in line with budget goals. Agree on a favorable start date.

Pitfalls and Potential Problems

The Virgo Full Moon on the 18th brings challenging aspects to your solar eighth house when Jupiter, Saturn, and Neptune interfere with smooth execution of a home loan or a contract for services. Missing documents may cause the delay, yet resolution occurs within a week. Minimize clashes at work with authority figures on the 21st.

Rewarding Days

3, 5, 12, 26

Challenging Days

10, 14, 21, 24

Aquarius | April

Overall Theme

The New Moon occurs twice this month—in Aries and your solar third house on the 1st and in Taurus and your solar fourth house of home on the 30th, the date of 2022's first Solar Eclipse. It's a no for travel when the Full Moon in Libra occurs in your solar ninth house on the 16th. Implement electronic upgrades to stay competitive.

Relationships

Friends and family members are your primary contacts this month. On the 1st, give a former colleague a job lead over lunch, and share an intimate dinner with your partner that evening. Network with members of professional groups on the 22nd. The last third of April brings quality rapport with officers in professional organizations, with timely support from Mercury, Venus, Mars, and Saturn.

Success and Money

An excellent day to apply for a loan or to ask for a raise is the 27th. Follow up on leads for an attractive position that features a significant raise. Apply if the opportunity is a good match for your skill set. Selection occurs after the Solar Eclipse in Taurus on the 30th.

Pitfalls and Potential Problems

Avoid peevish family members on the 4th, when the Moon in Taurus lands in your solar fourth house. Tension comes between you and your spouse on the 11th. A disappointed job candidate spreads gloom on the 20th during a lunch meeting. Pluto goes retrograde in Capricorn on the 29th, not a good day to bare your soul.

Rewarding Days

1, 22, 27, 30

Challenging Days

4, 9, 11, 20

Aquarius | May

Overall Theme

Decisions get tough on the 2nd when home repairs demand your attention at the same time that children expect you to deliver on promises to spend time at a special event. Hire someone to do the household work and happily attend the sports or entertainment venue with your children.

Relationships

Work deadlines call for adjustments by reassigning employees to cover staffing shortfalls. Relationships with staff generate trust when you see how well you can count on the winning combination of talent and commitment. Schedule a celebration lunch for the team around the 24th and acknowledge performance excellence.

Success and Money

On the 6th, hidden information comes to light and puts you in the running for a new job. On the 7th, Jupiter transiting your solar second house in compatible aspect to the Moon brings unanticipated cash your way at the end of the workweek. Take delight in the bargaining power of a job well done.

Pitfalls and Potential Problems

A potential work contract hits a disappointing snag on the 5th when you discover key elements were missing from the original bid you submitted. Mercury goes retrograde on the 10th, disrupting your schedule and delaying plans for the next three weeks. Demands on your time the morning of the May 16th Scorpio Lunar Eclipse escalate when you're asked to develop funding recommendations for a proposal ASAP.

Rewarding Days

2, 6, 20, 24

Challenging Days

5, 9, 11, 31

Aquarius | June

Overall Theme

While Mercury resumes direct motion in Taurus on the 3rd, giving you an opportunity to stabilize conditions at home, two other outer planets turn retrograde, affecting responsibilities and clarity of intentions. This month is ideal for accepting social invitations and spending time with relatives and children. Create opportunities to share a welcome change of pace that includes fun and innovative games.

Relationships

Romantic relationships sparkle with promise for Aquarians who discover passionate feelings for a significant other. Jupiter in Aries in your solar third house highlights socializing with siblings and neighbors. The quality time you spend with loved ones leaves a lasting impression, with expressions of loyalty and appreciation for your generous heart. Children and pets elicit warm feelings.

Success and Money

Mercury, Venus, and Uranus unite in your solar fourth house early this month, generating harmonious communication and adding spontaneity to interactions with family members. You're most effective in your workplace coordinating assignments and providing quality control for end products and services early in the month. Persistence pays off when you meet deadlines early.

Pitfalls and Potential Problems

Avoid starting or signing off on a project when Saturn turns retrograde in Aquarius on the 4th while simultaneously getting a hard hit from Mercury that interferes with smooth communication. Neptune in Pisces turns retrograde on the 28th in your solar second house, alerting you to look over confusing contract language in a financial proposal.

Rewarding Days

3, 20, 21, 27

Challenging Days

1, 5, 14, 30

Aquarius | July

Overall Theme

With your gregarious Aquarius nature, you could be at the center of holiday gatherings showcasing your patriotic spirit and encouraging participation of attendees after two years of pandemic-related social-distancing restrictions. Initiate intelligent conversations.

Relationships

You and your lover bond beautifully on the 1st, with Venus-Jupiter aspects driving momentum. You could meet a realtor at a holiday celebration who is interested in listing your home for sale. Expect lots of follow-up if you show encouragement. Rapport with business groups on the 10th yields important connections for future reference.

Success and Money

Money works for you all month except for the 2nd and 29th, when you and your partner are not aligned over expenses. A cash award allows you to pay off a loan or credit card debt, with enough left over for a nice vacation in August. Enjoy a high-energy day on the 17th when an authority figure talks to you about a new job or a promotion. Savor the rewarding cycle.

Pitfalls and Potential Problems

On the 28th, Jupiter in Aries goes retrograde in your solar third house, making its way back into Pisces and your solar second house. Don't move any money between accounts on the 8th or invest in stocks. You won't know the bottom line if you don't look over proposals carefully on the 5th.

Rewarding Days

1, 4, 10, 17

Challenging Days

2, 5, 9, 29

Aquarius | August

Overall Theme
With Mars occupying your solar fourth house from the 1st to the 20th, tension at home escalates and grows especially volatile on August 1 and 2, when Uranus in Taurus applies pressure and feelings erupt. Take a vacation if you can get away before the 15th. Use bonus money to fund your trip and enjoy the extra incentive to chill.

Relationships
In this people-oriented month, you'll bond with traveling in-laws and join them for a few dinners or sightseeing trips. Siblings invite you to a reunion or gathering around the 15th. Work connections extend invitations to barbecues and outdoor parties. You and your significant other make beautiful music together on the 26th and strengthen bonds.

Success and Money
Compliments about your performance and understanding of the process of reinventing work in the aftermath of the pandemic reach your boss from distant places. Rewards are in the plans to recognize the accomplishments and extra efforts. You could be setting up training programs to facilitate assimilation of new work processes that streamline innovative procedures for all employees.

Pitfalls and Potential Problems
Employees squabble over allocation of workspace on the 5th. The Aquarius Full Moon in your solar first house on the 11th disrupts the peace in home and work environments. If you're on vacation, disagreements could erupt over entertainment choices that displease some family members. Take steps to consider options that keep everyone happy and cover preferences to maximize fun.

Rewarding Days
2, 15, 23, 25

Challenging Days
5, 8, 11, 27

Aquarius | September

Overall Theme

Mercury goes retrograde on the 9th in your solar ninth house of long-distance travel, publishing, in-laws, and higher education, so maintain flexibility with plans and deadlines that could fall apart. Positive energy revolves around regrouping in private quarters, managing finances, bonding with family, and connecting with professional colleagues.

Relationships

Save the social networking for the 30th, when an end-of-month luncheon brings out notable contacts and a captivating speaker whose message speaks to your current career goals. Family members share exciting news about professional connections, and someone discloses details of a successful job interview on the 15th. Be encouraging and helpful.

Success and Money

Bargains make you happy when your money goes a long way toward purchasing tools and gardening equipment at a sale on the 10th. Earning power rises when the management team announces attractive incentives for increasing salary brackets scheduled for implementation in October. Look for a generous raise.

Pitfalls and Potential Problems

When the Moon in Scorpio on the 2nd reflects hard Venus-Saturn aspects, deflect awkward moments with your boss by preparing information for a meeting that relates only to your area of accountability, instead of adding references to another's responsibilities. The New Moon in Libra on the 25th opposes transiting Jupiter in Aries and your solar third house of communication, straining relationships with neighbors over local concerns.

Rewarding Days

6, 10, 15, 30

Challenging Days

2, 5, 17, 22

Aquarius | October

Overall Theme

If you've been stressing out over a number of important situations that have been on hold, celebrate October as a breakthrough month, when several planets shift course. Starting on the 2nd, Mercury goes direct in Virgo and your solar eighth house. Pluto moves forward on the 8th in Capricorn and your solar twelfth house, and Saturn turns direct on the 23rd after a four-month stall in Aquarius and your solar first house of self-expression.

Relationships

Some of your favorite people have a starring role this month, starting with your dentist, so make an important appointment. Then enjoy a romantic date with a love relationship on the 14th. Join children in favorite pastimes, a trip to the zoo, or a fall adventure like a corn maze.

Success and Money

Work collaboration brings successful outcomes that include earning more money. You turn a corner this month in breaking out of deficit mode, a holdover from painful pay cuts over the last two years. The Solar Eclipse in Scorpio conjunct Venus on the 25th occurs in your work setting, bringing a raise in line with last month's decision to increase pay levels.

Pitfalls and Potential Problems

A date on the 7th could be costly when car trouble ruins plans. The Full Aries Moon on the 9th could bring disappointing news about a child's grades. Mars in loquacious Gemini makes a retrograde station in your solar fifth house on the 30th, affecting social plans and triggering misunderstandings with a lover.

Rewarding Days

4, 14, 20, 30

Challenging Days

1, 7, 23, 25

Aquarius | November

Overall Theme

You're still celebrating a welcome infusion of cash this month and generously invite guests to your Thanksgiving feast, including friends who live far away. Although you enjoy hosting dinners and parties, you and your spouse could squabble over the menu or be at odds over the wine list on the 15th. Misunderstandings clear up quickly, resulting in a festive mood.

Relationships

Find your holiday spirit as you shop for special treats to share at the table. Jupiter in Pisces turning direct in your solar second house on November 23 reminds you to acknowledge a bountiful year, conveying gratitude to guests who dine with you. The New Moon in Sagittarius also on the 23rd signals the arrival of visitors to the feast. You recruit volunteers among celebrants to serve meals at the local community center, nurturing those experiencing economic constraints.

Success and Money

All the bills are paid as you enter November and start taking inventory of your holiday gift list on the 3rd. You're all set for holiday shopping on the 6th, so take advantage of attractive sales that stretch your gift-giving budget. Venus transiting your solar eleventh house attracts friends to your warm holiday gathering.

Pitfalls and Potential Problems

The last Lunar Eclipse of the year falls on the 8th in Taurus and your solar fourth house, making harsh aspects to Mercury, Venus, Saturn, and Uranus. Manage tension and stifle disruption. Hop on the treadmill and walk away the blues.

Rewarding Days

3, 13, 23, 29

Challenging Days

1, 8, 15, 22

Aquarius | December

Overall Theme

The universe has been working overtime to give you a happy holiday season. Spread goodwill and attend warm gatherings, uniting with those you haven't seen in a long time. Neptune turns direct on the 3rd and casts a glamorous spell on the vibrations of celebratory events. Invite your significant other to join you for relaxation and fun.

Relationships

Coordinate a party for a neighborhood shelter on the 3rd, providing food, bedding, and gifts for appreciative attendees. After the 17th, surround yourself with visiting relatives who arrive early to participate in holiday festivities.

Success and Money

Venus and Mercury line up cheerfully in your solar eleventh house in early December, creating camaraderie with favorite friends or members of a professional group at a lively holiday lunch around December 3 to 5. You'll find the perfect gift for a child around the 7th that appeals to the intellectual side of a youthful problem-solver, thus completing your holiday shopping.

Pitfalls and Potential Problems

A plan to look at the city's beautiful decorations fizzles just ahead of the Neptune station on December 3, when the location to meet up at is omitted from the organizer's invitation. A family member's nerves are on edge on the 5th. Order takeout to minimize stress and avoid a long wait for food. Avoid beginning or booking a trip on the 29th, when Mercury goes retrograde in Capricorn.

Rewarding Days

3, 17, 24, 25

Challenging Days

1, 5, 7, 23

Aquarius Action Table

These dates reflect the best—but not the only—times for success and ease in these activities, according to your Sun sign.

	JAN	FEB	MAR	APR	MAY	JUN	JUL	AUG	SEP	OCT	NOV	DEC
Move	21		5					2				17
Romance		7		30		27	1		30	20		
Seek counseling/ coaching			12		6			15			13	
Ask for a raise		2		22	2	20			10			
Vacation										14		24
Get a loan	7						17				3	

Pisces

The Fish
February 18 to March 20

♓

Element: Water

Glyph: Two fish swimming in opposite directions

Quality: Mutable

Anatomy: Feet, lymphatic system

Polarity: Yin/feminine

Colors: Sea green, violet

Planetary Ruler: Neptune

Animals: Fish, sea mammals

Meditation: I successfully navigate my emotions

Myths/Legends: Aphrodite, Buddha, Jesus of Nazareth

Gemstone: Aquamarine

House: Twelfth

Power Stones: Amethyst, bloodstone, tourmaline

Opposite Sign: Virgo

Flower: Water lily

Key Phrase: I believe

Keyword: Transcendence

The Pisces Personality

Strengths, Talents, and the Creative Spark

As the owner of a well-developed sixth sense that seldom guides you in the wrong direction when you're pursuing truthful answers, you enjoy ownership of the only mutable water sign in the zodiac. Your astrological symbol has a highly spiritual connotation: two fish swimming in opposite directions, representing compassion, imagination, and a strong desire to understand differences in others' views. Your luminous eyes reflect your probing mind and love for solving mysteries, pursuing romance, and following adventurous paths that open your intellect yet leave you plenty of personal space to explore metaphysical subjects. Neptune is your sign ruler and the natural occupant of the twelfth house of behind-the-scenes activity, charity, confinement, escapism, healing, hidden enemies, hospitals, meditation, mysticism, orphans, secrets, and widows. Since you like acting on hunches, some of you are excellent gamblers (Jupiter was your original sign ruler before Neptune was discovered) and enjoy playing the lottery or making trips to Las Vegas or Atlantic City.

Your mutable nature makes you versatile and adept at many types of careers. One of the signs most affiliated with the liquids of the earth is Pisces, which leads to employment affiliated with anesthesia, aromatherapy, alcohol, medicinal drugs (prescribed or illegal), perfume, and oil and gas commodities. You could excel at accounting and bookkeeping, join a convent, study medicine to become a doctor or nurse, write detective stories or poetry, or work in fields where confidentiality is a requirement, such as government intelligence, police work, or psychology. Your work could involve helping others through rehabilitation programs involving health issues, drug use, or probation. If you were born with Neptune in your first house, you might also have a dramatic flair and find satisfaction with acting, art, dancing, and design.

Intimacy and Personal Relationships

Stability is important to you in a love relationship, yet the path to finding it is often challenging. That's because you are a romantic, with a generous heart, who has sentimental values that get in the way of seeing potential partners for who they really are. Physical attraction means the world to you, and you often succumb to the outer package before recognizing that the inner works are not suitable for your emotional needs. You're a true believer of a happy ending and want that badly, putting a strong emphasis on love at first sight. If at first you don't succeed, you marry again. Pisces, you're one who may find the perfect mate in your opposite sign of Virgo, whose practical insight keeps you grounded in the relationship. The other earth signs, Taurus and Capricorn, make you feel secure as well and make plans around your interests. Empathetic water signs Cancer and Scorpio often make good matches, especially if their Moon signs are compatible with yours and they really understand you. If you have ever been with a Gemini or a Sagittarius, the experience may have been emotionally upsetting. As a parent, you cherish your children but may be a helicopter parent whose overprotectiveness interferes with their quest for independence. Close friends and small groups are your anchors.

Values and Resources

Clearing your head means ducking into the personally created sanctuary called your twelfth house of seclusion, where you regroup and come up with ways to share your generous spirit with loved ones. You seem to sense when someone you love needs your help and become a secret pal intent on bolstering confidence of a cherished connection. With your compassionate heart, you quickly assess pressing needs others have and send encouraging cards, notes, and gifts to lift them out of the doldrums. Unconditional love is one of the strengths you demonstrate by checking in with a phone call or text message, offering a ride, or inviting them to a movie comedy for a much needed laugh. It means the world to you for the recipient of your generosity to thank you for caring, whether they write it down or tell you how they feel. Lazy types who never acknowledge a kind gesture are a turnoff, and you'll eventually take them off your radar screen. You value bosses with organized minds who are interested in the quality of the work you perform and show appreciation for the value you add to the company.

Blind Spots and Blockages

Most of you are thoughtful, conscientious employees who take pride in your work, despite having a few sore spots. Whether it is learning how to cook or assimilating new computer technology, if it's not your jam, you balk at suggestions to take classes, perfect your application skills, or earn career-enhancing credentials. Often, spontaneity is not your strong suit.

A boss or coworker could ruffle your feathers with comments about your performance that you find demeaning, yet a response escapes you because you are caught off guard. Instead you're known for blurting out a defensive retort that gives others the impression you are hot-headed or uncooperative. Try asking for private time to discuss the incident after you're able to think things through. Some of you are known for withdrawing into Neptune's fog and daydreaming away valuable time that could be spent on meeting deadlines or learning a new skill.

Goals and Success

In this transition year, after coping with a worldwide pandemic, you are most likely revamping your goals or setting new ones. Where is the universe guiding you? What facets of work no longer attract you? Plan on securing your future with meaningful work. Depending on your stage of life, you might be ready for a new career or ready to retire, if eligible. Be sure to use your intuitive and visualization skills to develop a pictorial rendition of your hopes and desires (such as a treasure map or a vision board), and watch how fast you manifest your ideal job! Use your psychic gifts as the basis for setting up a practice to read for clients using tarot, numerology, runes, clairvoyance, mediumship, or related skills. Apply for work at CPA firms, banks, mortgage lenders, and small businesses to use your accounting skills. Satisfy your quest for privacy in your daily environment by pursuing freelance work to put writing, editing, entertainment, and customer service skills to good use. Your employer may offer you a telecommuting assignment that offers an attractive array of hours for completing the work that is compatible with existing family responsibilities and meets your expectations for happiness and your quest for job security.

Pisces Keywords for 2022
Charity, concern, confidentiality

The Year Ahead for Pisces

With Uranus in Taurus starting out the year 2022 retrograde in your solar third house, where it turns direct on January 18, you get the green light to resume matters that were put on hold last summer: moving into or out of your neighborhood, resuming civic duties in the community, enrolling in local or online classes, and making plans to see siblings or cousins that have been living under similar constraints. As the year begins, Venus, the love planet, is retrograde in Capricorn and your solar eleventh house of friendships, groups, and goals. If you're a single Pisces, you may find that a relationship with a casual friend takes a romantic turn. You had the company of several Capricorn planets in this house in recent years and have only Pluto in late degrees of Capricorn left there now to help you work through any karmic conditions associated with groups or friendships.

The first planet to turn retrograde this year is Mercury, the planet of communication, on January 14 in Aquarius and your solar twelfth house of seclusion, private matters, healing, and charity. The signal to move ahead with anticipated work plans will be muted, complicated by the presence of transiting Saturn in Aquarius while it also occupies your complex solar twelfth house. Saturn, the zodiac's taskmaster, comes with a set of personal restrictions that impede a fast recovery from either physical or mental health issues emanating from economic shortages resulting from the pandemic's toll on the planet. If your job was on the line or your hours were reduced, start a search for new employment opportunities as you broaden your field of expertise.

Jupiter

Lucky you, Pisces, since Jupiter, the planet of expansion, is in your sign all year. With the exception of a retrograde and a sign-change period, the mind-expanding planet occupies Pisces and your solar first house for most of the year, until December 20, when it moves into Aries for all of 2023. What a good place to be if you're launching an enterprise, inventing products, starting a new job, or improving your health or self-image. With a few entrepreneurial ideas in the pipeline, you could increase the value of your assets and add generous increases to your savings. Investors may catch the wave and come forward to sign agreements for your services. Travel may be part of the scene again. If you stay with your firm, enjoy recognition from authority figures for past efforts, even if work changes significantly. Give independent consulting a whirl or accept part-time assignments that help you pay the bills, especially if COVID-19 cutbacks reduced your salary and led to a change in duties and your work schedule. Jupiter travels rapidly through Pisces until May 10, when it moves into Aries and your solar second house of earned income. On July 28 Jupiter will turn retrograde in Aries, moving back into Pisces and your solar first house on October 28 until it goes direct on November

23 through the end of the year. Pisces born between February 19 and 28 experience the most impact from the shift when Jupiter is in Aries. Jupiter in Pisces connects with transiting Neptune in Pisces from April 7 to 14, favoring prosperity and an interest in mystical or spiritual activity.

Saturn

Saturn entered Aquarius on December 17, 2020, in your solar twelfth house of planning, regrouping, seclusion, private matters, healing, and charity. Planets in Aquarius often have little impact on Pisces placements, except for giving the impression that they are overly analytical and demanding. While Pisces does find the discipline, they like to travel at their own pace and don't like having their creative force squeezed out of them. You probably felt Saturn's tension over the past two years, especially if you dealt with health issues or depression due to overwhelming setbacks imposed by the pandemic. In this recovery year, you're forced to look at employment and living conditions, which could mean a move from your residence or the location of your job. It's possible that an employer owes you money for work you performed or you are waiting for unemployment benefits that have trickled in slowly. COVID-19 restrictions have affected the whole face of the work culture, and many of the changes will become permanent. Depending on the financial resources of your company, it is possible that some employees will lose their job, if they haven't already. Count on a boost from Jupiter in your sign this year to help you combat economic shortfalls, and take a critical look at revamping your resume to meet demand for skills shortages. Saturn in your solar twelfth house will help you stay on course. Work compatibly with team members to develop solutions that improve productivity. This year Saturn touches the lives most intensely of Pisces born between March 1 and 17. Saturn's retrograde period in 2022 occurs from June 4 through October 23.

Uranus

What are your strategies for managing transiting Uranus for another year in your solar third house of communication, contracts, education, electronic equipment, local travel, your state of mind, neighbors, relatives, and transportation? The planet of the unexpected disrupted specific goals you developed for these areas. You're ready to shed the persistent provocation of Uranus. Natal planets in Taurus, while friendly to Pisces, clash with hard-nosed Saturn in Aquarius, the aggravator that has put your solar twelfth house of recuperation in quarantine since 2020. Go after your spirit, Pisces, and trust the feelings you have about the volume and nature of intense communication, demand for help, confusing rhetoric, and outdated equipment that creates chaos. Retrieve your charismatic and intuitive mind and embrace this liberating force. With two eclipses in Taurus in 2022 in this house, sudden events shake up your world. If you're planning to travel, go back to school, study metaphysics, or change careers, Uranus and the constraints of COVID-19 will keep you on your toes. If you were born between February 29 and March 10, the planet of unexpected events has the strongest impact on you now. Enjoy the positive boost from Jupiter in Pisces and touch base with networks who connect you with others in your field. The rebellious planet moves retrograde on August 24 and goes direct on January 22, 2023. Get ready for a breakthrough.

Neptune

How are you enjoying Neptune's long residence in your solar first house, Pisces? Since April 2011, ethereal, mystical Neptune has taken center stage in this house, which represents action, assertive behavior, innovation, passion, the physical body, personality, self-image, and temperament. What's your secret for coping with the excessive daydreaming that Neptune brings, distracting you and making it harder to focus on your responsibilities and meet deadlines? During this ride, you have certainly had opportunities to cross paths with an eclectic group of people whose vast life experiences were inspiring, eccentric, and educational. In 2022, Neptune conjuncts your Sun, generating the most activity for those born between March 10 and 17, including new romantic relationships if you're single and business opportunities if you're looking for a new venture. Proposals of all types may come your way—business and romantic—so remember that if it looks too good to be true, it may very well be, coming in with a blast of Neptune fog, ready to be examined and cleared from your life. When Neptune transits your solar first house, you are exceptionally sensitive and feel every energy shift that crosses your threshold. Your interest in the psychic and intuitive realm intensifies and could even lead to work in this field if you are ready. If you contemplate surgery while Neptune is conjunct your Sun, choose dates carefully with the help of an astrologer. Use discrimination to dissolve illusions, cure addictions, or curb food binges, excessive gambling, or impulse shopping. The planet of dreams and illusions will be retrograde from June 28 to December 3. Align with Jupiter to use Neptune's insight to expand your intuitive mind when your Sun makes contact.

Pluto

Here comes Pluto, eager to spend another year in the paradise known as your solar eleventh house of associates, friends, club members, professional organizations, and peer groups. The karma cleaner of the zodiac made its first appearance in this house in 2008 and still expects to help you clear away the excess baggage associated with the themes of this house. You know what to do: eliminate anything that keeps you stuck. First identify your power struggles and problematic relationships. Pluto in Capricorn wants you to realize that without those fears, you'll be able to embrace personal freedom and take the lead in powerful groups or change careers to one that better suits your evolving preferences. Does fear of power drive the urge to push away invitations to lead? Pluto can help you grow confident and empower yourself to be more adventurous, expressive, and entrepreneurial. Take a look at situations where relationships or your work have become very intense, making everyday interactions contentious at times. Here's where you focus on letting go. Pluto is occupying the final degrees of Capricorn as it wraps up this long transit in 2025. The planet of rebirth forms a harmonious sextile aspect to your Sun this year if you were born between March 15 and 19, the dates most affected by this transit. Jupiter and Neptune in Pisces favorably aspect Pluto and give you the needed nudge and confidence to change the direction of your life. In 2022 Pluto in Capricorn's retrograde period begins on April 29 and lasts until October 8. Acknowledge your personal power and the depth of your commitment to change.

How Will This Year's Eclipses Affect You?

A total of four eclipses occur in 2022. Two eclipses are solar (New Moon) and two are lunar (Full Moon), which evoke intense periods that begin to manifest a few months before they occur. All four of these eclipses take place in cadent houses in your chart, in the solar third and ninth houses. Eclipses unfold in cycles involving all twelve signs of the zodiac and usually happen in pairs about two weeks apart. They are opportunities to release patterns and conditions that have outlived their usefulness. Never fear eclipses, since they often bring unexpected surprises and windfalls. The closer an eclipse is to a degree or point in your chart, the greater its importance. If you were born with a planet at the same degree as an eclipse, you are likely to see a high level of activity in the house where the eclipse occurs, and its impact may last six months to a year.

The first Solar Eclipse of 2022 occurs on April 30 in Taurus and your solar third house of communication, education, local travel, neighbors, siblings, and transportation. Activity in this house increases when assignments you perform from home become the new norm. Online courses interest you as a way to learn new skills suitable to changing work conditions. Expect a significant increase in communications between you and your siblings and increased interactions with neighbors and your community.

On May 16 the first Lunar Eclipse of the year takes place in Scorpio and your solar ninth house of the higher mind, education, foreign countries and cultures, in-laws, philosophy, religion, publishing, and long-distance travel. You could be struggling with financial setbacks that prevented you from moving for job advancement or recovering from a coronavirus-related career problem that affected job security. Contact with relatives at a distance continues to be limited. Reach out to online networks to find income options in compatible fields.

The year's second Solar Eclipse takes place on October 25 in Scorpio and your solar ninth house of the higher mind, education, foreign countries and cultures, in-laws, philosophy, religion, publishing, and long-distance travel. If you're thinking of relocating for work, you may find that transferring to a new city offers the perfect opportunity now. Discuss choices with family to address family goals. You may soon be able to visit family members at a distance or perhaps travel out of the country on business again.

The year's final eclipse is a Lunar Eclipse on November 8, again in Taurus and your third house of communication, education, local travel, neighbors, siblings, and transportation. At this point, your entire work routine may have changed, as well as those of coworkers who collaborate with you on assigned projects. You may be ready to retire or prefer to work fewer hours. The local mindset is unified to show compassion for those who need help. A job change may have you working for a neighborhood business or volunteering in schools to support community needs.

Pisces | January

Overall Theme
Your solar eleventh house of friendships, groups, and goals gets a boost with Venus and Pluto in Capricorn striking notes of altruism, embracing a humanitarian initiative, and visualizing wishes coming true. An after-holiday get-together with friends extends the celebration season on the 2nd and gives you a preview of confidential social plans that are in the pipeline.

Relationships
Mars in Sagittarius welcomes the new year with an energetic blast of passion in your career sector. Show leaders and team members the depth of your ambition as you pursue emerging goals. Give your romantic partner loving attention by making reservations for a special night out on the 21st. Long-distance travel late in the month aids business associates who need your input on a challenging policy.

Success and Money
Clearance sales around the 8th offer considerable savings incentives for purchasing household goods. Jupiter in your solar first house increases income, improving cash flow and generating funds to purchase handheld electronics or smartphones. Protect valuables while Venus is retrograde through January 29.

Pitfalls and Potential Problems
Mercury turns retrograde on January 14 in Aquarius and your solar twelfth house of secrets, planning, and regrouping while the Gemini Moon is in your solar fourth house—a day to avoid making a binding commitment or signing contracts. After months of social distancing, erratic Uranus goes direct on the 18th in your solar third house of communication, neighborhood activity, and local travel.

Rewarding Days
2, 8, 21, 26

Challenging Days
4, 11, 14, 20

Pisces | February

Overall Theme

Although full disclosure of upcoming plans is not yet available, management discussions on the New Moon in Aquarius on February 1 bring an optimistic vibe to your workplace, raising hopes that stability is on the employment horizon after painful adjustments to pandemic constraints. Schedule uplifting talks to acknowledge small victories in the interim.

Relationships

Children show affection and gather for bonding time and family entertainment on the 7th. Cherish meaningful moments. Get ready to enjoy an especially loving Valentine's Day, with Jupiter in Pisces in your solar first house. Plan a romantic celebration with your significant other.

Success and Money

Make job changes in response to job announcements after Mercury goes direct on the 3rd. Do more work privately on a creative idea for improving work efficiency. It won't be ready until next month, so don't be tempted to present it early. Your communication skills get a workout on the 26th when you're asked to take the lead in a critical presentation.

Pitfalls and Potential Problems

An unexpected conflict over expenses surfaces on the 2nd, shutting down discussions with involved parties. The topic resurfaces on the 10th, but family members are argumentative instead of open to talking. The Full Moon in Leo and your solar twelfth house on the 16th reveals hidden anger and confusion. Better aspects surface around the 26th.

Rewarding Days

1, 3, 7, 26

Challenging Days

6, 10, 16, 21

Pisces | March

Overall Theme

Bask in the sunny vibes on the 2nd when the new Moon in Pisces and your solar first house begins a new cycle of prosperity that affects your initiatives and gives a welcome nod to undertakings in play in your solar seventh house of personal and business partners. Plan a getaway with your sweetheart before work responsibilities pile up and stifle the opportunity.

Relationships

Give full attention to neighborhood issues during the first week of the month to provide input for adjusting homeowner association policies. Relatives at a distance connect to scope out availability for a summer reunion. Venus and Mars in Aquarius reflect romantic harmony that elevates your vacation plans to exciting levels.

Success and Money

Single Pisces meet new love prospects while traveling for business. Jupiter in Pisces in your solar first house brings an opportunity to use diplomacy to eliminate squabbles over problem-solving preferences. Business travel to a distant location proves successful around the 22nd, when strategic insights get the job done for a client.

Pitfalls and Potential Problems

Call it an early night on the 18th, when exhaustion crops up and the weekend Virgo Full Moon zaps your energy. Your money house displays unfavorable aspects if you ask for a raise on the 6th. Your boss already has something in mind based on recent accomplishments and wants to control the timing to add a surprise element to the mix.

Rewarding Days

2, 7, 22, 26

Challenging Days

6, 14, 17, 21

Pisces | April

Overall Theme

Savor the opportunities for new beginnings this month. Two New Moons occur, the first on April 1 in Aries and your solar second house of assets, income, and self-development, and the second—the first Solar Eclipse of the year—in Taurus and your solar third house on the 30th, accenting communication and travel. Make a review of your fiscal accounts a vital part of your schedule. Then enjoy downtime by visiting local fairs or exhibits.

Relationships

Interactions with financial planners or bankers take place early in the month. Keep promises with children for enjoyable outings over the weekend of the 8th. A dinner with friends on the 22nd is the start of a holiday weekend. Bond with visiting siblings and their children on the 30th by treating family to a favorite local festival.

Success and Money

Your money grew exceptionally well in the first quarter of 2022, as is reflected in your monthly financial report. Target savings dividends for children's summer camp or classes. Make reservations on the 8th. Members of professional groups applaud your innovative business ideas the last week of April.

Pitfalls and Potential Problems

Pluto in Capricorn goes retrograde for six months on the 29th, interrupting the flow of a group venture that supports a humanitarian initiative you started last fall. A related contract has a few glitches to work out, so don't approve it on the 4th. Ask key stakeholders to review problematic clauses and sign around the 27th.

Rewarding Days

1, 8, 22, 30

Challenging Days

4, 10, 14, 24

Pisces | May

Overall Theme
You're still reeling from the fallout of the April 30th Solar Eclipse transiting with Uranus in Taurus and your solar third house. Right on its heels comes the first Lunar Eclipse in Scorpio and your solar ninth house of travel on the 16th. The intensity and content of messages and information exchanges calls for revision of plans related to education, communication, and contracts that involve relatives living close by and those living out of town.

Relationships
Connections with family dominate the first week of May. Provide counsel to relatives living outside your home and listen carefully to their concerns for solving sensitive personal problems. Join friends or group members for discussions that center on revising incompatible school policies that conflict with current practices.

Success and Money
You or a child have a decision to make regarding college acceptance right after the Lunar Eclipse in Scorpio on the 16th. After Jupiter moves into Aries on the 10th, you'll soon receive a raise that has been in the cards. Review a new benefits package if you have returned to work after a long layoff period.

Pitfalls and Potential Problems
Mercury is about to go retrograde in Gemini on the 10th and affects household plans and family decisions. Be flexible and revise timetables for accomplishing renovations or starting a vacation. Be alert to cybersecurity information breaches. Validate facts that come from a coworker on the 9th.

Rewarding Days
2, 7, 20, 24

Challenging Days
5, 9, 12, 31

Pisces | June

Overall Theme

This month the Moon appears in Cancer twice in your solar fifth house, on the 3rd and the 28th, setting up social activity for diverse relationships that fill your calendar. Watch for several planetary stations. Jupiter is zooming through Aries and your solar second house for the next few months, giving you a preview of what is in store for you financially in 2023.

Relationships

Meet up with favorite pals at a trendy restaurant on the 3rd and get a jump on weekend relaxation while dancing to lively music. You and your significant other share deep feelings on the 7th. Children join you in favorite amusements to spend quality time on the 27th. Planets jar your equilibrium on the 30th if you accept a blind date.

Success and Money

Collaboration with business partners brings clarity for amendments to work projects on the 7th. Analytical expertise opens discussions for future agreements, and the CFO allocates startup funds. You feel secure with Jupiter in Aries occupying your solar second house showing promising income increases.

Pitfalls and Potential Problems

Mercury goes direct on the 3rd in Taurus. A day later, Saturn, the stickler, slips into retrograde motion in Aquarius and your solar twelfth house, demanding no lapses in work schedules, which will have to be changed due to an increased workload. On the 28th, Neptune in Pisces turns retrograde in your solar first house until December 3 and calls for distancing yourself from confusing relationships.

Rewarding Days

3, 7, 21, 27

Challenging Days

5, 11, 14, 30

Pisces | July

Overall Theme

New work assignments demand focused work until after the 4th of July. The Moon in Virgo on the holiday has perfect aspects for a happy celebration. You're fine with celebrating the holiday close to home. A desirable beach vacation works best between the 10th and 23rd, when you feel the call of the sun and the surf.

Relationships

Workmates, neighbors, and immediate family are star attendees at your holiday barbecue. Set up gameboards in the backyard and play softball if you have the room. Keep plenty of cold drinks on hand for participants. Play Independence Day Trivia to jog memories and entertain guests.

Success and Money

Work and family projects run smoothly thanks to excellent rapport and concern for professional and emotional feelings. Trust and confidentiality are critical to successful work accomplishments. Jupiter turns retrograde on the 28th in Aries and your solar second house of money matters. Keep adding to your savings account and control spending.

Pitfalls and Potential Problems

When the Full Moon in Capricorn in your solar eleventh house opposes Mercury in Cancer in your solar fifth house on the 13th, you'll have to decide whether to please friends or keep your significant other happy. Tension mounts when schedules clash. Invite relatives to a dinner on the 23rd, a lively date for a gathering.

Rewarding Days

1, 4, 10, 23

Challenging Days

2, 5, 9, 13

Pisces | August

Overall Theme

Mars and Uranus in sensual Taurus early in the month add strong romantic vibes to communication with your soulmate. The topic of conversation is the zone of intimacy, which ignites in your chart when you add Venus in Cancer to the mix with the Moon in Virgo in your solar seventh house. Ready for a trip to the altar?

Relationships

Investors, entrepreneurs, and financial specialists influence your thoughts to start your own holistic healing business when you attend a seminar on August 3 or 4. Bankers review your assets on the 15th. Discuss pending plans with your partner on the 23rd.

Success and Money

Invest in classes that add vital credentials to your resume and strengthen your value at work. The money is available for advanced studies if you prefer to start a side business instead of looking for a promotion in your current firm. Part with cash when you're ready, but not before weighing your options for a compatible career. The conditions on the 2nd, 7th, and 15th support your goals.

Pitfalls and Potential Problems

Forceful energy unfolds when Uranus in Taurus goes retrograde from August 24 until January 22, 2023, in your solar third house. Aspects to transiting Venus in Leo uncover painful discoveries about work matters. Depending on planetary placements in your natal chart, some Pisces may break up with a partner or learn of the death or illness of someone close.

Rewarding Days

2, 7, 15, 23

Challenging Days

5, 11, 17, 27

Pisces | September

Overall Theme

Be prepared before you venture into new territory. Four planets are retrograde this month, with Mercury in Libra about to join them on September 9, this time in your solar eighth house of joint income, assets and debt, wills, and estates. Examine work already in progress, return phone calls, and start new initiatives after Mercury, the messenger of the gods, goes direct next month.

Relationships

Bond with friends, work colleagues, and family over the Labor Day weekend. Pick a park or your own backyard for the festive setting and fire up the grill to treat guests to delicious food made with love. Provide outdoor games for children. On the 30th, accept a dinner invitation from your boss.

Success and Money

On the 6th, get involved with a worthy charity supported by your favorite humanitarian group. Purchase seasonal products at a clearance sale at nicely discounted prices. Sign contracts on the 15th after conferring with your attorney or financial advisor. Finance your new vehicle after negotiating a substantial trade-in and short loan term. Road-test your choice beyond the dealer's lot.

Pitfalls and Potential Problems

A team based at a distant location shows confusion over assignment details on the 2nd, making it necessary to provide unexpected training to staff before they can proceed with the work. Harmony at home base is disrupted on the 16th, when someone's sensitive feelings become overly emotional after an argument.

Rewarding Days

6, 7, 15, 30

Challenging Days

2, 5, 16, 22

Pisces | October

Overall Theme

Planets claim star billing this month, bringing a huge sigh of relief and optimism when they turn direct. The final Solar Eclipse of 2022 occurs in Scorpio and your solar ninth house on October 25. You travel more than usual for business to open a satellite office or recruit new hires for an expanding project. You're grateful for your knowledge of yoga and meditation to minimize stress.

Relationships

Members of a professional group meet on the 4th to launch recovery plans for an underfunded medical facility. Special bonding time with family starts with a night out on the 14th and turns the weekend into a memorable experience to help them build confidence due to lingering concerns over COVID-19 effects.

Success and Money

Work alliances show powerful shifts on the 18th when management cites the team for record-breaking accomplishments. Passionate Mars spends most of the month in Gemini and your solar fourth house, where communication bubbles with excitement over the pending purchase of new smartphones and electronic equipment for family members. Get ready for advances in the age of cyber power.

Pitfalls and Potential Problems

Three planets wrap up their retrograde periods this month: Mercury moves direct in Virgo on the 2nd, Pluto in Capricorn stations direct on the 8th, and Saturn goes direct on the 23rd in Aquarius. Mars in Gemini goes retrograde on the 30th through January 12 in your solar fourth house. Contain feistiness and squabbles.

Rewarding Days

4, 14, 18, 27

Challenging Days

1, 9, 17, 22

Pisces | November

Overall Theme
Your solar third house hosts the Lunar Eclipse in Taurus on the 8th, giving you a heads-up to prepare for visiting guests later this month. Make reservations, prepare a Thanksgiving menu, shop for ingredients for the tantalizing dishes you'll serve, and look forward to festive dinners with relatives who celebrate with you.

Relationships
Spend a lively Sunday with children on the 13th, treating them to an ice show or other favorite entertainment venue. Cherish your good fortune when parents and other relatives and friends arrive safely to spend the holiday with you.

Success and Money
On the 14th, your boss gives you a surprise holiday bonus, which you share with family and spend on remaining holiday gifts. Wanting to pay it forward, you write a large check to a local food bank to help defray costs for their annual Thanksgiving dinner. Be sure to mail holiday packages early.

Pitfalls and Potential Problems
The Lunar Eclipse in Taurus and Uranus are conjunct on the 8th, blocking smooth communication. Review work documents carefully on the 11th, when sloppy correspondence errors could lead to missed deadlines. A frazzled guest learns an arriving flight will be delayed on the 22nd. Jupiter in Pisces goes direct on the 23rd, just as you prepare to welcome out-of-town visitors to your Thanksgiving feast.

Rewarding Days
3, 13, 23, 28

Challenging Days
1, 8, 11, 22

Pisces | December

Overall Theme

Make this your most memorable holiday month yet by recreating special traditions that delight your whole family. Pay homage to Neptune, your ruling planet, by funding a Christmas celebration complete with gifts and a delicious dinner for a family in need. The planet of charity and compassion goes direct in Pisces on the 3rd in your solar first house.

Relationships

My, how you cherish your family and friends! Plan special gatherings during the period from the 24th to the 28th to show how much you love their company. Spend part of a day at a soup kitchen, having visitors and children tag along to share the holiday spirit with others in need. Feast on favorite meals and treats with your significant other and family on the 25th.

Success and Money

Jupiter in your sign occupies your solar first house until the 20th, reminding you of the prosperity and good health you regained in this healing year. Good fortune smiled on your checkbook, with steady employment and increased earnings and savings. You reduced debt and manifested security, the primary goal on your wish list.

Pitfalls and Potential Problems

On December 7 the year's final Full Moon occurs in your solar fourth house conjunct retrograde Mars in Gemini, reminding you to watch out for flaring tempers among family members. Mercury goes retrograde in Capricorn on the 29th in your solar eleventh house of groups and goals, a good time to reflect but not act on developing plans for the new year.

Rewarding Days

3, 24, 25, 28

Challenging Days

1, 7, 13, 21

Pisces Action Table

These dates reflect the best—but not the only—times for success and ease in these activities, according to your Sun sign.

	JAN	FEB	MAR	APR	MAY	JUN	JUL	AUG	SEP	OCT	NOV	DEC
Move		5	22		2				15			
Romance	21	26		8		3		23		4	3	
Seek counseling/ coaching							1		6			28
Ask for a raise					7		10			27		
Vacation	26		7			27					13	
Get a loan				22				2				3